PIML

595

BLUE NOTE RECORDS

Richard Cook has written about jazz and other music for some twenty-five years. He is currently the editor of *Jazz Review* and lives in West London.

BLUE NOTE RECORDS

The Biography

RICHARD COOK

PIMLICO

Published by Pimlico 2003

2 4 6 8 10 9 7 5 3 1

First published in Great Britain by Secker & Warburg 2001

Pimlico edition 2003

Pimlico
Random House, 20 Vauxhall Bridge Road,
London SW1V 2SA

Random House Australia (Pty) Limited
20 Alfred Street, Milsons Point, Sydney,
New South Wales 2061, Australia

Random House New Zealand Limited
18 Poland Road, Glenfield,
Auckland 10, New Zealand

Random House South Africa (Pty) Limited
Endulini, 5A Jubilee Road, Parktown 2193, South Africa

Random House UK Limited Reg. No. 954009

A CIP catalogue record for this book
is available from the British Library

ISBN 0-7126-3623-4

Papers used by Random House UK Limited are natural, recyclable
products made from wood grown in sustainable forests. The manufacturing
processes conform to the environmental regulations of the country of origin

Printed and bound in Great Britain by Mackays of Chatham

For Leonard Newman, a life-long New Yorker

CONTENTS

PREFACE

This is the story of a record label – originally black and pink, which was a printer's error, since they wanted it to be blue and magenta. From those first few 78s, Blue Note went on to become the most renowned and admired jazz-recording operation there ever has been. It's also the chronicle of a record *company*, and its trials and misfortunes, along with its successes. It's not a biography of Alfred Lion and Frank Wolff, and it's not a discography. I would have preferred to have called it 'notes towards a history' or something like that, but modern marketing forbids such modesty. It is a discussion, primarily, of the music which this company recorded and released, in the context of the culture of jazz and beyond, and a tale of what happens to the legacy of a tiny operation in the bigger, grander world of the global music business.

I haven't talked about every single album from Blue Note's golden age (hello, Grachan Moncur) since the story would then just be a string of record reviews. Nor is there much about boardroom politics, marketing budgets and annual projections: for more than twenty-five years of its existence, Blue Note was little other than two German guys putting out music that they loved. Companies don't have any kind of mystique, but record labels do, along with their covers, their papery inner sleeves, their thick black vinyl discs, and the music that comes out when you spin them under a needle. This is a look at how that mystique grew up, and how it endures.

These days, they don't have record labels any more. The titles and what have you are impressed directly on to little silver discs, which are offered to us by gigantic corporations, most of which operate as if they were selling breakfast cereal or shoe polish. I don't want this story to sound nostalgic, but it was a very different time.

ACKNOWLEDGEMENTS

This book was the idea of David Milner, my editor, whose patience and good humour seem inexhaustible. Whatever merit there is in it he must take much of the credit for; anything which doesn't measure up is entirely down to me. Thanks, David.

Bruce Lundvall and Michael Cuscuna – who will always know more about Blue Note than anybody else – gave unstintingly of their time in answering questions. Wendy Day, one of the great women in the UK record business, has always been a marvel. Gaylene Martin and Debbie Ballard were a big help. David Nathan at the Jazz Library in Loughton, Essex, gave plenty of cheerful assistance. My agent, Anthony Goff, is a definite good guy.

I have also drawn on conversations with the late Miles Davis, Benny Green, Johnny Griffin, Rick Margitza, Greg Osby, Dianne Reeves and John Scofield. Where uncredited, all quotes in the text stem from interviews with the author.

My wife, Lee Ellen, continues to put up with me and all the piles of LPs, CDs and papers which surround me and fill up our house. Thanks, honey!

ONE

At the end of the 1930s, jazz was a rich and powerful music. The record industry, once no more than a fledgling in the US business world, had grown healthily as American entertainment began to dominate the leisure time of the western world. If Hollywood movies were the most important export, American jazz – defined by the country's huge number of dance orchestras – was surely a close second. Although Europe could boast countless dance bands of its own, most of them took their stylistic cues from the great American orchestras – Duke Ellington, Benny Goodman, Tommy Dorsey, Count Basie. While such names are today thought of as jazz icons, then they were merely bandleaders, and they played, primarily, for dancers. It was jazz's golden decade, because it was the one spell in its convoluted history where jazz was the dominant popular music.

Even so, there were already plenty of reasons to be discontented with the way the music had evolved, as far as its commercial direction was concerned. If you were a committed jazz listener, you would have been dismayed to follow the recording career of, say, the trombonist-leader Tommy Dorsey, once a doyen of the New York studio scene of the twenties. Dorsey's band was a powerful entity in the swing era, and his record company, RCA, milked his popularity for all it was worth: in 1937 alone, he cut no fewer than twenty-two recording sessions. Yet many of these were routine workouts on undistinguished material, each date a search for a radio hit, with only a small strike rate of genuine success. Vocalists took their statutory chorus in the middle of each disc, undercutting whatever momentum the band might have achieved on its own. At least Dorsey had a small group drawn from the ranks of the big band, called the Clambake Seven, which contributed some of the fiercer performances to his discography; but the leader's nickname, the Sentimental Gentleman of Swing, deriving from his theme tune 'I'm Getting Sentimental Over You', was, as far as the music was concerned, often all too apposite (in reality, it was a sobriquet which scarcely suited Dorsey, a notorious martinet).

The black bands of Ellington, Basie and Jimmie Lunceford had considerably more to interest their listeners, although a hard look at their output and their popularity reveals that they had to cope with similar expectations. Ellington never stopped hankering after concert-music success, his Carnegie Hall appearances in the forties an apogee of black-tie black music in their day. Basie had the most exciting team of soloists of all the jazz orchestras, with the likes of Buck Clayton, Lester Young and Herschel Evans, but it was often singers Jimmy Rushing and Helen Humes who won the most attention. Lunceford, who believed that show business was above all a business, trained his men to entertain in chanceless, drilled performances.

In such an environment, it's hardly surprising that younger musicians began to feel fidgety with their lot: in a music supposedly built on a certain freedom of expression, the hallmark of swing-era jazz was its formality. The recordings by the freewheeling small groups of the 1920s, such as the Louis Armstrong Hot Five and Bix Beiderbecke & His Gang, seemed very different, almost primitive, next to the sophistications which now ruled the jazz mainstream. Yet small groups still played an important part in jazz in the 1930s, both in and out of the recording studio. In New York City, by then the acknowledged capital of the jazz world, the music had always been fostered in nightclubs, cafés, taverns, speakeasies and saloons, as well as in the larger theatres; and it was more likely to be a small group that performed there, rather than a big band. Some of the most successful series of recordings in the swing era, such as those by Fats Waller & His Rhythm, Teddy Wilson, Lionel Hampton and Bob Crosby's Bob Cats (another band-within-a-band), were by groups numbering no more than five, six or seven.

It was down to such groups to retain the element of 'hot jazz' in the day's popular music - even though, stylistically, there was a considerable gulf between the kind of jazz purveyed by the Bob Cats and the dapper music of Teddy Wilson. Rhythm sections, once the source of the two-beat pulse which drove most of the jazz of the twenties, had become smoother, and less obviously dependent on a stated rhythm. Where the improvising soloists were once anchored (often usefully) by their fellow players in the rhythm section, the more flexible patterns of the then-contemporary jazz rhythms created a greater democracy within the jazz small group, and encouraged leaner, more fluid, more integrated performances.

However 'modern' these groups aimed to be, their music was the bolt-hole of jazz listeners who felt that the big bands had taken too wayward a course. Although jazz, as a body of recorded work, was barely twenty years old at the height of the swing era, it had already formulated a band of followers who saw hot jazz as a romantic ideal, and those fans kept their faith by the small-group music of the second half of the thirties. Though the term 'revivalism' had yet to come into being, there was, by 1939, already a hankering after a more purist style of jazz performance, and an accompanying sense of a history that needed preservation. The major American record companies – Decca, Columbia, RCA and Victor – weren't altogether shy about recording such music. Victor's 1939 sessions by Muggsy Spanier's Ragtime Band, for instance, were a key example of the first wave of revivalism, a band of white Chicagoans playing repertoire which in many cases was drawn from the book of the Original Dixieland Jazz Band itself (ironically, although the records have always been widely admired, Spanier's group couldn't find regular work and was soon disbanded). But the majors were focusing their budgets on the big orchestras, and the small-group music existed as a kind of subculture which, then and now, seemed like a pendant to the main forces in the swing era.

In 1938, Milton Gabler, who at that time ran a music shop on Manhattan's 44th Street, decided to begin recording some of the music that appealed to him. A garrulous, enthusiastic character with enormous self-belief, Gabler began by working in what was originally his father's radio and electrical store, on Third Avenue. 'I was aware of jazz right from the beginning, because when I went to dances . . . the bands were like little bands, like Dixieland bands.'[1] By the thirties, Gabler was a fan and collector himself, then running a second store on 42nd Street, and smart enough to realise that a collectors' market was springing up for hard-to-find jazz records. In 1933, he even persuaded Columbia to reissue two otherwise forgotten sides by the Casa Loma Orchestra, which became an unexpected hit. The following year, he began leasing masters from the big labels and pressing them under the logo 'Commodore Music Shop'. As the shop became a mecca for local enthusiasts and out-of-towners, Gabler found himself at the centre of a burgeoning fan base for hot music. Although musicians like Condon and his circle were, in Gabler's word, 'scuffling' at the time, the music-store man began organising Sunday jam sessions featuring these players and drawing crowds of fans.

When Columbia began reissuing their own records, at John Hammond's instigation, in 1938, Gabler decided to quit reissuing material and start recording new music for Commodore, by now a firmly established label. On 17 January 1938, he produced the first session, seven titles by Eddie Condon's Windy City Seven and four by Bud Freeman's Trio. Commodore would last, as an active label, until the fifties, although Gabler himself subsequently crossed over and joined Decca. When the reissue company Mosaic released *The Complete Commodore Jazz Recordings* in the 1990s, it stretched to 128 LP sides. At one of the early sessions, Eddie Condon, a peerless hustler, persuaded a *Life* photographer to capture the session: 'It's an important thing, a little record store doing its own recordings. It doesn't like the records that the big companies make.'[2]

Commodore's emergence paved the way for a boom in independent-label jazz recording which has persisted until this day. It certainly inspired another fan of hot music. Something else happened in 1938 to galvanise that young man into action: the staging of a concert at Carnegie Hall, billed as 'From Spirituals To Swing'. John Hammond, the scion of a wealthy New York family, had taken quickly to jazz as a young man and was a member of Gabler's music-shop gang. He had whirled himself into all sorts of initiatives during the thirties, and one of them was an ambition to present a major concert featuring 'talented Negro artists from all over the country who had been denied entry to the white world of popular music.'[3] He got his wish on 23 December 1938. Carnegie Hall was completely sold out, to the extent that three hundred extra seats had to be placed on the stage itself to handle the audience overflow. Hammond had booked a huge programme of soloists, groups and singers – covering gospel, blues and swing stylings – with the Count Basie Orchestra as the climactic item. Recorded on acetate by Zeke Frank, some eighty minutes of music from the event has survived. It has the quality of a distant broadcast, and the fidelity has a remote feel to it, but the excitement of the occasion is still palpable. According to contemporary reviews, one of the most warmly received segments of the show featured three practitioners of boogie-woogie piano: Pete Johnson, Albert Ammons and Meade Lux Lewis. The two pieces which they played six-handed, 'Jumpin' Blues' and the tumultuous 'Cavalcade Of Boogie', Ammons's solo 'Boogie Woogie' and Lewis's 'Honky Tonk Train Blues' were cheered to the echo. It was an appearance which helped to commence a craze for boogie-woogie piano records that lasted into the forties.

In the Carnegie Hall audience, Alfred Lion was spellbound by the music that the pianists played. History has it as his defining moment. Most jazz listeners remember specific encounters as their personal way in to this music, and although boogie-woogie was a jazz style which would subsequently hardly feature in his catalogue, it was hearing these pianists which may have finally decided Lion on establishing his record company.

Unlike Gabler, Lion was not a born-and-bred New Yorker. He was born in Berlin in 1909. Many years later, he remembered how music played a role in his earliest memories:

> My parents took me on a vacation to a resort when I was five. The hotel had a ballroom with a large dance orchestra, and after my parents put me to bed, they went dancing. I'd get dressed and sneak down to the stage entrance of the ballroom. The musicians thought I was cute and let me in. They put me in the orchestra pit and I sat on the floor for hours next to the drummer. It meant something, to feel that rhythm.[4]

Ragtime and syncopated music had a strong hold on Berlin's popular culture:

it was not a bad place for a young man to hear the first stirrings of jazz-related music in Europe. However, opportunities to hear American musicians at close quarters were still rare, even for an inquisitive young man: very few black players made the trip to Europe in the twenties. It was something of a lucky break when Lion managed to hear the genuine article. In 1925, Sam Wooding's band, billed as the Chocolate Dandies, were playing in Germany. Pianist Wooding had come to Europe originally as part of a revue called *Chocolate Kiddies*, and he stayed on to play many engagements with his band. Although it was more of a showbiz orchestra than a genuine 'jazz band', Wooding had distinctive players, such as trumpeter Tommy Ladnier, among his men, and it was surely a more authentic jazz experience than anything else Berlin had to offer that year. Lion went to his local roller-skating rink one day and found that there was no skating that day, since Wooding's group were to perform a concert. He went in, and heard black American music in person for the first time: 'It was something brand new but it registered with me right away.'[5]

Lion began trying to find American records, and like many before and after him, found the pull of the new American culture irresistible. In 1928, barely out of his teens, he paid his first visit to New York. Although it was as tough for him there as it was for any other immigrant, with little command of the language and no money, he stayed long enough to absorb some of the city's music, even while sleeping rough and working in the docks. The city paid him back, though, since he was beaten by a fellow dock worker and ended up in hospital, an experience which eventually made him decide to return home. There, he sought work which might offer him the chance to travel back, and he managed to visit New York again while working for a German export firm. These were fleeting visits, but long enough for Lion to scoop up as many records as he could before going back to Berlin.

Lion's progress through the thirties is difficult to follow. His family moved to Chile in 1933, where Alfred undertook a variety of jobs, even attempting a spell as a lobster fisherman. But it was a permanent move to New York, in 1937, which signalled his future, after he landed a position with another firm of importers/exporters. Back in the capital of jazz, Lion began picking up where he had left off, and soon found out about places such as Gabler's Commodore Music Shop. The audience for 'hot jazz' was already beginning to resemble the motley, disenfranchised gathering which has, arguably, formed the core jazz audience ever since. A long-time record collector himself, Lion must surely have felt at home among Gabler's gang. Yet he must have brought some old-world business logic to even his first jazz-record enterprise. After their reception at the Carnegie Hall performance, any aspiring entrepreneur would have considered Albert Ammons and Meade Lux Lewis as likely targets for a record session. Both men had already recorded for other labels, but despite a slow buzz of interest in Lewis's work in particular, the earlier discs had yet to have any major popular impact. Lion was determined, first, simply to create a situation where he could record the two pianists, and two weeks after 'From Spirituals To Swing' he got his wish. On 6 January 1939, Alfred Lion supervised his first recording session.

It was a sunny winter's day. Lion had rented a small studio in the city for a single day, and he established a congenial setting for the two men to perform – mostly, through the provision of plenty of Scotch and bourbon. The producer was somewhat in awe of the situation and had no real idea how to direct the occasion, preferring to let the music and the musicians take their course. That resulted in a notable peculiarity which, in a sense, set the tone for Blue Note's future: instead of the three-minute duration which ten-inch 78s customarily enforced, Lion allowed both Ammons and Johnson to play longer solos, and the resulting masters had to be pressed as twelve-inch discs, a rarity in jazz terms. Ammons cut nine sides, Lewis eight, and Lion cajoled them into playing two duets on the single piano on hand.

At this distance, it's hard to understand the sensation which boogie-woogie piano created at that time. Lewis had cut one of the earliest discs in the style, his signature piece 'Honky Tonk Train Blues', in 1927, but the novelty of the steady-rolling style, built on its relentless walking-bass patterns for the left hand, took a strange grip on the popular music of that moment, taking its place as a rhythmic craze alongside some of the dance steps of the swing bands. Lion was perhaps rather more interested in the links between boogie-woogie and a more fundamentalist blues piano. At the date, Ammons had wanted to cut some tracks in a rather square 3/4 idiom, but Alfred persuaded him to try a more thoughtful piece, and 'Chicago In Mind', which might be his finest single recording, was the result. Distilling his familiar left-hand patterns into a stately, contemplative lilt, Ammons touched on deeper reserves of expression than some of his jollier recordings might have suggested. Even more exceptional was Lewis's five-part meditation, 'The Blues'. In later years, Lewis seemed to become disenchanted with his own powers, and by the idiom which he had helped to create, but here he explores one of the oldest and most worked-over resources and offers up a graceful resumé of the blues itself. In 1985, Lion recalled: 'He was so strong. No water, no chaser. Straight.'[6] It was an extraordinary idea, which suggested that Lion was already thinking in a kind of long-form, seeking to obtain a unique and significant result by thinking of a session as a complete entity.

There was enough material for several 78s (the entire session, pieced together from original acetates, was only released in full in 1985), but to start with, Lion pressed some fifty copies of two discs, one by each man. Hardly a major statement of intent, even from an audacious, independent operation. At the time, record distribution in America was probably at least as byzantine as it is today. The days of exclusive dealerships, where individual record stores would only carry either Victor or Columbia records, were long gone. But in such a huge country, there were regional hits tailored to regional tastes, whole styles of music which might sell in one area and be dead in another, and, in a culture where ephemerality was fast becoming characteristic, a subculture of traders who dealt in cut-out or deleted records. It was an environment that helped to create margins where an independent might tickle by. Lion could scarcely afford to promote his new label, but in a way he didn't have to. The coterie of admirers which Gabler and his United Hot Clubs of America represented would have made Blue Note persist, for a while at least. They also had a lucky break when the Philadelphia trader H. Royer Smith acquired some of the first pressings.

It was not as if Lion was about to give up his day job. But he clearly was ambitious for his new project. The legend of the Carnegie Hall concert as some kind of Damascan experience has been thrown into some question, since it now seems likely that Lion had already decided to set up his own company with two others, and had been discussing it extensively with various figures in the Commodore 'circle'. In the end, the Blue Note company was incorporated in 1939 with Lion and Max Margulis – who put up much of the initial money – as the two main figures. Margulis was a writer and committed left-winger who didn't want to be involved in making the records but ended up writing brochures and advertising copy for the music.

Lion, though, had been transformed by his first studio experience. Like anyone else who has attended a recording session, he had acquired a taste for the peculiar, pressure-cooker atmosphere of making records on tight budgets.

Though Lion saw himself primarily as a fan, and had no prior knowledge of producing record dates, he was soon caught up in the process, the unique mix of artisanship and high art, which is the sovereign state of the jazz-recording session. On 7 April 1939, he brought a larger, six-strong group of musicians into the studio, labelling them the Port of Harlem Jazzmen. Ammons returned, but this time with the two-horn frontline of trumpeter Frank Newton and trombonist J.C. Higginbotham. In the rhythm section, Teddy Bunn (guitar), Johnny Williams (bass) and the great drummer Sidney Catlett. Newton and Higginbotham each sat out on one tune, and there were three titles by the full sextet. This was accomplished, graceful small-group swing. Newton was a trumpeter who never seemed to have much luck in his career, and his few sessions as a leader barely fill up a single CD, but in his feature 'Daybreak Blues' (which turned out to be Blue Note's first ten-inch 78) one can hear his method of lining up clean, elegant playing with a chaser of behind-the-hand, wry asides. He was just the kind of major-minor talent which Blue Note – and, indeed, many other independent jazz labels – would consistently set down on record, as much with posterity in mind as for any commercial intent. The group returned to the studios on 8 June, and Newton was again granted a feature blues, 'After Hours Blues', abetted by Teddy Bunn's sinuous, funny solo. But the point of this date was the arrival of a seventh man in the studio, the soprano saxophonist Sidney Bechet. As a name, this was some catch by Lion, and Bechet gifted him an intense, singing treatment of 'Summertime' which presages the superb session he was to make with Louis Armstrong a year later. And it was Blue Note's first hit, issued as BN 6 and coupled with a septet performance of 'Pounding Heart Blues'.

Lion may have been making up the rules as he went along, but it was the idea of a hip, sympathetic mind to schedule these dates for the late-early hours of the morning, with one of the dates starting at 4.30 a.m., not long after the musicians would have got off from their regular 52nd Street gig (hence a title such as 'After Hours Blues'). Word began to get around that this was an operation that was doing something more than churning out record dates. Lion remembered: 'A lot of musicians had heard about these late sessions. At one of them, Billie Holiday and her entourage were on the sidewalk, shouting to be let up. But I was so nervous, because I didn't really know what I was doing yet, that I wouldn't let her up. I probably could have recorded her that night, but I couldn't deal with anything beyond what I was trying to do.'[7]

What was Lion trying to do? At first, it must have seemed like an exalted game, or fulfilling a dream. Men such as Bechet, Newton and the boogie pianists were scarcely the hottest properties in the record business, but they were exemplars of Lion's kind of jazz. He had set down his stated intentions already, in a paragraph which went out as part of a flyer for Blue Note's early releases, dated May 1939 (and probably penned by Margulis):

> Blue Note records are designed simply to serve the uncompromising expression of hot jazz and swing, in general. Any particular style of playing which represents an authentic way of musical feeling is genuine expression. By virtue of its significance in place, time and circumstance, it possesses its own tradition, artistic standards and audience that keeps it alive. Hot jazz, therefore, is expression and communication, a musical and social manifestation, and Blue Note Records are concerned with identifying its impulse, not its sensational and commercial adornments.

The lofty, professorial tone of the 'statement' is actually reminiscent of the publicity material which the gramophone industry used in its infancy, trumpeting their intent to bring fine culture into people's homes. But it does underscore the missionary zeal which men like Lion were starting to bring to a jazz scene that was already labouring under internal divisions. Sidney Bechet may not have thought of that 1939 date as anything dramatically different to anything else he'd recorded up till then, but the disc honoured his playing in the way that, for instance, his various dates for Victor didn't really match. Lion's dedication to 'hot jazz' and his determination to record it was in part a reaction to the music industry's homogenisation of the jazz culture. While home-grown American entrepreneurs valued the new popular music – be it jazz or pop – as an expression of post-Depression optimism, Lion, whose roots were in a European cultural value system, already had a conviction that jazz was an art music.

The period between 1939 and 1941 saw Blue Note inching forwards, one session and one release at a time. Lion had begun the label as a one-man band, but as the forties dawned, he had help from a friend who went back to his days in Berlin. Alfred had met Francis Wolff in Berlin as far back as 1924 and the two teenage boys discovered a mutual interest in popular music. While the Lions had few pretensions to being anything other than a working German family, Frank Wolff's background had more to do with affluence, good taste and Jewish bourgeois values. His father, a mathematics professor, had made money out of investments, while his mother had a taste for contemporary culture which she passed on to her son. Even so, Wolff proved to be, in the long term, the real business brain behind Blue Note.

Frank Wolff arrived in New York at the end of 1939 (by legend, on the 'last boat out of Nazi Germany'). He had worked in Germany as a professional photographer, a softly spoken, unobtrusive figure accustomed to discretion in his work. Once the Third Reich had taken a grip on domestic affairs, Wolff – although he left it curiously late in the day – realised that his tastes would have to take him elsewhere. In New York, he lost little time in making contact with his old friend Lion, and at the same time found a job as a photographer's assistant. Although both men depended on outside activities for their daily bread, their mutual love of jazz was enough to keep the Blue Note initiative alive, and they managed to sustain a tiny office on West 47th Street, Blue Note's first address.

Working together, they managed to set down eight further recording sessions before America joined the war. There were more piano sides by Meade Lux Lewis, and a session where he played harpsichord; five titles by guitarist Teddy Bunn; more music from Sidney Bechet, including an odd session where he played with the blues-folkie Josh White; and six titles by the boogie-woogie stylist who had previously eluded them, Pete Johnson. Clarinettist Edmond Hall was recorded in a quartet with Lewis on harpsichord, guitarist Charlie Christian and bassist Israel Crosby, a chamberish setting which might have owed something to the John Kirby group but which was innately flavoured by Hall's true grit: he was a New Orleans man who bridged rootsiness and metropolitan wit. Perhaps most interesting of all is the July 1939 session by pianist Earl Hines, his only recording for the label. 'The Father's Getaway' and 'Reminiscing At Blue Note' are full of the authentic Hines razzle-dazzle, skipping over rhythmic and harmonic conventions with insouciant abandon, the kind of solo he would live by in later years but which was rarely exposed, at length, in his prime. Lion let both masters run over four minutes and secured a priceless result.

If one was to characterise the label's profile on the basis of these early dates, with their emphasis on piano, boogie-woogie and blues, it might seem like an early example of revivalism. Frank Wolff would later reminisce that it was, really, no clearer to him what their style was:

> Jazz had gathered enough momentum so that an experiment like Blue Note could be tried. We could not round up more than a handful of customers for a while, but we garnered a good deal of favourable publicity through our uncommercial approach. Somehow we set a style, but I would have difficulty to define same. I remember though that people used to say, 'Alfred and Frank record only what they like.' That was true. If I may add three words, we tried to record jazz 'with a feeling'.[8]

Whatever the scope of their activities, they were suspended by the arrival of Lion's draft papers at the end of 1941. The Blue Note catalogue could boast twenty-seven records, but with the founder out of the way for a while, it was hard to see how it could have continued. Then their fellow label boss Milton Gabler re-entered the picture: he hired Frank Wolff to work at the Commodore Music Shop. Gabler had decided to begin a wholesale division to sell Commodore records more efficiently, and he let Wolff use the same network to distribute Blue Note 78s. It was a fortunate development, because it let the tiny independent hang on to an impetus which, surprisingly, came out of the war itself. Instead of depending on the fragile collectors' market, Blue Note found itself part of the business of entertaining the troops. Wolff: 'The soldiers wanted them – the Army wanted them. Records became hot, and Commodore sold a lot of them, mail and wholesale. Shellac was scarce, and only people who had been in business before the war could get a priority.'[9] With little need for promotion costs and no further recordings planned until after Lion was discharged, the label could even stockpile takings for a time.

Lion saw no combat duty and came out of the service in 1943. But before that, he passed a personal milestone. Around 1940 he had begun seeing a willowy, dark-haired girl named Lorraine, and while he was stationed in Texas, he persuaded her to come down and visit; and there they married, in 1942. When they came back to New York in 1943, they set up home in a tiny apartment in the Village. By November, Blue Note had begun recording again.

Lion cut a series of dates with James P. Johnson and Edmond Hall. This fresh start took place at a problematic moment in the recording industry's progress. The big-band business was being hurt by the war: a cabaret tax made booking orchestras expensive, and the rise of radio brought fears that live music was being further affected. In 1942, the AFM, the union of musicians, began talking to the major record companies about paying royalties to the union on every disc sold. When there was little progress, the AFM instigated a ban on all instrumental recording from 1 August. It was to last for nearly two years, but Blue Note came to an agreement with the union in 1943 and was able to stage a return to business when they wanted. They also opened a bigger office at an address which vinyl collectors revere to this day: 767 Lexington Avenue, the first 'proper' Blue Note headquarters, which features as a byline on the label of all the most sought-after Blue Note ten- and twelve-inch LPs.

The period between then and the end of the war saw the label's methods and activities take firmer shape. Instead of issuing only individually jacketed 78s, they also began sleeving some of their sessions in multi-disc albums. Although there were still occasional solo sessions, including dates by guitarist Jimmy Shirley and old faithful Meade Lux Lewis, Lion concentrated on small groups which leaned either towards Chicago-style revivalism, New Orleans authenticity or a new mini-genre, the swingtet. This was often two or three horns and a four-strong rhythm section, the kind of group a club could afford and call it an orchestra. Economics – the war, the call-up and inevitable changing tastes – had already begun to wind down the big-band era, and while the uproar of bebop was only a few paces away,

Blue Note was still more interested in 'hot jazz' than in documenting any revolution.

In the main, the hallmark of Blue Note's jazz at this point was an intelligent conservatism. The label still had the feel of a collector's indulgence. The sessions under the leadership of Chicago pianist Art Hodes, ten dates across 1944–5, are typical of Lion's good husbandry: tidy, relaxed music, the musicians apparently playing for themselves as much as for any perceived audience, but with a strong result at the end of the date. In his liner notes to a 1969 reissue of some of the sessions, Hodes, who was a gifted writer himself, recalled the atmosphere of each date:

> You walk in and there's a big bag full of food. Once we started playing, you didn't have to leave the building for nothin'. Alfred hung his hat in the control room, while Frank was all over the place taking pictures. After a while you got used to him almost in your lap. Took good pictures too. There was a feeling of 'at ease'. And considering the times, the bread was good. Eventually the records were released, and no one got hurt.

Hodes was also wry enough to run a small piece in the April 1944 issue of *Jazz Record*, the magazine he co-edited, under the heading 'Blue Note Goes White'. In the long history of the label, he was one of the very few white musicians to record for the company as a leader.

The Hodes sessions were also characteristic for their use of a repertory cast of players. Edmond Hall and Sidney Bechet were on some of the dates, and Hodes himself went on to play as a sideman on some other 1940s sessions. The Blue Note team spirit was already taking shape. It was mirrored in the sessions under the various leaderships of Hall, James

P. Johnson and trumpeter Sidney De Paris, some of which followed the swingtet format.

Johnson also recorded eight piano solos at two sessions in November and December 1943. In a publicity flyer for the discs, Max Margulis underlined the label's sense that they were upholding jazz culture against a tide of commercialism, a pretty bewildering stance for a record company to take: 'Now that for more than a decade jazz has been moving toward abstractness, and concerning itself with generating sheer excitement, we encounter fewer and fewer musicians who think and feel in terms of its traditional language. James P. Johnson . . . advances our view of the significant continuity of jazz.' The remarks might almost be akin to Stanley Crouch talking about the Marsalis family in the 1990s.[10] Whatever the intention, these were exceptional dates by a master whose visibility in jazz circles was rather erratic. Johnson was one of the few black composers able to realise some part of an aspiration to work outside jazz, having had one extended work, *Yamecraw*, played at Carnegie Hall. But his path eventually led him to the Eddie Condon circle, and despite failing health he recorded quite prolifically in the 1940s: there was a long sequence of solos made for Decca in 1944, for example.

The Blue Note solos, though, sound like real living history. Johnson was born in 1894 and had been around long enough to have played and written authentic ragtime. 'Carolina Balmoral' and 'Caprice Rag', which Johnson copyrighted as far back as 1914, are marked by their formal precision – the eleven choruses of 'Caprice Rag' are especially finished, close to a notated perfection – yet their syncopations and the personal touch which Johnson imbues belong to a later, jazz age. Ragtime, for all its cakewalking energy, is a largely impersonal strain. Johnson's sublime jauntiness is best brought out in 'Mule Walk', which may be an even earlier piece than 'Caprice Rag', and it exposes his links with the songster music of a performer such as Henry Thomas. 'Backwater Blues', the first of the eight pieces he set down, does not impress as 'authentic' blues piano, but that was not Johnson's forte: he shapes the idiom to his gentlemanly manner, a professional's resumé. Along with the early Lewis and Ammons solos, these beautiful sessions suggest that Blue Note might have gone on to compile a piano history of jazz.

Solo dates, though, were becoming the exception. The swingtet format polished the routine of small-group swing. The repertoire of the earlier dates is unremarkable: simple lines such as 'Blues At Blue Note' and staples of the new Dixieland such as 'Everybody Loves My Baby' and 'Panama' were the main vehicles, the kind of thing which younger musicians were already coming to despise. But the playing was notably crisp, while still expansive enough to justify the twelve-inch format which Lion continued to prefer. Scattered through these sessions were contributions from Sidney De Paris, Vic Dickenson, Ben Webster, Teddy Wilson and others which kept the music sounding fresh. Fortunately, the drummer on most of the dates was Sidney Catlett, subtle, propulsive and unmatched at differentiating responses to each soloist and occasion.

Fine as this music was, a more telling signing to the label was Isaac Abrams Quebec, a tenor saxophonist from Newark who had worked with Hot Lips Page and Roy Eldridge. Ike Quebec is a footnote in jazz history now, but he was important to Blue Note. Born in 1918, he was young enough to appreciate the direction that jazz was going in, even if his own style leaned towards the more classical approach of Coleman Hawkins, a big, mostly jovial sound that would have been comfortable in small-group swing or the surroundings which he seems to have eventually disappeared into, the R&B combos of the fifties. In July 1944, Quebec cut his first session for Blue Note, a quintet session with Ram Ramirez, Tiny Grimes, Milt Hinton and J.C. Heard. 'Blue Harlem', a luxurious blues, was one side of Quebec's manner; the other was the one to be heard in rambunctious settings such as that for 'The Masquerade Is Over'. Like Ben Webster, Ike had a tone which turned from thick and romantic to harsh and growling when the tempos went up. But at this point at least, he lacked either Webster's judgement or Hawkins's controlled finesse. His five sessions for Blue Note between 1944 and 1946 are some of the most unfettered music which the label had produced up to that point, and certainly some remove from the cloistered atmosphere of the solo piano sessions; but they also had a whiff of modernity, even if stylistically Quebec had little to do with bebop. He was, though, a young musician who knew instinctively that jazz was heading dramatically away from the classic feel of Blue Note's first period, and Lion and Wolff took note of what he had to tell them – that bop was the way forward for small-group jazz.

In 1946, Blue Note cut only four record dates (the last, on 23 September, was one of Ike Quebec's). By the end of the year, the label could boast a total of forty-nine recording sessions and a populous catalogue of records. But it was at something of a crossroads. Independent jazz labels had begun to sprout like mushrooms. It was not only Commodore and Blue Note that were recording New York jazz: there were Varsity, Musicraft, Keynote and Black & White. The hot jazz which Blue Note had apparently been founded to document was also in the hands of fundamentalist outfits such as Jazz Man and American Music, who recorded the New Orleans eminences Bunk Johnson and George Lewis. Most significant of all were the handful of labels that were rapidly recording the new music of bebop – Savoy, Dial, Manor and Guild.

Blue Note had already been noting many of the changes in the jazz of the forties. The more personal methodology of the late-night sessions and the string of swingtet titles suggested that. In a dramatic instant, they would gather in the most idiosyncratic figure in the next wave of jazz, and set down many of his defining moments. With Thelonious Monk, Blue Note entered its first modern phase.

TWO

Many of the most important documents of bebop's first wave had already been set down when Blue Note began their own documentation of the music. Charlie Parker's Dial and Savoy sessions, Dizzy Gillespie's small-group sides for RCA Victor, and the first dates by past and future masters such as Dexter Gordon, Serge Chaloff and Howard McGhee had been waxed and released, with the full impact of the new movement quickly becoming clear, at least to those keen enough to follow the independent jazz-recording operations. The new labels which had caught the first of this music, such as Savoy and Manor, were following some of the early cues of Blue Note, but the music was very different, and the old loyalty to 'hot music' was rather changed. It might also be argued that the next generation of label bosses were more like businessmen and rather less like the fans which Wolff and Lion always tried to be. But if there was one principle which Blue Note's founders stuck by, it was keeping an open mind as to where they should look for music to record.

Ike Quebec may have been unlike most of the first-wave boppers, in terms of his own playing, but like many of his immediate contemporaries he saw – reluctantly or enthusiastically – that bebop was an electrifying new charge in the music. The idea that he basically brought bop to Blue Note's attention is attractive, if hard to justify in reality: anyone with ears as inquisitive as Lion's would have been more than aware of bebop's appeal by 1947, and it would have taken a diehard retrogressive to have taken the line that the new music was beyond their ken (although that was the line Commodore largely pursued). Dizzy Gillespie had already been recording for almost a decade at this point. Parker's hurly-burly masterpieces had been set down. It was difficult to see who in the bop field could have created the kind of impact which Lion must have sought to create with his first bop records. But luckily, one figure, who had been in at the start but had cut no dates as a leader, was still in the picture: the pianist Thelonious Sphere Monk, who had just turned thirty when he cut his first Blue Note date on 15 October 1947.

It was not, in fact, the label's first step into recording the new music. Earlier in the year, Babs Gonzalez (despite the name, he was a male vocalist) cut two sessions with arrangements by pianist Tadd Dameron, who also played piano on the dates: one included the Gillespie favourite 'Oop-Pop-A-Da'. And Dameron led his own sextet session in September, with the mercurial trumpeter Fats Navarro, of which more later. But Monk's date is so individual and epochal that it changed Blue Note for ever. Lion was so intoxicated by the results that he hurried Monk back into the studios nine days later, cutting six more titles, with a further date (four titles) following in November.

Monk's music today is so lionised and readily frequented by musicians that he is generally acknowledged as the major jazz composer after Ellington. In 1947 – and, indeed, for years afterwards – he was deemed eccentric enough to seem like an aberrant crank to many, even in the unconventional playing field of bebop. Although he embodied many of bop's innovations, he stood apart from much of the language: the whirlwind tempos and virtuoso accuracy which typified most bop recordings are conspicuously absent from Monk's own.

His tunes, knotty with their own logic, often seem to have been jigsawed out of a combination of jazz past and Monk's own interior world, which his titles illuminate in a cunningly offhand way: 'Epistrophy', 'Let's Cool One', 'Well You Needn't'. He obliged his groups to play with a kind of martial swing, a loping forward stride, which became infamous for outfoxing unwary performers. Each of his records operates to a combinative intensity: they're famous not for their solo improvisations, but for their awkward and eventually triumphant unity, a collectivism which has much in common with the spirit of the first jazz performances.

The first Blue Note session is still startling to first-time listeners: as familiar as so much of Monk's music has become, the brisk, exacting treatments here are a reminder of how new – and unacceptable – so much of this was to the jazz orthodoxy. The strange descending line of 'Humph', the first master which Lion recorded, is already a country mile in distance from anything else Blue Note had set down. The assembled group was a sextet: Idrees Sulieman, a Southerner born in Florida, was the trumpeter, and two saxophonists, Danny Quebec West and Billy Smith, completed the front line. Besides Monk, the rhythm section is filled out by bassist Gene Ramey and the drummer Art Blakey. Two years younger than Monk, almost to the day, Blakey had already worked in the Billy Eckstine Orchestra which had featured so many of the front-rank young beboppers. Next to, say, Max Roach, Blakey's style seems almost heavy-handed, missing at least some of the fleetness and subtle accenting of Roach's work, but it sounds peculiarly apt for Monk's music: whatever else the pianist's jazz was, it wasn't especially subtle. It thrives on declarative players, not deferential ones. Blakey's thudding rimshots and lumpy swing would be gestures that he would refine over the next decade, but they already showed his insistence, which made him such a valuable contributor to Monk's Blue Note sessions.

Like most first-generation bebop, the titles cut at this date are over quickly – only the master take of 'Evonce' goes over the three-minute barrier – and they have the jolting, switchback feel of music which purports to live on its nerve ends. Still, this was hardly a case of a musician being rushed into the studio. Monk had been at work on his composing and his methods for years prior to getting this opportunity to record as a leader. Lion was facilitating the documentation of an already mature outlook. 'Evonce' and 'Suburban Eyes' are compositions credited to, respectively, Sulieman–Quebec and Ike Quebec alone. The saxophonist had clearly played a major part in making the session happen: Danny West was his cousin, only seventeen at the time of the date, and the 'original' material follows the bebop argot of using standard chord sequences to nourish new melodic lines. 'Suburban Eyes' is drawn over the chords of 'All God's Chillun Got Rhythm' (a special favourite, ironically, of the other Blue Note piano-bopper Bud Powell) but lacks any lasting character, relying on its solos to generate heat. In the background, Monk comps with bluff intensity, and when he emerges to take his solo on the master take, one can hear something very different to normal bebop practice going on (although Gene Ramey comes in for a half-chorus of his own at the end of the piano solo, Monk continues to 'accompany' so strongly that it's as if he was extending his own improvisation).

The masterpiece of the date is 'Thelonious'. While Sulieman, West and Smith are competent enough, they do little other than fill up space on the other sides. Although the horns offer a desultory harmonisation of the theme, 'Thelonious' is basically a feature for the piano, bass and drums. The theme itself is a see-sawing rhythmic motif on two chords, and as his extemporisation, Monk throws in a series of ideas of how that rhythm can be set off against the almost faceless playing of Ramey and Blakey. After thirty-two bars, he is stuck, seemingly, on a single chord, but then hits on introducing – of all things – a left-hand stride rhythm, an anachronism which might seem absurd in the ultramodern milieu of bebop but which works with placid logic in the context of this music. It must surely have made Alfred Lion's ears perk up, too, as a nod to his beloved 'hot music' of a jazz generation before.

Lion knew he was on to something, even if Monk hardly seemed the most likely type to be Blue Note's flag-waver for bebop. In 1985, he told Michael Cuscuna that 'Monk was so fantastically original and his compositions were so strong and new that I just wanted to record everything he had. It was so fantastic I had to record it all.'[1] For the 24 October date, the horns were absent and Monk, Ramey and Blakey were left to themselves. They set down six titles, four originals by the pianist and two standards. 'Nice Work If You Can Get It' and 'April In Paris' are quality popular songs and fertile ground for jazz improvisers. The Gershwin tune was already a jam session favourite and Monk's four choruses on each of two takes are jocular, pell-mell episodes. Experienced listeners might spot half-heard quotations from his own melodies – such as 'Well you Needn't', which he plays later on the session – but rather than any deliberate mining of his original work, they're more like a sequence of juxtapositions of phrases from his improviser's locker. 'April In Paris' was also cut in two takes: the alternate version is much faster and is over in 2:40, while the master runs for 3:17. Although he sounds a little harried by Blakey on the quicker treatment, each shows how much Monk liked the melody, since he actually chooses to stick closely to it for much of the way, inserting double-time runs and clattery repetitions without completely sundering the wistful feel of Vernon Duke's song.

The four originals are extraordinary. 'Ruby My Dear' is one of Monk's three great ballads, along with 'Crepuscule With Nellie' and 'Round Midnight'. He uses a four-note motif as the heart of the piece, modulating it to progress the composition, and the two takes, each a palatial investigation of the theme, have the mix of stateliness and playful bonhomie which distinguishes so much of his slow-tempo work. 'Well You Needn't' became one of his most-liked tunes. Over Blakey's bustle, he plays alternately full and then miserly lines. 'Off Minor' is one of Monk's most jagged ideas. 'Introspection' is one of the pianist's least-known pieces (it wasn't originally released until 1956) and one of his most oblique melodies, which seems, as Bob Blumenthal notes, 'to start somewhere in the middle'.[2]

The most striking thing about this music – then and now – is how different it seems to the rest of the jazz of its time. Bebop piano had already spawned such virtuoso players as Bud Powell, Al Haig, Dodo Marmarosa and others, but none of them approached the unalloyed newness of Monk's ideas and methods of delivering them. If bop was both a rhythmic and an harmonic advance on the precepts of the swing era, it still found it difficult to accommodate Monk's idiosyncrasies, even though the pianist had helped to create the theoretical base for the music, as an after-hours study partner of Dizzy Gillespie. Much has been made of Monk's allegiances to jazz principles already established, and it's possible to skeet-shoot through every bar of these records, noting bits of stride and boogie-woogie, as well as the influence of men whom Monk particularly admired, notably Duke Ellington. But they remain the products of a private realm, as humorous and full of vitality as it was. The music which Lion heard as 'so strong and new' existed almost in a parallel world to the bebop environment.

With ten sides already in the can, Lion brought Monk in for a third session, even though he had yet to release any of the earlier discs commercially. Blakey aside, the line-up was quite different: George Taitt (trumpet) and Sahib Shihab (alto sax) made up the front line, and Bob Paige came in for Gene Ramey.

'In Walked Bud', a particularly jaunty line based around Irving Berlin's 'Blue Skies', is rather blearily voiced by the horns, but Monk's peppery solo chorus is terrific. 'Monk's Mood' is mood music for an audience too hip to bother with mood music. Taitt and Shihab are required to follow the theme and not depart from Monk's instructions, and their main contribution – particularly Shihab, who might kindly be described as playing in a questionable tonality – is to create a sort of lounge atmosphere, which Monk's brief solo coolly undercuts. This is followed by the unexpectedly hectic 'Who Knows', which was difficult enough to have been attempted several times, although the first take was eventually deemed to be the master – despite Taitt's dreadful solo. But the jewel of the date is Monk's definitive ballad, 'Round Midnight', which had already been recorded by both Cootie Williams and Dizzy Gillespie. The horns again call attention to their own failings, even though they only have to spell out a countermelody, and it's Monk's exacting treatment of the theme and its possible elaborations which is memorable.

Not that everyone at the time found it so. The mysterious 'Tom', who reviewed new records in *Down Beat*'s new release column, had this to say about the single coupling of 'Well You Needn't' and 'Round Midnight':

> The Monk is undoubtedly a man of considerable ability but his abstractions on these sides are just too too [*sic*] – and I played 'em early in the morning and late at night. 'Needn't' doesn't require a Juilliard diploma to understand, but 'Midnight' is for the super hip alone. Why they list the personnel on a side where the whole band plays like a vibratoless organ under the piano is a mystery.

Quite a hip review, actually, confirmed by his judgements on two other Blue

Note 78s in the review pile: on four Sidney Bechet titles, Tom said: 'For that coterie of Dixie cats who love their two-beat pure and their Bechet throaty, this is just a couple of spits this side of the end.' And on an Ike Quebec coupling: 'It's practically bopless – not a descending minor seventh in sight.'[3]

In a way, the first three dates are all flawed masterworks: although Monk himself sounded crystal clear about how he wanted the music to be played, the inadequacies of his sidemen are exasperating. His reported rebuff to a complaint by Sahib Shihab – 'You a musician? You got a union card? Then play it!' – is the response of a tyrant, but having worked at his ideas for so long, he was entitled to his supremacy. No modern session would allow the presence of such barely competent players as Danny West and George Taitt, but in a sense their lack of individuality throws Monk's own playing into an even sharper relief. By the time of the Blue Note sessions, he had already distilled a difficult style. Mary Lou Williams, another distinguished jazz pianist, had heard him many years earlier: 'Thelonious, still in his teens, came into town with either an evangelist or a medicine show. While Monk was in Kaycee, he jammed every night, really used to blow on piano, employing a lot more technique than he does today. Monk plays the way he does now because he got fed up.'[4]

Alfred Lion finally began releasing the results of these sessions as ten-inch 78s after the third date, but the sales were not enough to set any world on fire. Monk's music had little of the explosive excitement of Parker and Gillespie. He was barely known outside New York's club environment. In his apartment on West 63rd Street, he would hold court with fellow players, and he was always generous with his musical wisdom. But he was rarely approached as an interviewee. Lion could hardly have chosen a more intractable character to launch his label's courting of the bebop audience.

History's consolation is that the music was magnificent, and immutably *sui generis*. On 2 July 1948, Lion recorded six further titles under Monk's leadership, with another new line-up. Bassist John Simmons and drummer Shadow Wilson played well enough, but it was the presence of vibraphonist Milt Jackson which really elevated the date (Blue Note would, in fact, reissue some of these tracks under Jackson's name when they released an album under the nominal leadership of the vibes player). Like Blakey, Jackson seemed to come to an immediate understanding of Monk's intentions, and he played some of his favourite Monk tunes for the rest of his long life. Jackson's work in this situation was a prelude to the enormous body of material he set down within the confines of the Modern Jazz Quartet, and it is tempting to surmise that, as an improviser, he did much of his best work when another musician was setting the context. But Jackson and Monk shared a similarly dry sense of humour, and perhaps Bags simply found his pianist's company particularly congenial.

Either way, the session begins rather less than ideally by opening with two ballad features for the vocalist Kenny Hagood. The singer had already worked with Monk in the context of Dizzy Gillespie's big band, and though his Eckstine-lite singing is not without appeal, it makes a jazz listener impatient to hear Jackson and Monk doing some intriguing business behind him on both 'All the Things You Are' and 'I Should Care'. But the four succeeding pieces are ample compensation. 'Evidence' was to become one of Monk's most familiar tunes, but the melody of this extrapolation from 'Just You, Just Me' is barely even mentioned in this tautly ingenious reading, which has a masterful piano improvisation at its heart. The almost contrapuntal interplay between piano and vibes which follows is made all the more compelling by the smooth momentum offered up by bass and drums - an act of righting which Monk's rhythm sections would be asked to provide for most of his career. All told, 'Evidence' only just breaks the two-and-a-half minute barrier, yet it is packed with detail.

'Misterioso' is perhaps even better. The theme is a cycle of parallel sixth chords, resembling a restless pacing up and down, and it's ingeniously elaborated on by both Jackson and Monk in their solos (in a briefer alternate take, Monk took one chorus less for himself). Jackson's solo is so fine, on each take, that one wonders why this most elegant and thoughtful of players is still comparatively remote on many commentators' lists of the best jazz improvisers. Jackson loved the blues underpinnings of Monk's music, and he never shirked the implicit connection. 'Epistrophy' had been previously recorded by Cootie Williams, and its dominant three-note riff has a characteristic bebop genealogy, turning up elsewhere and generally acting as a kind of tonic note in many bop structures. Although there are 'solos' by both vibes and piano, the entire three minutes is more like a duet, a constantly evolving interchange, between Monk and Jackson. 'I Mean You' is one of the composer's most boisterous pieces, and this almost respectful treatment lays its scheme carefully open, with the odd little coda at the end of the theme chorus intact. As with all these Blue Note sides, where Monk was setting down most of this music for the first time, the material seems both fresh and finished, its peculiarities – which have since become eroded by their constant use in the jazz repertory – intense and vibrant.

That was, however, the end of Monk's Blue Note duties for nearly three years. Lion had enough for a dozen 78s, had he so wished, but the market for them proved initially to be relatively cool. Blue Note's bop-recording dates actually numbered only eleven by the end of 1949. Besides Monk, the other leaders were scarcely minor figures: Art Blakey, Tadd Dameron, Howard McGhee, Fats Navarro, James Moody, Bud Powell. Yet most of them gathered more of a reputation among musicians than they did among the listening public. Blakey's first date, four titles in December 1947, was a relatively undistinguished quickie. Saxophonist Moody's two sessions, by James Moody And His Bop Men, were a mixture of assembly-line bop of the order of 'Moodamorphosis' and a nod towards the Afro-Cuban tinge then under way in the work of Dizzy Gillespie (Moody was at the time a regular Gillespie sideman). For the second, they even imported Gillespie's excitable percussionist-vocalist Chano Pozo for the band favourite 'Tin Tin Deo'.

The titles involving Dameron and Navarro, though, were of a higher order. Tadd Dameron counts as one of the more star-crossed figures in jazz, surviving bop's most iniquitous temptations (unlike Navarro) but losing his way in the fifties and hardly building on the promise of his earlier compositions. He wrote all eight of the originals set down at the two sessions with Navarro, and several of the tunes – 'Our Delight', 'Dameronia', 'Lady Bird' – are superb rationalisations of the bebop idiom within a composer's rigour. Dameron already had years of experience behind him, having been working as an arranger for Harlan Leonard in the late thirties, and subsequently for Gillespie. His two key sessions for Blue Note were recorded almost exactly a year apart – September 1947 and September 1948 – but both feature Navarro as principal soloist, the second taking place during a period when Dameron was leading the house band at the important 52nd Street club, the Royal Roost. Dameron's music wasn't something that sprang out of bop: while it is hard to date these compositions, several of them may have gone back several years, perhaps to a pre-bop situation. Certainly, it's possible to hear the voicings of such as 'Our Delight' in the ranks of one of the more progressive swing orchestras, and Dameron's gift for writing melodious lines set him apart from much of bop's abstraction.

When coupled with Navarro's electrifying playing, the results are heady indeed. Like Clifford Brown after him, Navarro lived too briefly (he died in 1949, ruined by both tuberculosis and heroin) and left a short but overpowering legacy. The four titles made at what was really Blue Note's first genuine bebop date have spirited contributions from all hands, but it's Navarro's solos which stay in the mind. Made three days after his twenty-fourth birthday, they show his precocity as a horn player – quick, ebullient, daredevil – yet suggest that he had a surprising maturity on his side too. The solos on 'The Squirrel' and 'Our Delight' are mercurial and dazzling, but clever in their balancing of excitement and logic; and listening to the alternate takes of each title suggests that, if he didn't exactly rely on a routine, Navarro had a plan in mind before he started his improvisation. 'I'd just like to play a perfect melody of my own, all the chord progressions right, the melody original and fresh – my own.'[5]

For the second date, Dameron assembled his outstanding Royal Roost band, with Navarro, tenor saxophonist Allen Eager and drummer Kenny Clarke, along with a guest in the shape of the swing-to-bop saxophonist Wardell Gray. Although Dameron's sessions are rather better remembered for Navarro's contributions, and often take second place in discussions to Navarro's later sessions with Howard McGhee, the music here is outstanding. 'Jahbero' is a Latinised theme, abetted by an appearance from conga player Chino (brother of Chano) Pozo. Navarro's solo bursts excitingly out of the crisp, mid-tempo setting. On 'Lady Bird' and 'Symphonette', with the tempos again not too demanding, the trumpeter is measured and skilful. There's a studious quality in his playing to go with the fireworks expected in bebop. Eager and Gray are no slouches, but their playing seems more facile, and Gray especially seems an inappropriately lazy partner to the trumpeter.

The session by the McGhee-Navarro Boptet was cut on 11 October 1948. Although there is an almost-novelty element to the two-trumpet front line, an instrumentation which has often been resolved into mere acrobatics in post-swing small groups, the pyrotechnics are actually quite contained, and driven by the adeptness of the two players. 'Boperation' is a typically convoluted bebop line which the trumpets swoop through, and is perhaps the least convincing thing on the date, but the two takes of 'Double Talk', each split over two sides of a ten-inch 78 for release, are superbly buoyant. The two horns amiably run rings round each other, especially in three choruses where they execute sixteen-, eight- and four-bar trades as the climax of what was effectively Part Two. If Navarro probably tops McGhee (they had earlier worked together in the brass section of the Andy Kirk Band), there's little in it, a spirited but basically friendly fracas.

These were good-humoured dates, and for all their various felicities they perhaps missed the crackling intensity of Monk's sessions. If Blue Note was proving valuable as a documentary resource for bop, the label was still finding its feet as an important source. But the last bop session of the decade, made on 6 August 1949, ushered in another major figure, Bud Powell.

Powell had already recorded as a leader for two other small labels, Roost and Clef – and with a group called the Be Bop Boys, for Savoy – before Lion brought him into the WOR Studios, where Blue Note did much of its recording. Lion enlisted Navarro and a nineteen-year-old tenor saxophonist, Sonny Rollins, as the front line, with Tommy Potter on bass and Roy Haynes on drums, and the group was noted on the Blue Note labels as Bud Powell's Modernists. Where Monk's bebop was always elliptical, Powell's was headlong. Though very different stylists, the two men held a strong mutual respect, and it was Monk who encouraged Powell early on. By the time he came to make his Blue Note debut, he had long been regarded as one of the masters of the 52nd Street scene, but his personal history was particularly troubled: hospitalised after a beating in 1945, he subsequently underwent ECT and for much of the rest of his life was troubled by mental problems (it has recently been suggested that he may have become epileptic, though if so it was never formally diagnosed). Powell's music teems with activity, his right hand at times seeming to explode off the keyboard, his close kinship with drummers emphasising his percussive delivery, while his clear thinking at high speed and the often lovely melodies he spun countermand any sense that he is running ragged. The four quintet titles are multifarious. 'Bouncing With Bud', a remote derivation of 'I Got Rhythm', is a harsh jog. 'Wail' is helter-skelter, the soloists flying. 'Dance Of The Infidels' is one of his most particular melodies, beautifully set up for the horns, with Powell's own solo a marvel. He then nods towards Monk by covering that composer's '52nd Street Theme', with an urgent Rollins followed by Navarro at his most immaculate and Powell himself, tearing impetuously through the changes and coming up without a stagger.

Roy Haynes was a splendid choice for the drummer on the date, and throughout these titles one can hear his mastery as both a percussionist, rattling and sounding out every part of his kit, and a provider of propulsion. But the two trio titles are in comparison almost gentle performances, with a plush reading of 'You Go To My Head' and two takes of 'Ornithology', the bop standard credited to Benny Harris. The tempo of the latter isn't actually all that fast, but it's sent skywards by Powell's quicksilver right hand. While his touch is light, contributing to the atmosphere of reflection, the detail in his long lines can intoxicate, if the listener follows closely. Speed wasn't the exclusive preserve of the bop musicians: Oscar Peterson was about to emerge as an exceptional technician. And Art Tatum had long been setting Olympian standards in jazz pianism. But Powell's mix of abstract urgency and an almost poignant lyricism was something daring and new.

He didn't, though, record again for Blue Note for almost two years. While Monk had his share of eccentricities, Powell was a deeply disturbed man, and unlikely ever to manage a rational recording career. In any case, it was not as if Blue Note had gone over entirely to bebop. During the same period, Lion and Wolff carried on recording music in the older style with which they had commenced operations.

Their main subject was Sidney Bechet. Out of all the jazz musicians who unequivocally belong in the first division of the music, Bechet remains the most neglected, the most difficult to focus on. He evades any easy classification. He set down the evidence of his being a master improviser even before Louis Armstrong, in the early twenties, and their occasional recordings together suggest that there is no clear case for either man being the superior musician. Although he recorded prolifically, there is no single block of recordings which scholars hold up as his masterworks. He played an instrument, the soprano saxophone, which few other musicians would even attempt to master, and his ingenuity went hand in hand with a sometimes furious insistence on his own premiership in whatever group he was playing in. He made few attempts to move directly with the times, playing Dixieland material up till the end of his life, but his interests were far from narrow: he even wrote a score for a ballet, *La Nuit Est Une Sorcière*, and an operetta. He spent many years away from America, restlessly wandering around Europe and ultimately settling in Paris for much of his last decade, but nearly all his best records were made for American labels.

Blue Note caught some of the best of Bechet, but whereas the label was accustomed to bringing out the best in its performers, Bechet seems to have been less accommodating. In all, he fronted ten sessions for the label over a span of thirteen years, which makes him one of the longest-serving artists for the company. His first date, four titles in March 1940, and the last, dating from August 1953, show little change in his style or approach: if he felt like giving his best, he did, but there are often times when his mind seems to be on matters other than the one in hand, a trait which may say something about his elusiveness as an artist.

On 10 March 1945, for instance, he cut a date with his old New Orleans colleague Bunk Johnson, then enjoying a halcyon spell as a revivalist figurehead. Playing clarinet, Bechet rather politely subdues himself next to the wayward Johnson, and on 'Milenberg Joys' and 'Days Beyond Recall' he only forces his issues when Johnson stops playing.

Bechet's last dates for Blue Note were made on two of his return visits from France, in November 1951 and August 1953. Still in the company of traditionalists such as Sidney De Paris, Jimmy Archey and Pops Foster (although the stylish swing trumpeter Jonah Jones is on the second date), Bechet blows with undimmed vigour, even if some of the combativeness has gone out of his playing. Compared to the sessions of the forties, which survive only as disc masters, these sessions have a rather cleaner, sweeter timbre, even if Bechet's soprano - like Charlie Parker's alto, on his many low-to-mid-fi survivals - tends to scythe through in the most piercing way. His fellow bandsmen are capable journeymen and each has his moment - De Paris on 'Original Dixieland One-Step', say, or Jonah Jones on 'Sweet Georgia Brown' - but Bechet's personality is enormous, even when playing at a lower throttle. On the second date in particular, he is an imperious orator, dirtying his tone on 'Sweet Georgia Brown' just to remind everyone how clean it is the rest of the time. An alternative take of 'Black And Blue' exhibits a startling and luxuriant revision of the melody that Sonny Rollins might have admired. When this date went into Blue Note's inventory, they had virtually made their break with his kind of jazz, but Bechet's grand individuality honoured Lion's old betrothal to hot music.

As the forties came to an end, Lion and Wolff were facing up to one of the ever-present problems of a small business: how to grow, without overreaching their resources. Blue Note's catalogue had grown to some significance, but they still had little to show for the label's efforts beyond a small coterie of fans – divided, in all probability, by the dichotomy between the label's original jazz recordings and its bop-inclined material. But a new issue was about to prove critical for every record company in America: formats. Although shellac-based 78 rpm discs had been the industry standard for close on fifty years, the inherent problems in the old-fashioned medium were obvious. The discs were fragile and susceptible to terminal damage; the hissing surfaces interfered with any notion of true high fidelity; the restricted playing time called for contained performances, although some might say that that restraint was no bad thing. The American industry had been working on a new medium, which had come about through the development of plastics. Instead of the old, coarse-grained shellac, a compound of PVC, which came to be called vinyl, offered a tough, virtually unbreakable disc which was nevertheless able to store more grooves and more sound frequencies than the old medium. Where 78s managed some forty grooves per centimetre, the new 'microgroove' discs could fit almost a hundred. Coupled with a much slower speed of revolution (the industry quickly fixed a new standard of 33⅓ rpm), the new discs suddenly sounded cleaner and fuller, and played – in the case of a twelve-inch record – much longer. So much so, that the discs soon became known as LPs – long-players – a sobriquet which exists to this day.

The major record companies initially had the new medium in mind for classical music. One famous publicity shot of the period showed a record executive with an armful of classical LPs, standing next to a leaning tower of 78s which comprised the same amount of music as he was carrying. But jazz was the first music to be profoundly affected by microgroove discs. As the format became the new standard, jazz studio performances began to change – solos became longer, the music grew more expansive. Although RCA Victor introduced a smaller microgroove disc, seven inches in diameter, in 1949, this was the format that would be ideal for the forthcoming charge of rock'n'roll, rather than jazz. As 'singles' replaced 78s, they became the preserve of singers.

There was another important change in industry practice: the use of tape over disc masters. After many tears of experimentation, a viable magnetic recording tape had been developed by the end of the war, and in 1947 Ampex were manufacturing tape-recording machines for studio use in the US. While Blue Note were still using disc masters in 1949, they were among the last, and by 1950 magnetic tape – with its ease of editing, storage advantages and cleaner sound – was virtually standard within the industry. Along with the new microgroove discs, it ushered in a new era of hi-fi.

The problem for Lion and Wolff was that it was also bringing about a new set of costs. Producing 78s in plain sleeves was cheap. But the start-up costs of the new idiom brought in a whole extra set of charges. There were covers to print and design, sleeve notes to write, photographs to develop. Although the mighty Columbia corporation fanfared its first long-playing records in 1948, Blue Note did not follow suit, releasing nothing on microgroove until 1951.

It was hardly a case of clinging on in the face of the march of technology, though. Just as it would later take many years for compact discs to supersede vinyl as the sound carrier of choice, so 78s outfaced their new competitors for a long time. For one thing, the new idiom was not yet the sonic revelation which the industry was trumpeting. Anyone who's played an early vinyl pressing next to its shellac equivalent will know how much bigger and stronger the 78 will usually sound, and with improvements in those pressings too, the old format was far from automatically dead. But even the surface sophistication of the long-players made a strong appeal to a generation of more affluent, more adventurous consumers; and the new format seemed ideally tailored to bop, which aspired to modern art as well as musical entertainment.

Nevertheless, the cost factor alone was enough to deter Blue Note at first. Its independent-label competitors, however, were more ready to take the plunge. Dial released *The Bird Blows The Blues*, Dial LP-1, in 1949, although it was at first advertised only in trade papers. Savoy put out its own ten-inch album of Charlie Parker material in 1950, and there was an important new outfit which began in 1949: Prestige, and its sister label New Jazz, which the entrepreneur and producer Bob Weinstock founded. It was surely only a matter of time before Blue Note followed suit; but the hard-working Lion and Wolff were more concerned about keeping the label as an active entity.

There had been another recording ban during 1948, instigated by the AFM and commencing on 1 January, but it had no real impact on Blue Note and only a lesser one on jazz itself, which continued its march away from big bands and a move towards small groups, either in the bop idiom or outside it. By 1950, bebop itself had been around long enough to have lost any sense of outrage that it may once have inculcated: Charlie Parker was recording with strings, and Dizzy Gillespie was making records such as 'You Stole My Wife You Horsethief'. In the first year of the new decade, Blue Note cut only two record sessions, a date with Sidney Bechet, and six titles by a Howard McGhee group including trombonist J. J. Johnson and tenor saxophonist Brew Moore. But the next few years would see the company reach a real stature as a force in contemporary jazz.

THREE

From their Lexington Avenue base, Lion and Wolff continued the slow process of turning Blue Note into a competitive modern label. Lion's life was given over entirely to his work: his marriage to Lorraine had foundered, and he now lived in a small place in Englewood, New Jersey. In 1951, they finally released their first vinyl issues, ten-inch LPs which were initiated as two distinct series. First, they commenced a Dixieland series with BLP-7001, which reissued tracks from Sidney Bechet sessions of 1949 and 1950. The companion series was headed 'Modern Jazz', and began, somewhat incongruously, with the not-so-modern music from the Ike Quebec, John Hardee and Benny Morton sessions of the mid-forties. In an amazing piece of prescience, that first LP was given the overall title *Mellow The Mood – Jazz In A Mellow Mood*, which – however unwittingly – anticipated the almost obsessive marketing of jazz as a 'mood music' in the 1980s and 1990s.

Their second 'modern' ten-inch, though, was far more important: it coupled eight tracks from Thelonious Monk's first three sessions, under the rubric *Thelonious Monk – Genius Of Modern Music*. The notion of marketing bop as art music was something which had gathered pace over the previous few years, as it became clear that bop was itself dissipating the popular audience for jazz. Words like 'genius' had long since been bandied around in reference to Charlie Parker. But Lion and Wolff, taking a view on the likelihood of selling Thelonious Monk to an unhip audience, decided to make every idiosyncrasy in their pianist's make-up into an enigmatic virtue. A press release which accompanied one Monk release described him as 'the genius behind the whole movement [of bebop]' and 'a strange person whose pianistics continue to baffle all who hear him'.[1] What Monk himself thought of this odd mix of hubris and deliberate obfuscation is not recorded. Either way, the gathering of several of these records into a single LP package underscored the impact of Monk's music: it was as modern as jazz was going to get at that time, and the opportunity to study it across the luxurious spread of eight tracks on a single disc conferred its own kind of importance.

Still, it was to be Bud Powell who fulfilled Blue Note's first new recording session for almost a year, on 1 May 1951. Although Powell's trio produced five different titles, two alternative takes of 'Un Poco Loco' were, unusually, added to the first twelve-inch LP release of the tracks (*The Amazing Bud Powell: Vol. 1*, BLP 1503) – a rare occurrence on original Blue Note albums. Listening to the three versions of the tune, they seem, though, like an inseparable triptych, with Max Roach's percussion part, centred around a clangorous cowbell line, evolving inexorably across the takes. Bassist Curley Russell and Roach had, at this point, already recorded frequently with Powell, and though Russell's bass parts are really no more than functional, one can only wonder how much more this trio might have achieved had they worked and recorded even more consistently. Powell's theme statement is almost too difficult – the little right-hand figure which caps each turnback is a finger-busting piece of pianism which even Powell doesn't execute consistently. In the improvisatory heart of each take, the pianist finds strange outbursts of sound, which are a hair-raising contrast to Roach's relentless cowbell (recorded in an almost ear-splitting treble). 'A Night In Tunisia', a great bebop anthem established several years earlier, gets a fittingly extravagant rendition. Powell was an early exponent of singalong piano, groaning a long, wordless counterpoint to what his fingers were playing, but where that became a trait of everyday ecstasy in the work of Keith Jarrett, decades later, it seems to signify a real turmoil in Powell's work. Compared to the trio tracks, two solos, 'Over The Rainbow' and 'It Could Happen To You', are quiescent, but the voicings of both melodies and the rhythmic liberties which Powell almost uncaringly takes with the tunes are peculiarly disturbing: listen to how he suspends the alternative take of 'It Could Happen To You' in limbo at its close. Yet the following tract, 'Parisian Thoroughfare', suggests a different side to Powell. It's a tribute to his imagination that the melody is an irresistible evocation of the city, even though the composer was not to settle there for several years hence.

Alfred Lion knew only too well that Powell was a difficult proposition as a recording artist. Lion, with his usual dedication, had taken to following as many appearances of his bebop favourites as possible, and having observed Powell's behaviour at close quarters, he was well aware of Bud's unpredictability. The night before the 1951 date, Lion asked Powell to stay over with him at his apartment in Englewood, to keep an eye on him if nothing else. Over breakfast on the morning of the date, Lion's cat jumped on the table and Powell 'went crazy, absolutely crazy. He took a big knife from the table and tried to kill the cat.'[2] On the drive to the Manhattan recording studio, Powell insisted that they stop at a doctor's office, only to find a waiting room with fifteen people in there. Lion persuaded Powell that they had to make the date, and eventually they arrived at WOR Studios. While Roach was setting up his kit, Powell vanished into the men's room. After ten minutes, he had failed to reappear, and when

Roach checked, he found Powell had disappeared. Lion asked the others to wait. An hour and a half went slowly by, and then Powell suddenly charged into the studio and sat down at the piano – 'OK, we're ready, let's go!' From there, they flew through the session.

It was to be Powell's last studio date for more than two years. He subsequently spent seventeen months in an institution and the only surviving music from this period consists of unauthorised airshots. Although Lion would record him again in 1953, it's arguable that his greatest music was already behind him.

At almost the same moment, Blue Note's other piano master, Thelonious Monk, ran into trouble with the law, allegedly taking the blame for a friend in a drug-possession incident, which led to his losing the cabaret card which he needed to work in New York clubs. Effectively barred from the live scene until 1957, Monk had the consolation of recording: but he actually led only two further sessions for Blue Note, since he was to be signed by the rival independent, Prestige, in 1952. The first was cut on 23 July 1951, and it featured a quintet of Monk, Sahib Shihab, Milt Jackson, Art Blakey and the bassist Al McKibbon. Five originals and one standard ('Willow Weep For Me') make up the results. Even with the several earlier sessions full of extraordinary music, this one is outstanding – so much so that it is tempting to set it alongside certain other occasions, from different eras in the music, as examples of how jazz has been perfectly caught and celebrated by recording microphones. One of the paradoxes in jazz's unruly history is that for all its dependence on spontaneity and in-person creativity, its most resonant influence has been through the medium of surviving records.

Here, for instance, is one of the most bountiful three minutes in modern music, the master take of 'Criss Cross'. The melody is, in its first measures, a kind of muttered aside, before the ringing notes which follow as a response.

It's all set over a pacing 4/4 beat which the superb Blakey (and McKibbon, who cleverly uses pedal points in his accompaniment) refuses to lose sight of. One of the reasons Monk's own recordings endure so well is that his finest collaborators are unfazed by his supposed eccentricities, and approach them accordingly. Shihab, who sounds like a different man next to the hesitant figure of the 1948 date, plays a melodious solo and the glittering Jackson steps through the minefield without faltering. Clear and open but profoundly mysterious, it's a paradigm of Monk's jazz.

The difficult, skipping 'Four In One' is one of the composer's most labyrinthine melodies. 'Eronel', which sounds more like a conventional, if slightly askew bop line (its original authorship is somewhat disputed), is crisply delivered by the group, and illuminated from within by Monk's solo. 'Straight No Chaser' reworks the blues. Monk states the melody by himself, every figure just slightly soured by dissonance, before Shihab and Jackson join him, then a piano solo economises the blues essence still further, ending on a mischievous quote from the composer's own 'Misterioso'. Shihab and Jackson sit out the trio number 'Ask Me Now', which was remade since the first take was too long for a ten-inch 78. Then Jackson returns for 'Willow Weep For Me', and the tune really belongs to him, turning in a chorus and a half that underlines how much blues feeling this master improviser could inject into any quality popular tune. It was astute husbandry on Lion's behalf to get so much out of a single date. There are four hardcore Monk originals, each a connoisseur's delight, but the relatively straightforward lyricism of 'Ask Me Now' and Jackson's feature would satisfy any producer's desire to get a couple of 'easy' pieces out of the occasion too.

Monk's final date was cut a year later, on 30 May 1952, and is perhaps the least familiar of all his Blue Note appearances. Only four of the six titles emerged at the time, the front line of Kenny Dorham, Lou Donaldson and Lucky Thompson added conventional bebop weight to the ensemble, and Max Roach's fast, chippy rhythms tend to push past any idiosyncrasies which the pianist might have been tempted to essay. But the originals are still a remarkable lot: the knotty 'Hornin' In' and 'Skippy' are another pair of Monk themes that suggest the composer at his most algebraic, but 'Let's Cool One' encapsulates the moody soliloquising of cool jazz in a single piece, and 'Sixteen' (not actually issued until the 1980s) is one of his oddest pieces, setting the most cryptic of melodies against a much-used chord sequence. The most shocking thing on the date was the interpretation of the Davies–Burke standard 'Carolina Moon'. Monk seems to be trying to play it as a waltz, while the horns spell out the melody in broken-up blocks and Roach plays the theme choruses at either end of the performance in a furious double time. As ever, Monk's own brief solo – more a break, really – at the end of the sequence of improvisations seems to right a lopsided vessel. Lastly came another standard tune, Turk–Ahlert's 'I'll Follow You', played without the horns, an almost ordinary piano-trio piece. If Lion felt that this was his pop side safely in the can, he must have changed his mind later, since this was another master that stayed unissued until the 1980s.

As a body of work, Monk's Blue Notes might feasibly stand alongside Louis Armstrong's Okehs or, perhaps more pertinently, Charlie Parker's Savoys. It is not timeless music, because it does sound very much of its period – an extrapolation of bebop and the early days of that music's successor, hard bop, yet done by a man who resisted any kind of particularisation. These original Monks still, for the most part, sound like the most effective interpretations of themes which have become some of the most overworked materials in jazz. Yet they were not making Blue Note's fortune.

Lion had a fan's admiration for Monk. But with the pianist soon to be barely visible on the New York scene, and with his imminent move to Prestige Records, he was hardly the kind of property that would have financed the rest of the label's operations. The final session made no appearance on vinyl until 1956, and though the two ten-inch volumes of *Genius Of Modern Music* were in the racks, they had only a modest impact outside the immediate community of Monk's admirers.

Blue Note were having difficulties getting any kind of hit. Jukeboxes with black music – whether R&B or jazz – wouldn't have rung up too many plays for a Thelonious Monk 78. Something as old-fashioned as a Sidney Bechet session would have fared better in that situation. But Lion began to address that problem. They are not much remembered, but two important early sessions were those cut by Wynton Kelly, a pianist from Brooklyn (though originally born in Jamaica), with Oscar Pettiford on bass – replaced by Franklin Skeete on the second date – and Lee Abrams on drums. Kelly was still only nineteen, and had been working as accompanist to Dinah Washington, but he had some important engagements ahead of him – a stint with Miles Davis in the early sixties is what he's best remembered for. These early sessions, though cast in a somewhat utilitarian style, may surprise many for their inventiveness and lack of routine. The Latinised feel of 'Where Or When', the dramatic intro to 'Moonglow', the freewheeling delicacy of Al Haig's 'Opus Caprice': these are modestly spoken pieces, as was Kelly's wont, but the young man had beautiful poise at the keyboard. He often sounds like a Bud Powell reborn as a model citizen.

This style of piano trio was starting to become a central part of the jazz-recording regimen. Previously, the guitar substituted for either bass or drums in a piano-based threesome, but improved recording techniques enabled any potential muddiness to be sidestepped, and the piano-bass-drums trinity began to sound and feel like something integral to modern jazz – not only in the high-end bop recordings of Powell and Monk, but in the less ambitious styles of a more deferential player such as Kelly. In the end, Kelly made only two sessions for Blue Note, and Lion squeezed three 78s and a single ten-inch LP out of them. Yet they clearly hint at what was soon to emerge in Horace Silver's recordings, and, a decade later, those of the Three Sounds, all of which would be crucial to Blue Note's business.

Kelly's ten-inch album was BLP 5025, *New Faces – New Styles: Piano Interpretations By Wynton Kelly*, and was one of a string of titles which went under that general heading, 'Blue Note's Modern Jazz' series. The cover art for Kelly's album featured a small photograph of the pianist, just slightly upper-left-of-centre, framed in a protoplasmic two-colour dreamscape with a melting staircase and a bare-branched tree. It was a design by Gil Melle, himself a saxophonist, and a fellow Blue Note artist.

Gil Melle is among the more picaresque characters jazz has encountered. Born in New Jersey on New Year's Eve, 1931, Melle became an archetypal Greenwich Village bohemian when he was still in his teens, playing saxophone, painting and composing in a style which he came to describe as 'primitive modern'. Having enlisted in the Marine Corps at sixteen, after lying about his age, he started playing saxophone in what he described as 'countless gin joints'.[3] He had put together a huge collection of Duke Ellington records as a boy, mostly from second-hand sources, and at thirteen was captivated by the music of Thelonious Monk. Lion heard Melle at one of his gigs, and it led to no less than four ten-inch LPs for the label. Melle was perhaps more interested in ensemble direction and composition than improvising, and he was a capable but less than riveting soloist. Ironically, he made probably his most interesting music for Prestige later in the decade, with the excellent *Primitive Modern*, *Quadrama* and *Gil's Guests* albums.

Melle did, though, prove to be of enormous importance to Blue Note. He was one of three graphic artists who began to design covers for the ten-inch LP series. Although the 78 format had already accommodated the 'album' idea for many years, the art of cover design was very much in its infancy. Previously, a number of 78s had been jacketed together into what was literally a bound album - rather like a scrapbook - of individual discs, with a suitable cover picture. But the advent of individual microgrooves called for an entirely new aesthetic, where records would be racked for browsing in stores, and the old uniform appearance of plain-sleeved 78s would eventually disappear.

If the industry had been prepared for this new design opportunity, the evidence would have been more impressive. As it was, until well into the 1950s most companies issued their LPs in the most functional of jackets. The majority of covers - in whatever genre - were at first a simple variation on typography. But Blue Note, as late as they were in entering the microgroove arena, decided to follow a more adventurous route.

Lion and Wolff were patrons of their arts as well as record businessmen. In the 1940s, their trade advertising in *Down Beat*, the leading American jazz magazine, and their give-away flyers, sometimes suggested the feel of the great Bauhaus school of design. 'Industrial' blocks of type were a simplistic but effective means of demonstrating what they were selling, with 'Blue Note' always the huge, predominant phrase. For their first series of ten-inch sleeves, the company employed three designers to establish the look. Besides Melle, whose designs were the most fanciful, they had John Hermansader and Paul Bacon. Each employed 'interesting' typography, or simply fanciful design: for all the subsequent suggestion that Blue Note was blazing a trail in jazz design from the first, though, the ten-inch covers actually offer little evidence of any coherent strategy. The unifying factor was, rather, a separate ingredient: the photography of Frank Wolff.

Wolff's passion for taking pictures had never left him. From the earliest Blue Note dates, he had had his camera with him, and his penchant for the medium was if anything strengthened by the opportunities which the recording sessions offered. Most jazz-studio photography had hitherto been based around posed pictures of groups in performance or of formal line-ups for publicity purposes. Wolff sought to take truthful and unpremeditated photographs, more for himself than for any commercial use (this was all some time before LP sleeves began to appear).

What was extraordinary about Wolff's black-and-white photography, aside from the candour which seems to lie in the expressions of every musician, is its sensitivity to light and dark. This is actually rather difficult to divine from the many pictures which adorn both the front and back of so many of Blue Note's ten- and subsequently twelve-inch album covers. Indifferent printing on relatively poor-quality, paper-covered cardboard jackets offers an image which is usually several generations away from Wolff's original in terms of its visual impression. It was probably not until the publication of *The Blue Note Years: The Jazz Photography Of Francis Wolff* in 1995 that the breathtaking depth of Wolff's pictures became obvious to all.

Recording studios tend to exist in a kind of twilight world. Deprived of natural light and ruled by a clock which pays no particular attention to day or night, the studio environment often has the eerie feel of a separate universe, a place remote from regular time. For many musicians, studios can have an almost narcotic attraction, with their ability to reshape and remodel sound. It is a contemporary trend for any musician who can afford it to build a studio for themselves. In the curious antechamber of the recording room itself, a performer can feel completely alone, yet constantly aware that their every action is being monitored. The modern studio, with its starship's worth of technology, can seem a cool, neutral place, but even in the studios of the forties and fifties the mix of quiet, dark and confinement could make for a tense cocktail, intimidating for anyone new to the setting.

Wolff's photography, which only rarely steps away from the studio, catches that atmosphere at least as well as it memorialises the musicians. The players sit on stools, at keyboards, singly or in twos and threes; listening intently, or playing, or sharing a laugh. They seem to emerge from complete darkness: only occasionally can one glimpse a background wall, or the slats of a blind. Beautiful faces and expressive eyes and mouths dominate the frames. Saxophones glint like polished weapons; trumpets and trombones muster a metallic shine. Whether in repose or in full-on motion, each man has a meditative stillness imposed on him. Curls of cigarette smoke, a trait which dominates so much 'classic' jazz photography, are often there, but while such atmospherics play their part, Wolff is uncannily sensitive to the human beings in each shot.

At first, Wolff's photography was used only sparingly in both advertising and on record sleeves. The dictates of design came first, and artists' names, tune titles and whatever else jockeyed for position on the front of an album jacket. In the context of Melle's peculiar design for the Wynton Kelly album, Wolff's photo of the pianist – eyes almost closed, mouth open in an appreciative smile – is an oasis of calm.

Melle's importance to Blue Note was, however, not limited to what he could bring to the company as either saxophonist or designer. He also introduced Alfred Lion to the man who would become the next most important contributor to Blue Note's identity. Hitherto, nearly all of Blue Note's recordings from the late forties and early fifties had been set down in the WOR Studios in Manhattan, usually under the supervision of engineer Doug Hawkins. During the period of transition between metal and tape masters, Blue Note's fidelity was about as good as could be expected - no better or worse, really, than most of their independent colleagues. While there's a dustiness about many of the late forties dates, the pressing and mastering conditions were at least as responsible for that as was the original engineering. With the advent of tape masters, the issues of room acoustic and microphone placement became rather more sensitive than they had been, especially for the kind of small-group, interactive music which Blue Note specialised in.

Rudy Van Gelder typified both a new generation of sound engineers who would accompany the march of microgroove technology, and a determined spirit and believer in excellence for its own sake that made him kindred to Lion, Wolff and their company philosophy. A former radio ham and someone with a technology bug, the young engineer was by profession an optometrist. He had a little practice in Teaneck, New Jersey, but lived in nearby Hackensack. And he was a jazz fan. Melle had made his acquaintance and had discovered that the professional Van Gelder had set up what was effectively a little recording studio in his living room. Van Gelder remembers:

> He [Melle] had a nice little band, and came to me through this other label, I think it was Progressive Records. Alfred acquired that record, he bought it and released that on Blue Note as a ten-inch LP, and then he wanted to make another one. At that time, Alfred was going to a studio in New York which was incidentally also a radio studio, WOR Studios, and they had a business of making their recording facilities available. So, that's where Alfred went and he took that album to the engineer

there and he said, 'I want it to sound like this.' So the engineer listened to it and told Alfred, 'Look, I can't make it sound like that, you better go to the guy that did it.'[4]

Melle himself remembers it slightly differently: 'Alfred was very reluctant to meet Rudy Van Gelder. He went out there, looked around, and Rudy played some things for him, and showed him how it all worked. And Alfred came out and went, "Yah – we do the date here."'[5]

Still, Van Gelder did not take on all of Blue Note's work immediately. During 1952–3, Lion continued to work at WOR Studios, and began to expand his roster of performers. On 7 April 1952, he cut a session with what was soon to be the Modern Jazz Quartet (Milt Jackson, John Lewis, Percy Heath and Kenny Clarke), with alto saxophonist Lou Donaldson added for four titles. Donaldson was another who would figure in the label's 'New Faces – New Sounds' series, and in June the saxophonist cut four titles with Horace Silver, bassist Gene Ramey and drummer Art Taylor. In many ways, Donaldson was the archetypal Blue Note saxophonist. He never felt that jazz developed very far beyond the work of Charlie Parker, an opinion he cheerfully holds to this day, and as a Bird disciple he was a worthy follower. Unfailingly spry and energetic in his playing, he had a tart, cutting tone that found a surprising elegance on ballads, while his affinity with blues playing soaks through most of his work. His book featured a rock-solid choice of standards, blues and jazz tunes that were easy-going enough to appeal to any casual jazz audience. Donaldson was no slouch – his appearance with Monk proved that – but he wasn't one to carry the torch of innovation.

Somewhat unwittingly, Donaldson helped to lift off the career of another Blue Note stalwart. He was booked to record a second quartet session on

9 October, but was unable to get to the studio on the day, and Lion instead asked Horace Silver if he would go ahead and make some titles featuring the trio (Silver, Gene Ramey and Art Blakey) by themselves. Silver had three days' notice, but he still managed to fit in a rehearsal before the date, and the group put down three titles, returning eleven days later to complete five more.

If one artist exemplifies Blue Note's music, it must be Horace Ward Martin Tavares Silver. He was born in Norwalk, Connecticut, in 1928, of a Portuguese father and an American mother. He took up piano at ten – a spinal condition obliged him to give up on his saxophone-playing ambitions – and after deciding to make a go of being a musician, he worked mostly in his local area, especially Hartford. Stan Getz hired him in 1950 – their early recordings for Roost, another jazz independent, are marvellous for their fast, exciting synthesis of the bop and cool languages – and he made his debut and eventually his home in New York. Then he ran into Lou Donaldson, who remembered: 'I used to go to a little studio called Nuby's on 116th Street. You could rent a rehearsal room for fifty cents. Horace and I met there, and we played and got friendly. Both of us were trying to learn how to play bebop. Then we got together with Art Blakey and Gene Ramey and worked up some tunes and got some little gigs here and there.'[6]

At this point, Silver had absorbed an unusually wide range of music. His mother, who sang in church, inveigled gospel music into him. As a teenager, he had listened to a lot of blues records from the thirties and forties, a surprising departure for a young man of the time; and he liked the bands playing on Manhattan's Latin club circuit too. In the fast company of Getz, he had learned how to support a master soloist. At twenty-four, he was just about ready.

Backed by Blakey's explosive playing, Silver's own confident methods make for a tremendous amount of excitement. He uses both hands extensively, his left-side lines adding notes of darkness to the innate bounce that he liked to put into his bass parts. Instead of the sometimes fulsome decoration of bebop piano, Silver preferred a simpler, more open playing in the right hand, with little riffs and figures making playful entries and exits as a solo would progress. He always played percussively, rarely suggesting excessive force on the keys but mustering a crisp and upward sound. Dance rhythms seem to underpin everything he plays. Instead of the helter-skelter forward rush of original bebop, there's a swaying, circular motion to much of Silver's jazz. And he reasserts swing.

He was also starting to write some naggingly memorable themes. 'Horace-Scope', 'Ecaroh', 'Silverware' and especially 'Opus De Funk' are all early instances of the style, dating from his first three trio dates, all with Blakey. Their songful snap was the sign of a new style emerging within Blue Note's house. Lion listened and realised that, while Powell and Monk were the master innovators, Silver was showing how smart, contemporary jazz could be more immediately attractive. While it lacked nothing in profundity, it was earthy enough to fit plausibly alongside R&B records on black jukeboxes, something that one couldn't always say about Powell's music. It wasn't long before Silver was taking the ear of more than one horn-playing leader, particularly Miles Davis: 'he put a fire up under my playing.'[7] Davis, though, didn't use Silver until 1954, after the trumpeter had already set down two sessions for Blue Note.

Perhaps Blue Note were unlucky with Davis. His first date for the label took place on 9 May 1952, right in the middle of what was a desperate year for the trumpeter: he was without a regular band and suffering from a chronic heroin addiction. Lion labelled the session as by the 'Miles Davis All Stars', but with the unremarkable Gil Coggins at the piano and the young and raw Jackie McLean on alto, the appellation was wishful thinking. 'Dear Old Stockholm', the first title, goes off at a lugubrious pace which even Oscar Pettiford and Kenny Clarke seem unable to lift. 'Chance It' is a fast bop line which Davis seems harried by. He turns Dizzy Gillespie's usually ebullient 'Woody 'N' You' into an almost funereal episode, and though the ballad features 'Yesterdays' and 'How Deep Is The Ocean' have some of the cracked melancholy which Davis's admirers set the greatest store by, they're nothing like as good as his comparable playing in his forthcoming Prestige years. For one thing, Davis plays too many notes: the baleful economy which he would later bring to bear on his music is notably absent. As little space as he gets, it's arguably J. J. Johnson's trombone playing which offers the most interesting music.

If Lion was disappointed with these results, he still convened another 'All Stars' session nearly a year later, on 20 April 1953. This time, everything turned out much better. Art Blakey is his normal purposeful self at the drums. Tenor saxophonist Jimmy Heath replaced McLean and brought one excellent theme, 'C.T.A.', to the date. Johnson also came in with two pieces, the dryly effective 'Kelo' and a stark ballad named 'Enigma' which actually features very little improvising – the only solo is given, surprisingly, to Coggins. Davis is excellent on 'Ray's Idea' and Bud Powell's 'Tempus Fugit', constructing fast, clear lines that have none of the preening quality which masks so much of his later playing. Blakey's superb drumming on both surviving takes of 'Tempus Fugit' underscores how important this musician was to Blue Note: he seems to raise the musical conversation on every date he plays in this period.

What is also striking is how sharp and well-drawn the ensemble playing is. It was a feature which Alfred Lion set great store by. Perhaps Blue Note's most renowned characteristic of all was their pre-session preparation. At this point, most jazz recording was done on a more or less ad hoc basis, as far as readying the musicians for the date was concerned. This was as true for the new breed of jazz independents as anywhere else: the resources available for planning and rehearsal were modest at best, given the inevitable budgetary strain. But Lion was adamant that he had to allow for just that kind of preparation if he was going to get the kind of results he was after. He offered musicians paid rehearsal time, sometimes for a couple of days, to ensure that any sloppiness – particularly on any ambitious and original music – was going to be ironed out before the players got to the date. Lion also delighted in excellent ensemble playing. The English producer Tony Hall, who befriended Lion in the fifties and remained in touch with him until Alfred's death, sought out the Blue Note boss's advice on matters of production, and was told to always make sure that the themes and ensembles were played right: 'Alfred would always prefer a take which had the best playing by the band as a whole, even if the solos were better on another take.'

Bob Porter, who worked as one of the regular producers for Bob Weinstock's Prestige operation, crystallised the feelings about this approach in a celebrated remark: 'The difference between Blue Note and Prestige is two days of rehearsal.'[8] Blue Note's approach to this situation rather goes against the grain of the romantic ideal of jazz as a spontaneous, unfettered art, but it must have impacted on the players' ability to be more expressive with material they had already grasped. While that may have mattered less to some of the true giants who recorded for the label, the second division of players must have benefited enormously from that discipline. It also contributed to the mutual respect which Lion and Wolff enjoyed with so many of the musicians. In an era when most performers were easy prey for record-company humiliation and manipulation, Blue Note at least offered respect, if little prospect of making any fortunes.

Jazz musicians are often presented as a family, which tends to ignore the competitive and ill-tempered sides of the music – yet seems more plausible when one thinks of how dysfunctional and argumentative the family unit often is. It might be more accurate to see them as an embattled community of largely disenfranchised artists, certainly in every jazz epoch following the height of the swing era. Lion and Wolff recorded musicians they liked and admired, and although there are examples of significant players who made only isolated appearances in the Blue Note catalogue – notably Davis and John Coltrane – as the contemporary movement of the fifties progressed, it was clear that a school of New York players was emerging that would create a new kind of jazz repertory, on which Blue Note was in a position to focus. The idea of a label of kindred spirits has become a commonplace among the jazz labels of today's era, but in Blue Note's fifties period it was a rare philosophy. For the most part, labels were opportunistic and in search of hits. Building a catalogue was a consideration – Commodore had set such an example years earlier – yet the notion of a house style, with players intimately aware of each other's methods, and consistently playing on each other's records, was something which the more or less chaotic small-label scene of the forties had neither the wherewithal nor the breathing space to accommodate.

This, though, was the picture which began to emerge on Blue Note during 1953–4.

FOUR

The period defined by 1953–4 is one of the most critical in Blue Note's history, since so many of the characteristic qualities which define, for many, the Blue Note style, were set in place. The company was beginning to record with a regularity which would have surprised the two young German émigrés back in 1939. After only six recording dates in 1951 and eight in 1952, there were fifteen in 1953 and thirteen in 1954. The leaders involved included Bud Powell, J. J. Johnson, Miles Davis, Art Blakey, Clifford Brown and – a nod to the old hot music once more – Sidney Bechet and the New Orleans clarinettist George Lewis. It was an experimental period as much as one of achievement. Along with the names listed above, there were also dates for guitarists John Collins (eight rejected titles), Sal Salvador and Tal Farlow, the trombonist Urbie Green, and the pianists Kenny Drew, Elmo Hope and George Wallington. There was even a session made under the leadership of Julius Watkins, one of the few jazzmen to try and make a go of the French horn as a bebop instrument.

Lion's curiosity for new music was enthusiastic and wide-ranging. As Blue Note's business began to grow, he and Wolff realised that they had to have a regular turnover of new material if the label was going to keep its place in the newly expanding world of jazz microgroove records. They were still stuck with their 78 rpm and ten-inch LP formats, still reluctant to go over to twelve-inch albums; but at least, at the beginning of 1954, they released their first 45 rpm seven-inch single, BN 45-1626. Bizarrely, it featured two titles from a Horace Silver session, 'Message From Kenya' and 'Nothing But The Soul', which were features for Art Blakey's drumming: on the first title he duetted with percussionist Sabu Martinez, but the other was all Blakey (a nice tribute, though, to the drummer's importance in the Blue Note hierarchy). As jukeboxes began to go over to the new seven-inch format, singles would assume an increasingly important place in Blue Note's visibility in the marketplace.

Quality control, which was a preoccupation of Lion's, saw to it that there were very few duds among Blue Note's release schedule, even as the pace of their recording increased. Among the 1953 sessions, the two led (or, in the case of the first one, co-led) by Clifford Brown stand out as exceptional, even as they hint at greater things which were not to be realised on Blue Note. Brown is one of the great 'lost leaders' in jazz. Killed in a car accident in June 1956, he didn't live long enough to fulfil a widely held conviction that he was becoming the pre-eminent trumpeter in the music. Rather than offering anything much in the way of innovation, he pacified the influences of Dizzy Gillespie and Fats Navarro into a beaming, exceptionally lucid style of playing. His playing blended both the staccato – the way he hit notes, with a rather slow and even vibrato – and the curvature of the long, flowing phrase. He was one of the key musicians in the mollification of bebop: he liked to swing, in a way which might even have seemed old-fashioned to some of the hardcore boppers, but which had its own kind of fiery beauty. There are few better examples of Brown's greatness than the three choruses he throws off on 'Brownie Speaks', the fourth title cut at the 9 June 1953 date, which the trumpeter is accredited as co-leading with Lou Donaldson (Elmo Hope, Percy Heath and Philly Joe Jones in the rhythm section). While full of bonhomie, the solo shows acute control, a good deal of thinking ahead – at the end of it, the alert listener can seem to see back to where Brown had decided to set out from to get to this point – and enough of the daredevil element to remind us that the soloist was still taking plenty of chances. Yet it was a first-take performance.

Next to Brown, the other players on the date – even the oddball pianist Hope – seem merely proficient, yet here and there are hints that he was helping them to play above themselves, particularly in Donaldson's solos on 'Dee-Dah' and the altered blues 'Cookin''. Still, Brown's later session achieved a finer result. With the saxophonists Gigi Gryce and Charlie Rouse, he formed a particularly interesting front line, with the tonal colours of the horns offering a range of pastel hues as well as the expected brilliance. 'Hymn Of The Orient' is a handsome setpiece for the ensemble; 'Cherokee', the old test piece for a player's executive powers, dazzles with Brown's improvisation. But the ballad 'Easy Living' suggests how Brown still had development left in him: graciously done, but not moving or even especially feelingful, it hints at areas he had yet to master.

These were not Brown's only Blue Note dates, although the music he made for Mercury/EmArcy, with Max Roach and others, offers the fullest picture of his talents. He also figured on the first of three outstanding sessions by J. J. Johnson, the trombonist who more than any other had made that instrument a plausible part of bop's landscape. Johnson had quickly established his eminence in the forties on 52nd Street, his sober, deliberately gloved tone partnering a rapid-fire execution that allowed him to hold his own with the trumpets and saxophones of the bebop small group. He was also a thoughtful composer. At the time of this date – 22 June 1953 – he was feeling the downturn in bebop's fortunes as much as anybody, having spent much of the previous year as a blueprint inspector in a factory on Long Island, yet the music has a surprisingly finished and accomplished quality. The originals, 'Turnpike' and 'Capri' (the latter by Gigi Gryce), are a bit clipped, but the sound of the group is individual, and it derives from the simpatico pairing of Brown and Johnson. They both enjoy the very quick rush through 'Get Happy', but seem equally at home in the far less congenial setting of John Lewis's piece 'Sketch 1'. Lewis, who went on to mastermind the music of the Modern Jazz Quartet for much of the next forty years or so, was only just starting his experiments with baroque and other classical forms, and this piece is probably well enough titled. Yet it has a serene tranquillity which both Brown and Johnson appear to relate to, a reflective side in opposition to all the energy playing elsewhere. Their improvisations throughout the date seem joined to each other, a matter which the saxophonist on the session, Jimmy Heath, never intrudes on.

Brown also appears on one of the most significant occasions in Blue Note's fifties catalogue: the live recording of the Art Blakey Quintet, from Birdland, one of the leading clubs in New York. Birdland was just north of 52nd Street, at 1678 Broadway, and had opened in 1949, soon assuming a position as one of the premier bebop locations. Broadcasts from the club were frequent and recording there was straightforward, but Lion decided to capture an entire evening's work – five sets – by Blakey's band, and he hired Rudy Van Gelder to make it happen. Van Gelder by this time had done half a dozen studio dates for Blue Note from his Hackensack location, but nothing yet of this importance.

The original edition of *A Night At Birdland With The Art Blakey Quintet Vol. 1* (BLP 5037) starts with the voice of Pee Wee Marquette, Birdland's diminutive MC for many years:

Ladies and gentlemen, as you know we have something special down

> here at Birdland this evening . . . a recording for Blue Note records . . . when you applaud for the different passages, your hands go right out over the records there, so when they play them over and over, throughout over the country, you may be some place and say, well, uh, that's my hand on those records there, that I dug down at Birdland . . . We're bringing back to the bandstand at this time, ladies and gentlemen, the great Art Blakey and his wonderful group featuring the new trumpet sensation Clifford Brown, Horace Silver on piano, Lou Donaldson on alto, Curley Russell is on bass . . . Let's get together and bring Art Blakey to the bandstand with a great big round of applause here, how about a big hand here for Art Blakey! Thaaank yaoow!

From there, Blakey and his group kick into what would have been a typical night's work. Except this wasn't a regular working band. Already mindful of the idea of a Blue Note school, Lion had hired Blakey to front a made-up working band of Blue Note regulars. In the sleeve note to the twelve-inch issue of this session, even Leonard Feather described it as 'what might be called the Blue Note family'.[1] Just before the concluding track on the second volume of the original recordings, Blakey opines, 'Yes, sir, I'm going to stay with the youngsters . . . when these get too old, I'm going to get some younger ones . . . keeps the mind active.' It was a philosophy that would serve him for the rest of his working life, even though he was still only thirty-four at the time of the recording.

Van Gelder's work is critical to the success of the recording. Most location recordings had, up until this point, survived on the basis of an airshot quality, of something that might have been taken down from a rogue radio broadcast. Here, finally, was a live recording that gave some impression of a proper ringside seat. Compared to some of Blue Note's studio dates it was still rough and ready, but the fidelity mixed immediacy and fidelity in a way which was almost unique in live jazz recordings up until this point. Nearly half a century later, one can almost imagine oneself at a table near the bandstand. The American critic Ira Gitler, in a subsequent sleeve note, also caught something of the moment: 'Horace gets down with the blues in his inimitable style. I can almost hear Alfred Lion, as he stood by the bar, saying, with that rolled "r" typical of the native Berliner, "Yeah, dot's *fenky, cherchy – grroovy*."'[2]

The music is consistently marvellous. Brown and Donaldson were a congenial pairing, with plenty of experience of each other's work, and if Lou's Parkerisms are often not much more than that, he makes an effectively tart contrast to the lyrical streams which pour out of Brown's trumpet. Some of the material is actually rather old-fashioned for 1954: Gillespie's 'A Night In Tunisia' and Parker's 'Now's The Time' and 'Confirmation' belong to a decade earlier. But they suit an atmosphere which often seems to lie midway between a formal club set and a jam session. And in their roles, Blakey and Silver continued to develop a partnership which was beginning to seem central to New York's new jazz.

The more expansive setting of a live situation made for longer pieces. Hitherto, most of the tracks Lion recorded were still capable of fitting on to ten- or twelve-inch 78s, but with some of the Birdland material moving up towards the ten-minute mark, this was Blue Note's first real long-playing date. It was first released as three ten-inch LPs, some tracks also appearing on singles, but none in the 78 rpm format, which Blue Note was finally preparing to abandon. The last 78 rpm releases on the label would be four titles by Bud Powell.

The pianist had returned to Blue Note for a session on 14 August 1953, with George Duvivier (bass) and Art Taylor (drums). After his most recent spell of wretchedness, Powell had come back to the local scene, although under a kind of supervision. He had a regular Birdland gig, and the club put him up in an apartment, in a situation which Lion characterised as 'house arrest'.[3] The Blue Note man had to ask Oscar Goodstein, Birdland's manager, for access to Powell, and one day the pianist played Lion some new pieces:

> One piece really stood out. I asked him what he called it. He looked around the apartment and said, 'Glass Enclosure'. I knew that we had to record that. Morris Levy insisted that everything that we recorded had to be written out because they had all of the publishing rights. So the bass player George Duvivier wrote out Bud's tunes. We rehearsed at Birdland in the afternoon. And Goodstein was there, making sure that Levy got the written music. That's how that went down.[4]

Powell was easy prey for a man like Levy, who basically controlled Birdland and various small-label interests, and who later in life was honoured as a great record-industry figure, even as he was subsequently convicted for various business misdemeanours. Levy was all too typical of the exploitative crooks who at that time filled several powerful positions in what was still a relatively small and inexperienced world, the American record business. Controlling publishing rights, taking composer credits and offering royalties that smacked of a plantation system were almost routine procedure for several of the so-called pioneers of the post-war American music machine. On what amounted to the other side of the tracks stood figures such as Alfred Lion and Frank Wolff, yet it should be remembered that they were not alone. The impresario Norman Granz, who began the renowned 'Jazz At The Philharmonic' concerts and would go on to both manage several key jazz artists and run some important record labels of his own, may have been a tough businessman, but he was utterly dedicated to the jazz idiom. George Wein, himself a capable Dixieland-swing pianist, had founded a club and record label (both called Storyville) in Boston, and in 1954 was about to launch one of the most important of all jazz festivals, at Newport. Bob Weinstock may not have directed his recording regimen at Prestige with the same acuteness that Blue Note mustered, but he unquestionably looked up to what Lion and Wolff were doing, and with signings such as Monk, Davis, Sonny Rollins and John Coltrane, Prestige's catalogue would subsequently prove to be Blue Note's principal rival in the independent jazz label arena. On the West Coast, Richard Bock had founded a new label called Pacific Jazz in 1952, to document the work of the Californian school of players that were presenting a cool alternative to the emerging hard bop of the East Coast. And Lion's original mentor, Milton Gabler, continued in his work at Decca, although by this time the Commodore label had more or less faded away. For every Levy figure, jazz could still claim a supporter that had the music as much as the business in mind. Without this small corps of figures, it seems likely that the intensely creative period of the fifties in jazz would have gone largely undocumented and unpromoted.

The mainstream record business would certainly have left a figure such as Bud Powell in the cold, although he did, surprisingly, go on to record some sessions for the giant RCA Victor later in the fifties. The August 1953 date for Blue Note yielded a remarkable nine titles – a mix of standards, Powell originals and Oscar Pettiford's 'Collard Greens And Black-Eyed Peas' (sometimes known as 'Blues In The Closet'). Curiously, it took six takes to get a finished master of the first piece of the date, a rather wan reading of 'Autumn In New York', but the other pieces went no further than two takes apiece before Lion was satisfied (a reading of 'I've Got You Under My Skin' was rejected and is apparently lost).

Powell does much here that is thrilling – the intricate work on both takes of Barry Harris's 'Reets And I', the unexpected counterpoint with Duvivier on 'Sure Thing', and the previously cited 'Glass Enclosure', which has the feel of a completed composition, needless of any improvisation, and is despatched in less than two and a half minutes – yet some of his playing is blemished, and the session follows a path which would be taken every time he returned to a studio. 'Polka Dots And Moonbeams' is a moribund ballad reading, and the blues shapes on both 'Collard Greens' and 'Audrey' seem ready at times to fall apart. Whatever the state of Powell's interior world, he was not the dazzling executant that he had been at the height of his powers.

Despite Lion's concern for Powell, he didn't record him again for another four years. There was much else to occupy him during 1954. A month after the Birdland date, he recorded Miles Davis again, this time as the sole horn, with Horace Silver, Percy Heath and Art Blakey behind him. It was some of Davis's best playing on record up to this point. The quicker pieces, 'Take Off' and 'The Leap', are untypically bright and bubbling for the Davis of the fifties, and will surprise many who only know his later records. 'It Never Entered My Mind', though, complete with his patented cup-muted sound, is archetypal Miles, the kind of ballad performance which still finds the most affection with admirers of the nocturnal Davis. Silver, Heath and Blakey prove a most effective backdrop for the trumpeter, with Silver especially energising the leader. But it was too late: Davis had already signed for Bob Weinstock, and aside from his superstar-cameo role on Cannonball Adderley's *Somethin' Else*, this was his last appearance for Blue Note.

Rudy Van Gelder recorded the session from his Hackensack front room. At this point, Van Gelder had effectively become Blue Note's in-house engineer. He never worked exclusively for the label, and he still retains his independence from any particular allegiance, but there's no doubt that Van Gelder's most important and characteristic work was done for Blue Note: 'Alfred knew exactly what he wanted to hear. He communicated it to me and I got it for him technically. He was amazing in what he heard and how he would patiently draw it out of me. He gave me confidence and support in any situation.'[5]

What was special about Van Gelder's sound? In modern terms, the fidelity of Blue Note's fifties sessions sounds tied to an aesthetic of warm, analogue sound, the principal difference between then and now in musical and socio-cultural terms. With modern digital techniques, the size and volume and glare of modern soundmixes are designed largely to overpower listeners. The bulk of today's music is created for functional purposes, usually either to fill the airtime quota of the numberless music-based radio stations around the world, act as a soothing 'wallpaper' in the vast number of retail and service environments which play music, or deafen dancers in the many places where so-called club culture does its business. In other words, most recordings are no longer designed in the first instance for the pleasure of individual listeners to focus on and enjoy. When compared with their present-day successors, even a comparatively urgent recording such as *A Night At Birdland* seems gentle, almost reposeful.

Van Gelder's method was to secure a sound which respected both the timbre of the group and the singularity of the players. The different characteristics of individual players are magnified by Van Gelder's methods because he seemed to take pains to create a consistency of house sound. The softer, pastel tones of Hank Mobley are given no more or less prominence against their background than are those of a fiercer stylist such as Sonny Rollins. The inimitable sound of Art Blakey's press roll and the flash of his cymbals are pushed no further forward than the far less thunderous figures of Art Taylor.

Van Gelder's most particular trade mark is his piano sound. The piano has had an extremely mixed history in the way it has been recorded in a jazz setting. Art Tatum, for many the master of all jazz pianists, was never graced with a truly effective sound in a studio, even though he recorded well into the LP and tape-master era. Many others have also fared poorly: one thinks of giants such as Jimmy Yancey, Jelly Roll Morton and even some of the boogie-woogie masters who recorded early on for Blue Note. Van Gelder positions the piano centrally, as the tonal anchor of the ensemble, but he gentrifies its attack, smooths the pathway between octaves. The bass sonorities are less cavernous and the treble end has no clink or glassiness. A Van Gelder piano chord is even more instantly identifiable than the style of the pianist who's playing it. Comparing, say, Horace Silver's first trio session (cut by Doug Hawkins at WOR) with any of his later Van Gelder sessions makes the difference clear.

It's tempting but misleading to hear this as a more 'truthful' sound. Every record made in a studio offers no more than an impression of the music made on that day, and it is a truth made manifest only in the skills of the engineer, producer and whoever else was in on the documentary as opposed to the creative process. But it is not unreasonable to hear Van Gelder's sound as one which respects the human toil which brought this music about in the first place. Nothing ever seems to be magnified at the expense of anything else. It is as 'democratic' as one imagines a soundmix can ever be.

Van Gelder had a broad range of opportunities with which to explore his technique during 1954. Aside from the Birdland and Davis dates, he recorded guitarist Tal Farlow leading a quartet with another guitar player, Don Arnone; quintets led by Frank Foster and Elmo Hope; the Julius Watkins date, which featured French horn, tenor sax, piano, guitar, bass and drums; a J. J. Johnson group, which this time featured Johnson as sole horn, but with none other than Charles Mingus on bass; a Lou Donaldson sextet, with trumpeter Kenny

Dorham and trombonist Matthew Gee joining him in the front line; and a further quartet date by his friend Gil Melle, this time playing only baritone sax. None of these sessions have really stood the test of time in terms of either popularity or historical significance, and perhaps at this point Lion was rather casting around for some real success.

The most interesting of these dates might be the session by pianist Elmo Hope. Born in New York in 1923, and named for the patron saint of sailors, St Elmo, Hope was perhaps rather more significant as a composer than as a pianist, and with the rash of interest in reviving the music of such previously neglected figures as Herbie Nichols (himself a Blue Note artist), it's rather surprising that so far Hope has evaded any posthumous comeback. Van Gelder had already recorded a trio session with Hope a year earlier, but this time, with Freeman Lee (another completely forgotten figure) on trumpet and Frank Foster on tenor sax, he framed Hope's music in a quintet setting. Hope's music is a jumble of harmonic notions and convoluted melody lines, owing (as every history has said) much to Monk and Powell but really resembling both only in his awkward departure from pianistic convention. Hope was another musician who ended up doing his best work away from Blue Note, in his case for both Contemporary and Riverside. Originals such as 'Chips', 'Later For You' and 'Maybe So' have flashes of ingenuity bedded into a twisting, even shambling sequencing of ideas. Aside from the ever-reliable Art Blakey, once again at the drums, the group approaches this music with energetic but mostly unhappy facility, as if they couldn't wait to get off the themes and into the solos. Hope was another casualty of narcotics, his career interrupted by a prison term, and he died in obscurity in 1967.

Admirable though it may have been for Blue Note to be recording musicians such as Hope, such ventures were unlikely to pay the company's bills: if

Thelonious Monk couldn't do it, how could figures such as Elmo Hope and Gil Melle? By the end of 1954, Lion and Wolff were really feeling the pinch of a difficult, unpredictable jazz marketplace. According to Michael Cuscuna, Lion 'actually got a very piddling offer from Atlantic records to buy him out in 1954, and he was almost prepared to take it'.[6] Just as jazz musicians have frequently been tempted by the offer of a handsome remuneration for less than honourable work, so must jazz entrepreneurs often feel the same way. Atlantic, run by Ahmet Ertegun and Herb Abramson, had some links with jazz – Ahmet's brother Nesuhi was a jazz fan, and in its earliest years it had signed Pete Johnson and Joe Turner – but at the time it was basically a rhythm-and-blues label, with performers such as the Clovers, Ruth Brown and Fats Domino. That Lion even considered taking an offer from Atlantic says a lot about the health of Blue Note at the time. It's fascinating to conjecture on what such a merger might have resulted in, but it would surely have sidelined many of Lion's interests.

At the back of his mind must have been the concern that, eventually, Blue Note would have to rethink their formats. The 78 rpm disc might have been eliminated from their plans – although this was actually rather an early decision to take, as in England, for instance, pop 78s were still being manufactured as late as 1960 – but the label had still not gone over to the twelve-inch LP format which was beginning to look like the natural idiom for the jazz album. That would mean preparing fresh masters, pressings and jackets for the entire catalogue.

Lion badly needed some kind of hit. Although accurate sales figures for records in this period are difficult to come by, it seems likely that an initial sale of a typical ten-inch set might do no better than one or two thousand copies. After that, catalogue sales might put two or three times on that, slowly, or it might not, which would account for the extreme scarcity of the more obscure

Blue Note ten-inch pressings to this day. Like any small business that tries to expand in a competitive field, Blue Note needed one successful thing which would cover overheads in a way that would at least keep their heads above water while they continued to build their catalogue.

The answer began to emerge in the shape of the Blue Note family. As the bebop scene had begun to atrophy – after ten years of following a very similar methodology, what music scene *wouldn't* suffer from its familiarity? – its ad hoc nature grew to seem like a curse. Although there were some more or less regular formations, the faces in the musical community were familiar but not working together in ways which let ensemble identities gel. As Art Blakey would later remember: 'Guys then would throw together a band for one night and play standard bebop tunes, just stand there and jam. And people got tired of that. Everybody was just copying.'[7]

The usual genealogy of jazz history follows a sequence of individual names. Actually, it is groups rather than individuals which people tend to remember, and follow. The landmark ensembles are the real conduits of jazz. Louis Armstrong's Hot Five, the Duke Ellington and Count Basie orchestras of differing vintages, Dizzy Gillespie's big band, the Modern Jazz Quartet, the Gerry Mulligan Quartet, the Miles Davis Quintet with John Coltrane, Cannonball Adderley's band of the sixties, the Jazz Crusaders . . . while the names of individuals stick in people's minds, it is the sound of a band which stays in the collective memory. Perhaps that is the proper legacy of a music which relies as much on group interaction as it does on individual, spontaneous creation.

Another Blue Note record date brought together the blueprint for perhaps the greatest small group in post-war jazz. Alfred Lion offered Horace Silver another date as a leader and this time the pianist asked if he could add horns to his trio. Silver had been leading a group at Minton's Playhouse with the tenor saxophonist Hank Mobley and bassist Doug Watkins, and he brought both men to the date, along with the ubiquitous Blakey and a second front-liner, trumpeter Kenny Dorham. On 13 November 1954, they cut four titles at Van Gelder's Hackensack studio. The session went so productively that Lion reassembled the same group for another date the following February, which again resulted in four titles.

Aside from Mobley's blues line 'Hankerin'', made at the second date, all the compositions were by Silver. Each of them seems cut from the same cloth: rocking beats, nothing too quick but nothing that dawdled; sashaying minor melodies, voiced in clean unison by tenor and trumpet with riffing interjections from the piano; gospel and the blues seeming to soak into every eight-bar passage. Compared to the careening tempos and linear charge of 'true' bebop, this music might have seemed almost too simple, a reduction rather than a development. But Silver's group opened up possibilities in other ways. His themes had a melodious side to them, which the slash-and-burn tactics of bop had little time for. It was listening music, but it opened the door to backbeats, a grooving motion which audiences tired of abstraction were ready to welcome. In the new black popular music – typified by the kind of output which Atlantic, as noted above, was making money from – bebop had no real place. But maybe this blend of funky sophistications could take a seat at the table.

Even Lion was sceptical at first. He OK'd 'Doodlin'', the key tune on the first date, a slinky twelve-bar blues with a deliciously catlike beat. But when he heard the first run-through of 'The Preacher', from the rehearsals for the second session, Alfred was dismayed. Why did Horace want to record such a cornball piece? It sounded like a clip-cloppy nursery rhyme, just as Charlie Parker's blues 'Now's The Time' had been twisted into the dance tune 'The Hucklebuck' (in fact,

Silver had based it on the old English music-hall song 'Show Me The Way To Go Home', an after-hours anthem for juiceheads everywhere). Couldn't Horace just fill in with a straight blues instead? Blakey overheard, and advised the pianist to stick with the tune. But Silver knew Lion well enough by now to know what to do. He told Alfred that, all right, he could come up with another tune - but that would mean more writing, and more rehearsal, and they would have to delay the date. Lion might have guessed that he was being hoodwinked, but he let them go ahead anyway. Many years later, he told Michael Cuscuna: 'I still think it's corny.'[8]

Coupled as a single, 'Doodlin'' and 'The Preacher' were irresistible. The two albums, *Horace Silver Quintet* (BN 5058) and *Horace Silver Quintet Vol. 2* (BN 5062), at last gave Blue Note some best-selling status. Relatively speaking, at least. Silver's records didn't trouble *Billboard*'s R&B charts, which were the principal business yardstick for black music sales in the US, but then very few jazz records - singles or albums - of any description did (a situation which, amazingly enough, continues to this day. It is interesting to note that, despite its almost iconic status as one of the greatest and certainly most 'known' jazz albums of all time, John Coltrane's 1964 recording *A Love Supreme* was not accorded *Billboard*'s gold-disc status, acknowledging sales of 500,000 units, until the beginning of 2001). But the coupling of 'Doodlin' and 'The Preacher' might be the first example of a jazz hit single going on to boost sales of its source album - or, as here, albums. It was perfectly at home on black-music jukeboxes, which would have soaked up most of the initial pressing, and in this case would probably be at least as effective as radio-play in bringing the music to its core audience's ears.

It wasn't only the beat that was selling this music. The group felt like a real, integrated unit. Kenny Dorham, who had just turned thirty, was a veteran of the original bebop school, but he had a lyrical bent not unlike Clifford Brown's, and his presence suggested a thoughtful amiability which was at ease in the more easygoing surroundings of a Silver group. Hank Mobley, who was much younger at twenty-four, had started out in R&B bands, but had then had a spell in Max Roach's groups. Although his great work lay ahead of him, he was already an individual. His tone was hard to pin down - sometimes light, sometimes foggy, or hollow - and his solos had an evasive air, yet he was superbly light on his feet when it came to dodging past clichés, and other musicians greatly admired him. They were an ideal front line, because their personalities were not so domineering that they would unbalance the group, even when their playing was peppery enough to perk up a listener's ears. Silver and Blakey had become an indomitable team by now, and Watkins fitted right in. It felt like a real, identifiable band.

They had a name too. Blakey himself had used it back in the forties, for both a big band and his smaller ensemble, and it had already featured on a Blue Note session, the first under his name in 1947: Jazz Messengers (although Silver subsequently claimed that it was his idea to use the two words together.)[9] It was a band that would also stick around, for a time at least. Blakey: 'We decided to put something together and make a presentation for the people. We stayed basically around New York, but made some gigs in other cities. This helped the clubs and the whole scene because other guys would form real bands and start working.'[10]

To some extent, this was true. Besides the Jazz Messengers, there was Max Roach and his line-ups (which at various points in this period included Dorham, Clifford Brown, Sonny Rollins and Harold Land), and the all-conquering - at least as far as posterity is concerned - Miles Davis Quintet with John Coltrane, which also came together in 1955 (one regrets that no documentation exists of the group Davis briefly led which, according to the trumpeter, featured both Coltrane and Sonny Rollins; as he once put it to the author, 'Damn! I have no tapes of that band!'). But it was not quite yet the age of the familiar hard-bop group.

Even the term 'hard bop' had not yet come into being, and its nativity seems difficult to pin down. As far as history is concerned, it might as well be those two dates which codified the paths that would then be taken by Horace Silver, Art Blakey and the Jazz Messengers; and Blue Note was going to document it, every possible step of the way.

FIVE

The success that the Horace Silver records would enjoy had yet to have any impact, since they weren't released until the end of 1955. Looking through the recording schedule for that year - there were fifteen sessions in all - it reads as if Lion and Wolff were still ready to sing for their supper rather than turn Blue Note towards any kind of specifically commercial bent. There were further sessions for Gil Melle and Julius Watkins, one (perhaps the most obscure Blue Note date of all time) for a guitarist named Lou Mecca, and even two led by the New Orleans clarinet man George Lewis. Their decision to release a record by Lewis (with a band of Crescent City émigrés such as Kid Howard, Jim Robinson, Alton Purnell and others) was another sentimental link with Blue Note's first few years, but in 1955, long past the heyday of a New Orleans revival, it was a strange decision.

Nevertheless, the label continued to build on the results of the first Jazz Messengers dates. Hank Mobley made his debut for the label as a leader with a session cut on 27 March. Silver, Watkins and Blakey were in attendance, but the front-line duties were left to Hank himself. The six titles were never released on any American twelve-inch record, but they were one of Blue Note's last ten-inch discs (BLP 5066). Two days later, Kenny Dorham helmed a date featuring no less than eight players, including a four-horn front line. J. J. Johnson made his final date for the label on 6 June, with Mobley, Silver, bassist Paul Chambers and drummer Kenny Clarke. This is perhaps the least successful of his three sessions, the least individual and most reliant on bop ready-mades. The two ballads, 'You're Mine You' and 'Portrait Of Jennie', are played with the utmost grace and sure-footedness, but leave little impression in their wake, and perhaps only on the spirited 'Daylie's Double' does the group really snap into something beyond itself. Johnson's improvisation on this piece illustrates something of the difficulties he faced head-on, with the trombone's reluctance to be expressive undermined by the performer's ingenuity – he uses a sort of stop-time trill and nuances of attack which entirely overcome any sense that the horn is tonally bland.

The most important recording sessions of the year came during May and August, when Lion almost breathlessly set down as much as he could of a pianist named Herbie Nichols. For many years, Nichols was little more than a hidden paragraph in jazz history, but in the 1980s and 1990s he was comprehensively rediscovered, through the advocacy of long-time admirers such as Steve Lacy and Roswell Rudd. His complete Blue Note recordings were reissued, at first in a limited-edition boxed set issued in 1988 by Mosaic, the independent company run by Charlie Lourie and Michael Cuscuna, and then, when that set caused such a positive reaction, by the new Blue Note itself. A band called the Herbie Nichols Project recorded some of his tunes, and one or two of them nudged the borders of the more frequented parts of the jazz repertory. Yet there has been no full-blown Nichols revival. Perhaps his music is too strange for that.

Born in New York in 1919, Nichols was something of a late developer. Away from his few Blue Note sessions, he is enigmatically ordinary. He played in R&B bands, swing groups, even Dixieland settings, and the few glimpses of his sideman work are unimpressive. Yet Nichols was entirely aware of the contemporary direction of jazz and, extraordinarily enough, he even wrote the earliest extant journalism on Thelonious Monk for a black magazine called *Music Dial* in 1947. He began sending compositions to Alfred Lion, but it wasn't until 1955 that Lion finally offered the pianist a date. In fact, Nichols had already recorded some titles for Savoy, in 1952, but if Lion had heard them they scarcely galvanised him into a response. The session of 6 May 1955, though, must have electrified the Blue Note boss. Along with Al McKibbon (bass) and Art Blakey, Nichols set down six titles which asserted something that was, at the very least, completely his own. Lion quickly engaged him for further dates. In all, Nichols recorded thirty different titles across five sessions, each in the trio format.

Even a glance at some of his tune titles – 'Cro-Magnon Nights', 'Amoeba's Dance', 'Orse At Safari' – makes clear that Nichols was no straightforward thinker. He wrote the notes for the first twelve-inch release on Blue Note (BLP 1519), where he claims inspiration from Jelly Roll Morton, Beethoven and Villa-Lobos, and he ends them with 'I am in a constant race to make my "classical theories" catch up to my "jazz theories". It used to be the other way around.'[1] Lion called the two ten-inch releases of Nichols tunes *The Prophetic Herbie Nichols*, but in the end they prophesied nothing, other than the singularity of Nichols's talent. He was a storytelling player: the matter of 'House Party Starting' or 'The Gig' is, as he explains in his own notes, programmatic. But his style is hard to pin down or describe. In the notes to Blue Note's new edition of Nichols's music, the suggestion is to 'Imagine a Dixieland beat, a diatonic, hummable melody, and the harmonies of Bartók all woven together and you'll get the idea. Nobody's music grooves quite like Herbie's.'[2] Perhaps – but, as with Monk, Nichols was fortunate with his drummers. The superb playing of Blakey on the first two dates and Max Roach on the next three makes the pianist's waywardnesses palatable. The solidity of the drummer's groove keeps Nichols from slipping into inscrutability.

Nothing in the compositions and their treatment is ever quite as one might expect, even as they often follow conventional AABA patterns. The Ellingtonian feel of 'Step Tempest', where Ducal harmonies flit in and out of view, has an enigmatic extra six bars added to the last measures of the theme chorus. 'Cro-Magnon Nights', an impression of a caveman's Saturday night, is at once dark and jovial, stentorian left-hand figures danced over by the right. 'The Gig' is one of his most ambitious conceptions: a sixty-seven-bar construction, with an eight-bar drum coda (which Roach jumps all over, as if in relief), it seems to roll crazily forward as if steadily climbing a platform and falling back again. When Roach ends the piece, one feels bewildered: what were we just listening to here?

Each of these sessions proceeds in the same way, and the steady mid-tempo which Nichols seemed to like best is the most familiar setting. But the music asks a lot of the listener: even more than with most piano-trio jazz, which often sounds 'samey' to half-attentive ears, Nichols's ideas dart past so quickly that he can seem abstruse – certainly next to Monk, who seems easy in comparison. In this regard, Nichols has become a musician's favourite.

Alfred Lion clearly liked him too, but there are some strange aspects to his Blue Note tenure. Lion had planned a series of ten-inch albums, yet only two were issued, with a single twelve-inch album following on. Only one title from the pianist's fourth date was ever issued until the 1980s, when Michael Cuscuna discovered the eight missing tracks and no less than eighteen alternative takes. Nichols was isolated within Blue Note too: he never recorded as a sideman for the label, and he never heard his music recorded with horns. While one can understand Lion's reluctance to cede Horace Silver's chair to Nichols on the kind of standard Blue Note session that was beginning to emerge, that was still the kind of gig that Herbie was playing on most of his working nights. Sheila Jordan, who sometimes sang with Nichols as an accompanist, remembered him well:

> He was a very good-looking man, very tall and mysterious, and always well dressed. I remember one time he was standing outside of the club and he saw me getting out of a car driven by a man who needed a shave. He asked me what I was doing with a gangster. I said, Herbie! That's the drummer in the trio that's here on Mondays, your night off. He couldn't imagine a musician not being well groomed.[3]

Nichols never found much limelight again: he became ill with leukaemia, dying in 1963.

At the end of 1955, Lion again set down a recording by the Jazz Messengers, this time recording four sets from their night's work at the Café Bohemia. This was a relatively new venue on Piper Street, which had only opened earlier in the year. On 23 November 1955, the same personnel which had recorded the two crucial sessions with Silver and Blakey set down nineteen pieces for the microphones, of which all but three survive. While the Birdland sets with Brown and Donaldson had been carefully prepared, this was more like a typical night's work for a band which had had plenty of exposure since the beginning of the year. There's a charm to the recordings, with Kenny Dorham and Hank Mobley both rather shyly introducing their ballad features, and the expansive Blakey beginning to work up his philosophical raps about how jazz works for all of us – how we're all swinging. Although the band was still notionally under Silver's direction, it was Blakey that appeared more like the frontman, doing most of the talking and, of course, setting his volcanic tempos for each piece. When the results were eventually released, as part of the first sequence of twelve-inch Blue Note dates, they were credited to *The Jazz Messengers At The Café Bohemia*, although on the artist byline it was Blakey's name which appeared first.

The star performer on the date is probably Kenny Dorham, who by this time had taken great pains to advance his own playing: still as fleet as any bebopper, Dorham had worked hard on the construction of his lines, and had developed a sense of an interior, rather muted emotion underpinning the expected fireworks. He was fast, but not flamboyant. There is a severity about Dorham's playing, as if he is unimpressed by mere pyrotechnics, and going in hand with his lyricism – he had some ambitions to be a singer as well as a trumpet player, and though he never sang on a Blue Note date there is one 1958 session for Prestige, *This Is The Moment*, which highlights his powers as a vocalist – it gives him a markedly individual stance.

If Lion was taking stock at the end of the year, he must have still been uneasy about the label's continuance. They were about to face up to the inevitable, and refashion their catalogue to fit with the twelve-inch medium. But he had had a happier year in other respects, forming the relationship which would last him the rest of his life. Ruth Lion remembers how, as a rather brash and self-confident young woman, she had her own PR firm and a gig on the side as a DJ at the Palm Café, when she saw the forever preoccupied Lion one night, sitting at one of the booths. When introduced, 'I said something to him about records and how I was kind of business-minded. I said, "How much is a record date? How much do the artists get?" He thought it was too personal. He really closed up because he didn't like me in the first place, and here I come asking him a business question. But I finally did get to Alfred.'[4]

Although their relationship would not lead to marriage for a number of years, the Lions soon kept the business in the family, with Ruth working in the front office while Alfred and Frank had their lairs in the back. 'Alfred was doing everything. He was taking care of getting the records out. He was getting to rehearsals. He was getting to auditions. He put in at least a seventy-hour week. Days off were very rare.'[5] Perhaps the Blue Note team weren't doing anything different to any small and under-resourced business which its founders loved. But they were becoming central players, rather than marginal small-label guys. The imminent success of the Horace Silver albums paved the way for the investment in the twelve-inch medium, and saw the company through at a crucial moment in jazz progress.

Lion and Wolff never really looked outside New York for their raw material – as inveterate scene-makers, they lived the jazz of their city. There are a handful of sessions in Blue Note's early catalogue which emanate from elsewhere. The Leipzig-born pianist Jutta Hipp was offered a release *(New Faces – New Sounds From Germany: Jutta Hipp Quintet*, BLP 5056) of a session taped in Frankfurt with local musicians. Hipp had made it to New York and was trying to break into the scene (she later had a further Blue Note release which also featured Zoot Sims's only session for the label, and then vanished from jazz history). Two ten-inchers had been released (BLP 5059/60) made up of three dates recorded in California, featuring players from the new Los Angeles session crowd. Made under the patronage of Leonard Feather, *Best Of The West – Modern Sounds From California, Vols. 1 & 2* was surely representative of what was coming out from that side of American jazz. But it hardly belonged on Blue Note. The house style was very different.

Not only that: the house style was becoming the central idiom in the new jazz. As the new school of hard bop gathered pace, fresh faces and anticipatory stylists began to emerge from elsewhere in the US, and head for New York, still, inevitably, the jazz capital of the world. From Chicago came saxophonists Johnny Griffin, Clifford Jordan and John Gilmore; from Detroit, the 'motor city' that would spawn so much of the soul of the sixties via the Motown imprint, came pianists Barry Harris and Tommy Flanagan, trumpeters Thad Jones and Donald Byrd, and guitarist Kenny Burrell; from Philadelphia emerged Benny Golson, John Coltrane and the Heath brothers; from Pittsburgh, the Turrentine brothers, Stanley and Tommy. Art Farmer started on the West Coast but moved east. These and many more like them added to the already intense jostle of top-flight players who were stirring up the New York scene.

Nobody was better placed than Blue Note's operation to begin documenting the new jazz although plenty of other labels were either already in place or soon to set up shop: Prestige, Riverside, Contemporary, New Jazz, Fantasy, Vee Jay, Roulette. The accepted wisdom is that none of these had the commitment to excellence which Blue Note had by now taken as a hard-won necessity; but that would be unfair to dedicated practitioners such as Riverside's Orrin Keepnews, and it tends to belittle many superb albums which appeared outside the Blue Note enclave. This was also the era of – to choose a mere handful – the Miles Davis Quintet albums on Prestige (and his subsequent first discs for Columbia), Sonny Rollins's *Worktime* and *Saxophone Colossus*, Art Pepper's *Meets The Rhythm Section*, and *Thelonious Monk With John Coltrane*, any one of which could stand comfortably alongside the best of Blue Note's output.

For their first record date of 1956, though, Blue Note put down a significant marker which had eluded the other labels. Babs Gonzalez, who'd made some sides for the Blue Note of the middle forties, told Lion and Wolff that they had to go down to a Harlem club called Smalls' Paradise and hear their latest attraction. Ed Smalls had been running jazz clubs for literally decades, and the Paradise was one of the longest-lived places of its kind, first opening in 1925 and lasting until the mid-1980s. One February night in 1956, the Blue Note bosses went to hear Jimmy Smith at the club. Smith was a novelty: although he'd started out as a pianist, he had turned instead to the Hammond electric organ, an instrument whose impact on jazz had thus far been negligible. Despite some fairly polite work on record by Milt Buckner and Wild Bill Davis (the latter actually being Smith's original inspiration), no vocabulary had yet been invented for what was, in jazz terms, a new instrument.

Smith changed all that. One of the Philadelphians who had arrived to try their luck in New York, he took the New York jazz stage by storm. Frank Wolff's recollections of their visit to Smalls' are justly celebrated:

> He was a stunning sight. A man in convulsions, face contorted, crouched over in apparent agony, his fingers flying, his foot dancing over the pedals. The air was filled with waves of sound I had never heard before. The noise was shattering. He came off the bandstand, smiling, the sweat dripping all over him. 'So, what do you think?' 'Yeah!' I said. That's all I could say. Alfred Lion had already made up his mind.[6]

In an era saturated with rock and its attendant hysteria it is hard to look back and envisage the kind of upsetting excitement Smith must have created. There were still very few amplifiers in jazz clubs and electricity was confined to guitars for the most part (and guitars without any added effects beyond their open tone). The 'shattering' noise which electrified Frank Wolff was something absolutely new to jazz. Fortunately, Smith was no mere effects merchant. He was a skilful bebop player, who could introduce musical substance just as he could enthral an audience looking for showmanship. There are several legends surrounding his initiation into jazz performance, but among them are that he didn't even touch the organ until he was twenty-eight, and that he spent an entire year practising at home and mastering the complexity of the Hammond and its various possibilities before he ventured into performance. Whatever the truth of it, Smith's mastery of both the instrument and the style he'd decided to employ was so complete that his earliest recordings are almost as 'mature' as those of his seasoned later years. The methodology was relatively simple: a tireless walking bass in the pedals, the crucial 'third hand' which allows organists to dispense with the need for a bass player; thick, juicy chords in the left hand; tingling, rapid-fire decoration with the right hand; and an awareness of how the various Hammond stops could alter the attack, decay and tonal variation of whatever was being played. A guitarist added further electricity to the group, and a drummer set down a simple, stinging groove (no need for the dynamic variations of an Art Blakey here: the drummer was bedrock, not volcano). As a musical formula, it was both simple and open to seemingly endless variation when applied with sufficient imagination.

Smith has kept with this kind of constancy ever since. Even today, in his seventies, while the energy levels are a good deal more constrained, the fingers still fly and the face, mouth agape, still shows at least the ghost of the convulsions which transfixed Wolff and Lion. Their first recordings with Smith were suitably fanfared: *A New Sound – A New Star: Jimmy Smith At The Organ Vol. 1* (BLP 1512) was the first of Blue Note's twelve-inch series which was a debut release (the previous eleven albums had been reissues of material by Monk, Blakey, J. J. Johnson, etc.). At the first session, on 18 February 1956, Smith was reportedly nervous, and an attempt on one of his live set pieces, Dizzy Gillespie's 'The Champ', was rejected. They cut some standards, but Frank Wolff later remembered that 'they didn't quite project his new sound', which seems a surprising judgement, especially since the rest of the session was deemed good enough for Smith's first release. If there's a difference between this date and the one cut on 27 March, it's that Van Gelder seems to have figured out a better way of recording the organ – it sounds fatter and a good deal less waspish than on the first session. This time they redid 'The Champ', a seething performance that goes through a relentless eight and a half minutes, with Smith swarming all over the keyboard. There is fine work throughout both dates by guitarist Thornel Schwartz, who's hardly on a par with the great bebop guitarists but has an ideal repertoire of licks and fills, and the two drummers, Bazely Perry on the first session and Donald Bailey on the second. When Frank Wolff began offering the first Smith albums to the trade, 'the distributor said: "Who's Jimmy Smith? What's this – sounds like birds twittering. Very, very strange. Well – give me ten pieces."'[7] Sales reps everywhere will nod in recognition of that kind of response to a new jazz record, but Smith's music was genuinely something unprecedented. Before long, the organ combo would be something that distributors would be clamouring for.

There was one more piece of the puzzle to be fitted in. While Frank Wolff continued to snap his photographs at every session, the design of Blue Note's covers was less codified than it might be. While they are seldom remembered for their work, the two designers whom Lion had used up until this point, Paul Bacon and John Hermansader, were actually a good deal more gifted than has been given credit for. Hermansader in particular balanced the twin issues of photography and type in a way which would mirror many of the concerns of the Blue Note of the years ahead. If one looks at, for instance, Hermansader's covers for the Jazz Messengers *Café Bohemia* dates, most would imagine that they were the work of the man who succeeded both Hermansader and Bacon as Blue Note's designer-in-chief: Reid K. Miles.

There is something poetically appropriate about the involvement of Miles. While the sponsors of any artistic movement are often almost dangerously close to their subject matter, it has often been the case that the designers are far more detached from the matter in hand. Miles wasn't particularly interested in jazz, and professed to being much more of a classical music fan. He worked in the art department at *Esquire* magazine, and Wolff hired him to handle some of the early twelve-inch covers (Hermansader did the first eight). Miles began with the Milt Jackson and Monk reissues, BLP 1509, 1510 and 1511. Although the Jackson cover is conventional enough, the Monk artwork is initially startling. 'Thelonious' is split across two lines, with a hyphen between 'o' and 'n', in stark black type, while 'Monk' is in clear white against the one-colour backdrop – an ochre-yellow on the first volume, and an orange-red for the second. A Wolff photo of Monk is cropped into a small rectangle at the top of the frame. 'Genius Of Modern Music' is run, lower case and in a small font size, to the left of 'Monk'. 'Two colours didn't hurt that product at all. The few full colour covers I did were not as strong as the ones with black and white and red.'[8] Miles disliked fussiness or crowding, but there's a ruthlessness about his designs. Though Wolff's photography is mostly elevated by the sleeves, Miles always put the design ahead of the picture (as, indeed, any designer would). While Hermansader's sleeves for *The Amazing Bud Powell: Vol. 1* and *Vol. 2* take a line of least resistance and have the typography humbled by Wolff's magnificent head-and-shoulders of Powell, Miles's subsequent designs for the later Powell releases are much less subservient.

Although his style seems immediately identifiable, that is often as much to do with Wolff's photos as Reid Miles's designs. Miles never settled into a particular typeface or system. Upper and lower case, personnels sometimes and sometimes not listed, track listings occasionally, and many styles of typeface. Sometimes he even used the calligraphic style of *Lee Morgan Indeed!* or Dizzy Reece's *Soundin' Off*. When Miles chose not to use photography at all, the results were sometimes startling. Jackie McLean's *Jackie's Bag* (1959) resembles a string-tied document file. Hank Mobley's *Peckin' Time* (1958) looks like the master case holding the session tape. Others, such as Sonny Clark's *Trio* (1959) resemble canvases from a familiar contemporary gallery – blocks of colour, lines, shapes, abstraction. But always the impression is of a certain starkness, even when Miles filled a sleeve with material. Whatever he thought of the contents inside (and Miles usually traded in the records Blue Note gave him for classical albums), the designer made sure that his fronts were as heavyweight as the music inside was intended to be. Nobody, looking at the cover for Andrew Hill's *Smokestack* (1963), with Hill peering impassively through the space in a sculpture, could have been in any doubt that the music within was some serious stuff. If Miles cracks any jokes, they must be very private ones: the only trace of any humour is in the smiles on some of the musicians' faces. But perhaps Miles and Wolff did have a line in deadpan wisdom. The cover of Eric Dolphy's sole Blue Note date, *Out To Lunch!* (1963), shows a small adjustable clock face framed in a doorway, headed by the legend WILL BE BACK. Instead of showing the time of return, the clock has six hands, pointing to a range of possible times of day or night.

'Fifty bucks an album,' Miles remembered. 'They loved it, thought it was modern, they thought it went with the music . . . one or two colours to work with at that time and some outrageous graphics!'[9] He said he 'got the pictures from Frank and integrated them with the design of the moment'.[10] It might have pleased Blue Note's small amen corner of followers, and many of the musicians must have been surprised that their work was being retailed in such solemn, artistic-looking jackets. But Ruth Lion's comment seems particularly sharp: 'They were sure that with these new artists they were introducing, so many of them were leaders for the first time, so maybe the public in Harlem knew about them, but across the country they didn't . . . and they felt it was very important to put these men's photos as prominently as possible on the covers, and they got a lot of flak from distributors across the country who felt a pretty girl would have been better.'[11] Frank Wolff, who had to battle with distributors every working day, must have felt at times that they were suffering for their art as much as the musicians. But he kept on taking pictures at every date.

Although the first eleven of Blue Note's new twelve-inch 'Modern Jazz' series were reissues (there was also, briefly, a 'Traditional Jazz' series, which extended to only eight issues and was dedicated to the sessions by Sidney Bechet and George Lewis), Lion and Wolff began issuing new material in the bigger format almost immediately, starting with the first Jimmy Smith album. The year 1956 would prove to be their most prolific to date: there were twenty-five separate recording sessions, with all the new mainstays of the label busily at work, and additions to the roster coming in seemingly all the time. Thad Jones, in seniority terms the middle man of the three Detroit Jones brothers, cut his first music for the label on 13 March, resulting in BLP 1513, *Detroit–New York Junction*. Later in life, Jones would be best remembered for his bandleading. He co-led a famous orchestra with the drummer Mel Lewis for many years, was a gifted writer (one of the most-recorded jazz tunes is his ballad 'A Child Is Born') and a demanding arranger who secured formidable performances of very taxing charts from his groups. His talents as a trumpeter have sometimes been forgotten, but that is what Lion recorded him as, and each of his three small-group Blue Notes has much merit. *The Magnificent Thad Jones*, issued second, is distinguished throughout by Jones's big, gorgeous sound, and by taking his time – only 'If I Love Again' could be called brisk – he lets the listener see all the byways and sidelong glances in a sequence of long, impeccably detailed solos. The opening glide through 'April In Paris', swung off Max Roach's brushes, is the sort of track which is destined for best-of anthologies of the artist and the label alike.

On the previous day to Jones's first session, another Blue Note stalwart made his debut. Like Jones, guitarist Kenny Burrell was from Detroit, and had won some attention while working as a sub in Oscar Peterson's trio. Placid and unflappable, Burrell is another musician who seemed to function in the full confidence of a mature style from his earliest appearances. There is little change from the clean, bluesy, supple lines of his first Blue Note dates to anything he did in his middle and senior years. He wasn't a superfast technician in the manner of, say, Tal Farlow, but listening to 'This Time The Dream's On Me' from *Introducing Kenny Burrell* or 'Mexico City', an out-take from Kenny Dorham's Café Bohemia recordings which was used on *Kenny Burrell Vol. 2*, makes one realise that he could hold his own at the quickest tempo. More of a bebopper in the Charlie Christian tradition, harmonically acute rather than adventurous, Burrell is one of those rare jazzmen – like Zoot Sims or Jack Teagarden – who never seems to play below par, whatever the setting. That also means that his work rarely peaks, which has led to his albums being somewhat undervalued, but the results of his first two Blue Note sessions (their release was somewhat jumbled, most of the music from the first date coming out on the second disc) are consistently fine. Burrell enjoyed the same rhythm section which backed Thad Jones on his first session – Flanagan, Pettiford and Wilson – but the second, where Paul Chambers and Kenny Clarke arrived on bass and drums and Candido Camero played congas, was hotter still. There are few tracks from the era more terrifically grooving than their treatment of 'Get Happy'.

Four major horn players made their debut on Blue Note in the same year. Johnny Griffin, the 'little giant' from Chicago, cut a sensational debut, *Introducing Johnny Griffin* (BLP 1533), which was a calling card for one of the fastest saxophonists in jazz. Griffin plays with such mercurial force that it sounds as if Max Roach is yelling at him to slow down on a cavalry charge through 'It's All Right With Me'. It is doubly effective because Griffin had a nuts-and-bolts accuracy to go with the quickfire phrasing. You could break the solos down and they don't sound disjointed, or full of mere showboating. The price for that, inevitably, is a loss of nuance, which Griffin would in his later years address more fully, and some of the record seems to show time being filled up (Griffin's partners, Wynton Kelly, Curley Russell and Roach, were a somewhat uncomfortable mix). But the point of it is to hear the saxophonist's sheer abandonment, his unquenchable exuberance.

Although it isn't much cited, given that it was his sole appearance on the label and he is hardly a familiar jazz figure anyway, the album by J. R. Monterose was also a very considerable statement. Frank Anthony Monterose Jr (the 'J. R.' was a nickname drawn from the 'junior') was another refugee from Detroit, but he had arrived in New York some years earlier and had played in Buddy Rich's groups, among others. In 1956, he also joined Charles Mingus's Jazz Workshop group. *J. R. Monterose* (BLP 1536) was a tough and individual quintet record. Monterose doesn't perhaps make quite the impression that he might have done, given that his front-line partner, trumpeter Ira Sullivan, is often at least as powerful as he is in the improvisations. But Monterose cuts a singular figure nonetheless. His gruff and hard-bitten tone is used for expressive effect, but he is an opposite to John Griffin: where the Chicagoan is all helter-skelter outpouring,

Monterose is miserly with notes, disjointed, staccato. All of his solos are hard to predict, in the way they'll go from phrase to phrase, and although it often feels like he's not really swinging – against the excellent grooves set down by Wilbur Ware and Philly Joe Jones – the saxophonist handles himself with such authority that he convinces the listener. The material is an unusual bunch of themes – no standards, bop-like extrapolations out of familiar chord sequences, a variation on a minor blues by Donald Byrd, a Paul Chambers original – and the record does have a one-off feel to it. Lion went no further with Monterose – who did, indeed, make relatively few records altogether afterwards – but his sole entry is an intriguing footnote in the Blue Note catalogue.

Lion's great catch of the year was Sonny Rollins. The saxophonist had already cut a string of albums for Prestige which asserted his claim as the master of his instrument, and his first Blue Note date (*Sonny Rollins*, BLP 1542) came at the tail end of an extraordinary twelve months of activity, which included the albums *Work Time, Plus Four, Tenor Madness, Saxophone Colossus, Plays For Bird* and *Tour De Force*, a sequence which has little parallel elsewhere in the LP era. But with his Prestige contract at an end, Rollins was available.

Compared to what had immediately preceded it, the first Blue Note album was unremarkable. Although Rollins's frequent cohort Max Roach was on drums, the rest of the group – trumpeter Donald Byrd, making one of his first appearances on the label, Gene Ramey on bass and Wynton Kelly – were rather too conventional for this most unconventional of musicians to function at his best. Although Rollins brought four originals to the session, there's a sense that he is playing to a kind of routine rather than his own music. At this point, he was straining against the shackles of whatever idiom was coming to displace bebop, and other horn players tended to get in his way. On the rather ingenious minor blues 'Decision', which opens the record, he has to make way for Byrd just as his own solo seems to be ready to start going places, perhaps for another twenty choruses or so. And so it goes on, through the record, with the ballad 'How Are Things In Glocca Morra' a typical Rollins surprise sprung midway through (in his original sleeve notes, Leonard Feather calls it 'a ballad . . . which has often appealed to modern musicians', although if that were true there are mystifyingly few recorded versions of it).

Bringing Rollins into the fold proved, in the end, to be only a temporary thing. But Lion's other major signing of the year was far more important to the label, since the musician concerned would be associated with Blue Note for literally the rest of his life. The Philadelphia-born trumpeter Lee Morgan was still only eighteen when he made his first records for Blue Note and Savoy, for whom he also recorded during 1956. At first, he had a gig with Art Blakey, but moved on to the Dizzy Gillespie Orchestra later in the year, before ultimately rejoining Blakey in 1958. If Horace Silver, Hank Mobley and Art Blakey were all in the quintessential Blue Note line-up, then Lee Morgan would have to be in there too. He was a child of bebop trumpet. His masters were Fats Navarro, Dizzy Gillespie and Clifford Brown, but he added a personal, cocksure spark of his own to whatever he had learned from them.

As a boy, Morgan had heard the original bebop giants, and his sister encouraged his interest, finding him a trumpet at the age of fourteen. He got his hands on a lot of records, and his home town was full of music, with clubs and jam sessions and informal workshops all over the city. Word quickly circulated about this accomplished young man, and Morgan was a good self-publicist too, outgoing and personable. While many of his friends were content either to keep music as a part-time thing, or at least stay in the city, Lee was more ambitious, and he was in New York before long.

Lion recorded him twice before the year was over, with a quintet on 4

November and with a sextet on 2 December. Neither session is among the immortal Blue Note dates, yet neither betrays any nerves on behalf of the young trumpeter: he is the most impressive player on both sessions, even with Silver and Mobley in the line-ups. The first session, variously known as *Presenting Lee Morgan* and *Lee Morgan Indeed!*, features one of his Philadelphia cohorts, Clarence Sharpe, on alto, with Silver, Wilbur Ware and Philly Joe Jones. The material includes themes by Benny Golson and Owen Marshall, two more Philadelphians, and throughout Morgan plays with an engaging mix of vitality and lyricism. He doesn't have much of, say, Clifford Brown's almost regal delivery, and his tone has a kind of sneaking quality, as if he is surprising his own ideas before pushing them out through the horn. Where Sharpe almost loses his way on his solo on 'Gaza Strip' (although his attempts to recover are exciting in themselves), Morgan's equally chancy solo is completely secure. On the second date, *Lee Morgan Sextet*, where Hank Mobley and another young Philadelphian, altoman Kenny Rodgers, join the front line, the ensembles are gracefully led by the trumpeter, yet in at least two solos – the chuckly muted outing on 'Whisper Not' and the tart, almost mocking one on 'His Sister' – Morgan steps aside from what might be expected of a youthful fellow trying to copy his idols.

Morgan's early flowering is a salutary reminder to many who think the getting of wisdom in jazz is the preserve of older hearts and minds. In the hard-bop 'revival' of the 1980s and 1990s, criticism was frequently levelled at performers who were considered, basically, to be too young to be any good. Yet the history of the music is full of players who were already masterful at an indecently early age, and Lee Morgan is only one of many. Besides, the Morgan of these first two dates *did* have much development to come, even as one listens back to this early music and wonders at the elusive brio of this brilliant young man. It was to Alfred Lion's credit that he took down so much early Morgan, and he would continue to follow him in later – and not always so bountiful – years.

At the end of the year, Art Blakey and Horace Silver went their separate ways as bandleaders. Blakey retained the 'Jazz Messengers' name (and kept it for the rest of his days), while Silver settled for the Horace Silver Quintet. But otherwise the two premier spirits of the hard-bop movement continued to follow the same path. *Six Pieces Of Silver* (BLP 1539) was, initially, just another studio date for the pianist and some of his regulars, although the with-hindsight sleeve notes suggest that it was already a regular band. The faces weren't unfamiliar: Hank Mobley, Donald Byrd (who had been in the Messengers a year earlier) and Doug Watkins, with only the eighteen-year-old Louis Hayes as a truly new arrival.

The session (cut on 10 November) features some of Silver's cleverest writing to date. 'Cool Eyes' manipulates a four-part, thirty-two-bar theme before leading to blowing sections for the horns over the familiar changes of 'I Got Rhythm', interspersed with eight bars of ensemble. 'Shirl', played only by the rhythm section, is typical of Silver's other side, the composer who would come up with such ballads as 'Lonely Woman'. Over unexpectedly dark changes, the enigmatic melody is beautifully elaborated on. 'Camouflage' uses stop-time figures to underscore both ensemble and solos. 'Enchantment' is characteristic of Silver's rather sly use of a kind of down-home exotica: the rumble of Hayes's mallets and the vaguely mysterious theme have a touch of kitsch about them, which this leader always liked.

The key track, though, is 'Senor Blues'. A consummate example of how Silver could push a twelve-bar blues through its trickiest paces, the piece manages to be exhilaratingly catchy at the same time as deploying complex rhythmic ideas. It's hard to even say what time it's in, somewhere between 6/8 and 12/8, and the cool smoke of Byrd's and Mobley's solos prefaces a further change in the rhythm, leading to Silver's own epigrammatic solo. With the bass line amounting to an ongoing vamp, the piece lacked for nothing in terms of memorability. Lion cut an alternative take of the tune for a single release – although, at more than six and a half minutes, it's hardly any shorter than the seven-minute album version.

It was destined to be another hit for Horace Silver. Still without a regular working band, the pianist was called by agent Jack Whittemore, who had a Philadelphia club-owner begging for the group since the track was getting a lot of local airplay. Silver was reluctant, still unsure of whether he wanted to run a regular band or not, but Whittemore pressed him. 'So I hired Hank Mobley, Art Farmer, Doug Watkins and Art Taylor. We rehearsed, and went down and packed the place. Then the guy wanted us back in two months. In the meantime, I got another gig and it snowballed.'[12]

It was another good day in the Blue Note office.

SIX

As the fifties progressed, it became clear that while jazz had largely lost its popular support – hardly any records by recognisable jazz artists made the *Billboard* album or single charts in the period covering 1955–60 – it had built up a committed, hip audience of both blacks and whites in the urban areas that were still nurturing the music. The club culture of 52nd Street may have declined since its pinnacle of the first bebop era, but New York City was still full of places which had a jazz booking policy, from young venerables such as Birdland and the Village Vanguard to mayfly cellars and bars that lasted a while before switching policy or changing hands. Just as significant were the many other cities, cited in the previous chapter, which could boast similar, if less populous, local circuits. While urban real estate was still cheap and low-rent accommodation plentiful, there remained the margins which could almost comfortably support the jazz musician and his or her working life.

It was also a time, in American culture, of a new bohemia. The beat poets, writers, film and theatre people, artists and just a general gaggle of people who liked to hang out were temperamentally attuned to the idea of jazz, even if not always the substance or actuality of it. Most of the hard-bop musicians plied their trade in hard-core circumstances: their daily work was what it was. Unlike the situation on the West Coast, where a climate of session work had built up for many of the local jazzmen, playing on pop records or for TV and film music, the idea of being a 'session musician' hadn't so far emerged in the hard-bop life. Yet any sense that this was some kind of balmy period with plentiful work and agreeable conditions should be quickly set aside. The pull of New York began to hurt local scenes, as the most talented musicians in the end left for the principal jazz city. Clubland was still substantially in the grip of gangsterdom. And just as so many musicians a decade earlier had found themselves with remorseless narcotics habits, so heroin still exacted a considerable price among young musicians. Many of Blue Note's roster were acknowledged heroin addicts. Instead of the squalor which came to be associated with hard-drug dependence, the ugly reality of heroin chic sucked in many in this new bohemia, jazz musicians making up a plentiful proportion of their number.

For all that, it was an intensely creative moment in jazz, perhaps even more so than the original bebop era, because the language had been established and was available for anyone to speak, if they had the will to do so, and a new record industry was rushing to grow up around it. Where bebop had once seemed almost outrageous, to some of the more settled swing-era musicians, hard bop was now familiar. The neurotic climate of bebop had been traded for a more studied intensity. As the LP format became standardised, the music, now available in a medium which approximated the length of a typical club set, was documented in a way that sought a new audience. Followers of the music began to build collections – without necessarily becoming mere 'collectors'. If microgrooves encouraged a more leisurely, contemplative approach to jazz listening – no more rushing to change the record after three minutes – they also helped to educate tastes, and develop serious appreciation.

All of which might suggest an atrophying – or at least a gentrification – of this new jazz mainstream. But there were too many individuals, too many singular and identifiable voices at work in hard bop to allow anyone even to imagine that the movement could go stale or turn grey. For many listeners (although not all critics, of which more later), each fresh record spelled out an exciting new development. The further away one was from the local scene the more compelling it seemed. Tony Hall, at work in the thick of the new British jazz of the fifties, recalls how eager local musicians and fans were to seek out the new recordings, on Blue Note in particular. 'They were so hard to come by, and even if you could have got import copies, they were very expensive. I used to try and persuade people who were going over on the boats to bring some back.'

Who was buying this music? It has never been easy finding a profile of the jazz audience, or any typical jazz fan. Photographs of New York club audiences during the forties and fifties suggest a predominantly white middle-class clientele, but they were not the only people buying the records (visit a leading jazz club even today, in New York, London or Tokyo, and you may find that a considerable proportion of its patrons are people who don't buy jazz records). A modest number of white aspiring intellectuals – the kind of 'bohemians' alluded to above – would have invested some of their money in records. College students, who today are still seen by industry demographics as an important audience for several different kinds of 'alternative' music, might have added to some of the numbers. But most of the record buyers came from black neighbourhoods. Joe Fields, who worked at Bob Weinstock's Prestige outfit during the fifties, told David Rosenthal: 'Our sales were overwhelmingly to blacks – not just tenor and organ stuff but hard bop too. That's why what we sold in Boston was *nothing* compared to Chicago, St Louis, Cleveland.'[1]

Away from New York, certainly, hard bop was still easier to find in black environments – on jukeboxes where it might be cheek by jowl with R&B and doowop sides, and in ghetto clubs and bars. If the microgroove album did anything to create a hip audience of white jazz fans, it would be outrageous to suggest that it did anything less for black listeners. If a black audience could afford to buy any records, then they would be as likely to buy jazz albums as anything else.

Still, the music had to have an entertainment value that could make it stand alongside the best of the rest in black popular culture: its potential audience was as demanding as any other. Recording the likes of Gil Melle and Herbie Nichols might have satisfied the Medici conscience inside Alfred Lion, but it would be Jimmy Smith and Horace Silver who paid most of his bills. When important records such as 'The Preacher', 'Senor Blues' or *Jimmy Smith At The Organ Vol. 1* began to rack up significant sales, it was the making of Blue Note as a commercial entity.

The year 1957 was the one that saw Blue Note's recording activity really explode. No less than forty-seven sessions were recorded for release during the course of the year. Considering that the company was still basically being overseen – including all matters pertaining to A&R, recording, packaging and distribution – by the original two-man team, the pace was extraordinary. It was not, though, the label's finest year in terms of quality: if anything, a look through the session book for the year suggests that a sense of routine was already starting to set into the company's activities. But the strongest Blue Notes of the year were good enough to rank with the greatest jazz albums of the era.

A few players who'd already recorded as sidemen were offered their first Blue Note dates as leaders: Curtis Fuller, Sonny Clark, Clifford Jordan, John Jenkins. But the most important 'debut' of Blue Note's year was the sole record to be issued on the label under John Coltrane's leadership, *Blue Train*.

The existence of the album offers one of the most tantalising might-have-beens in jazz. At the beginning of the year, Coltrane, already attracting great attention through his work with the Miles Davis Quintet, paid an informal visit to the Blue Note offices around seven o'clock one evening, ostensibly to ask Alfred Lion for some of his Sidney Bechet records (Coltrane had not yet recorded on the soprano saxophone, an instrument which had been all but outlawed in modern jazz). Lion was there on his own, Wolff having left for the day. The two men talked about the possibility of a record deal, but with Wolff – the man who looked after the contractual side – absent, there was not much more than talk. Still, Lion sensed that he was on the verge of a deal with the saxophonist.

The chronology here is a little difficult to figure out. The meeting took place either late in 1956 or early in 1957, but Coltrane signed a deal with Prestige early in 1957 and made his first date for them as a leader on 31 May. On 6 April, though, he participated in the Johnny Griffin Blue Note date *A Blowing Session*. Did he discuss the earlier proposition with Lion once again at that session? Either way, the first office meeting concluded in somewhat bizarre circumstances. Lion offered Coltrane a small advance for the making of at least one record, which Coltrane took and agreed to. Just as things were about to be even further formalised, the cat which resided in Blue Note's office leaped out of the window and into the street (they were not very high up). Concerned for its welfare, Lion ran to the window, looked out, and saw the animal being shepherded into a taxi by a woman who'd just opened the door of the cab. Alarmed that someone was trying to steal his cat (the second time a feline had played a part in Blue Note history, after the incident with Bud Powell!), he ran down into the street, and apparently managed to recover the animal. But on his return, Coltrane had disappeared. The contract remained as no more than a handshake agreement.[2]

However, even though he had a new deal with Blue Note's great rival, Prestige, Coltrane didn't forget his promise. On 15 September he led a top-drawer Blue Note line-up through five compositions at the Van Gelder Hackensack studios. *Blue Train* has acquired an enormous reputation through the years, and after *A Love Supreme* and *Giant Steps* it is surely Coltrane's most renowned and frequently encountered record. It sits in collections which otherwise have none of Coltrane's Prestige or later Impulse! recordings, the most convenient and tolerable example of the first period of a difficult musician.

It's not hard to see why the album has been so successful. As the sole Blue Note by one of the most famous musicians in jazz, it has always staked a comfortable place in browser bins. For once, Reid Miles did little messing around with Frank Wolff's cover shot, cropping closely in on Coltrane's head and shoulders: he looks down, apparently lost in thought, saxophone hanging off his sports shirt, his left hand caught in the crook of his neck, his right raised to his lips as if he is musing on an imminent question. The title, *Blue Train*, almost suggests a kind of mood music, bolstered by the warm blue tint which Miles put on the photograph.

The music is beautifully delivered. Bob Porter's adage about Blue Note having two days of rehearsal where Prestige had none is borne out better by *Blue Train* than by any other session. As big and powerful as many of Coltrane's Prestige recordings are, none has quite the precision and polish of his Blue Note offering. Even so, the album is, in many ways, a high-craft, functional hard-bop record. Coltrane brought four original compositions to the date, of which at least two – 'A Moment's Notice' and 'Lazy Bird' – became frequently used parts of the jazz repertory. But there's a sense of impeccable routine about the music, which perhaps prophesies the way hard bop would go. In the notes to the latest reissue of the record, Curtis Fuller, who plays trombone on the record, says that 'I've been with younger musicians trying to work out that tune ["A Moment's Notice"]. And I tell them that that's just how we did it . . . on a moment's notice.'[3] That prosaic summary says much about the occasion.

The opening four minutes of the record are still electrifying. The stark, sombre blues theme of the title piece is elaborated through Coltrane's opening solo, beginning with long notes but quickly departing into a characteristic labyrinth where the chords are ransacked for many-headed motifs and trails of melody. It's a quite magisterial statement which Van Gelder captured in a sound more handsome than Coltrane had hitherto been blessed with. Yet from there, the performance becomes almost a matter of playing a blues until its end. Lee Morgan and Curtis Fuller were plausible choices for the front-line roles, and ones which the leader was responsible for, yet neither does anything other than, well, play the blues. Morgan, still finding his way, could be excused (what might Kenny Dorham have made of the role?), and the dyspeptic Fuller sounds far better as an ensemble colourist than as a soloist. It is always Coltrane himself one waits to hear. Paul Chambers and Philly Joe Jones are men he knew well, and they play with exemplary attention, although pianist Kenny Drew is again perhaps too bland a presence. All that seems forgotten once one hears the proud beauty of the tenorman's interpretation of 'I'm Old Fashioned' and the fast, controlled excitement of 'Lazy Bird'.

In the currently available CD edition of *Blue Train*, the originally issued version of the title track, take nine, is placed alongside take eight - with the added complexity that Drew's solo on take eight was the one featured on the familiar version, thanks to some tape splicing at the time of the first LP release. Some may be shocked that Lion's Blue Note would do such a thing, but as Tony Hall remembers Alfred telling him, it was not an uncommon practice for them to adopt, particularly where an ensemble head was much cleaner than on a take where the solos were hotter. Since the advent of tape mastering, jazz had become no more immune to post-production than any other kind of recorded music, and while such matters are often thought to have grown up in the sixties and seventies, it was a convention that started early. One of the more famous examples in fifties' jazz was Thelonious Monk's *Brilliant Corners* date for Riverside, where a finished version of the title piece had to be spliced from three different takes.

Curtis Fuller might not have been the star of the record, but he had a very good year with Blue Note. Three of his four leadership dates were cut in 1957. Another Detroit man, Fuller was, inevitably, a J. J. Johnson disciple, but was less focused and terse than Johnson, tending to bluster a little at fast tempos. His Blue Notes have seldom been widely available and are rather little known – his Savoy recordings from the end of the decade are more familiar – but they have their attractions. What Fuller excelled at was the ballad form. The English trombonist and bandleader Andy Prior has pointed out that 'in films, during the pillow talk, it's always the trombone you hear on the soundtrack', and Fuller's debut set *The Opener* commences with a languid and perfectly judged walk through 'A Lovely Way To Spend An Evening'. Fuller's first solo is meltingly lovely, and when Art Taylor uses his brushes to kick up the beat a little on his return, the mid-tempo croon of the horn is delightful. On the blues lines 'Hugore' and 'Lizzy's Bounce' he has less to say. Hank Mobley, the other horn player on the date, tends to outplay him on the quicker pieces, particularly with the sinuous tenor solo on Oscar Pettiford's rather tricky 'Oscalypso'. *Bone & Bari*, Fuller's second date, paired him with the baritone saxophonist Tate Houston, a fellow Detroit musician. Trombone and baritone was a combination which had secured some familiarity via the Gerry Mulligan-Bob Brookmeyer partnership, but this gruff, almost surly one-two sounded nothing like the mellifluous smoothness of their West Coast counterparts. When Houston gets out of the way and Fuller has the stage to himself for 'Heart And Soul', it sounds better. The best of Fuller's Blue Notes is *Curtis Fuller Vol. 3*, cut on 1 December with Art Farmer, Sonny Clark, bassist George Tucker and Louis Hayes. 'Little Messenger' does, indeed, sound like a pocket-sized Jazz Messengers workout, with Clark's solo particularly outstanding, and the group sounding more like a genuine band than those on Fuller's other dates. Art Farmer proved a particularly compatible associate of Fuller's and they would soon work together in the Jazztet, with Benny Golson.

Fuller's other important date of the year was his work on, of all things, a Bud Powell date. Powell had drifted out of Alfred Lion's orbit, but eventually Lion did ask Powell to make some more records, not realising that he was actually under contract to Norman Granz at the time. (Lion had to pay Granz a visit: 'I walked in and after he saw what kind of person I was and what my label was about he let me go ahead and release the albums with a credit to Verve.')[4] Fuller remembers that he was on the subway with Lion when out of the blue Alfred asked him to make the date with Powell. Subsequently, Lion wondered 'why we did not get another horn. It would have sounded better with two horns.'[5] Released as part of *Bud! The Amazing Bud Powell* (BLP 1571), the three quartet tracks seem to hark back to an older bebop period. Fuller acquits himself well enough, both on the ballad 'Don't Blame Me' and the up-tempo 'Idaho' and 'Moose The Mooche'. But it's a strange occasion, like so many of Powell's later sessions. Bud seems to take the most peculiar course through 'Idaho', eventually settling into a kind of stride piano. He is curiously mundane on 'Moose The Mooche', a piece he must have known inside out. The trio pieces have some excellent moments –

and 'Bud On Bach' is an amusing bit of probably unconscious hubris - but much of the playing sounds either effortful or under-powered, and Powell loses his way altogether on 'Some Soul'. Lion released all the music, but he knew that the playing was no match for the Powell of a few years earlier.

If Powell had lost his way, there were other pianists for Blue Note to record, and the one who made the biggest impression in 1957 was Conrad 'Sonny' Clark, who began recording as both sideman and leader for the label that year. Clark was twenty-six and had been around, playing first as a teenager in Pittsburgh, and then gleaning experience in both San Francisco and Los Angeles, where he was one of the relatively few black players to work steadily with the leading West Coast jazzmen. Returning east, he soon found himself in demand, and Lion recorded him prolifically: he is on twenty-nine sessions as either leader or sideman. The solo cited above, on Curtis Fuller's 'Little Messenger', is typical Clark: buoyant, neatly articulated, with idiosyncratic little left-hand figures counteracting long and ambitiously complex lines in the right. Clark at one point expressed a perhaps surprising admiration for the New York piano guru Lennie Tristano and for George Shearing, and one can hear, if not an influence, at least a kinship between their sometimes baroque methods and Clark's long, unspooling melody lines.

Dial 'S' For Sonny (BLP 1570) was his first record as leader, cut on 21 July 1957, with Art Farmer, Curtis Fuller, Hank Mobley, Wilbur Ware and Louis Hayes. This and its follow-up, *Sonny's Crib* (BLP 1576) - with a completely different line-up of Donald Byrd, Curtis Fuller, John Coltrane, Paul Chambers and Art Taylor - are accomplished but ultimately interchangeable hard-bop records. Clark sounds too much like an accompanist when he's with horns - and he was an excellent accompanist - to really authenticate his leadership, and unlike Horace Silver he tended to defer to rather than direct his front line. The best place to hear him is on his one trio date for the label, *Sonny Clark Trio* (BLP 1547), with Chambers and Philly Joe Jones. Disappointingly, there are none of his originals on the record, but over the encouraging and not too intrusive playing of the other two he sounds outgoing and full of ideas. The improvisations on 'Two Bass Hit' and a very long workout on 'Be-Bop' make full use of Clark's expressive powers. He has an impish side to him: the 'Be-Bop' solo in particular seems to have lots of nearly-but-not-quite quotes tossed into it, with funky little interjections, phrases repeated just for the fun of it and others used almost as paragraph endings in an improvisation that is rolled out over many choruses. At his peak, as here, Clark was a match for any pianist of his day. It was to be a melancholy truth that first heroin and then alcohol would seriously impede his progress.

Sonny Rollins made three further dates for Blue Note in 1957. *Sonny Rollins Vol. 2* (BLP 1558) followed, to some extent, the formula of his first session, with the saxophonist sited in the middle of a regulation hard-bop quintet – although, considering that the others were J. J. Johnson, Horace Silver, Paul Chambers and Art Blakey, there could hardly be any complaint about the leader outclassing his colleagues. Still, it did tend to sound like another hard-bop outing, with Rollins poking his head above the parapet every so often. On two tracks, though, there was an unexpected extra: the presence of Thelonious Monk, to whom Rollins had already given much credit for his own conceptions. Silver and Johnson sat out for 'Reflections': Monk expansively sets down an introduction, and follows it with his own solo before Rollins's huge sound wrangles its way around the theme. Better yet is 'Misterioso', where Johnson and Silver return, the latter to actually share the piano part with Monk (Silver comes in under Johnson's solo and stays for the rest). Rollins absolutely mows down Monk's changes during his three-chorus solo, yet the whole thing is also a tip of the hat to the master: so much of his shaping, toying with time and irascible exuberance seems to have been handed on from Monk himself. After only a brief interlude from Monk, Johnson barks his way through a couple of choruses, bluff but hearty, before the inimitable Silver shows how even 'Misterioso' can get funky. Behind it all is Blakey's stunning playing, shifting between regular and double time and proving beyond doubt that he was Monk's ideal drummer. A nine-minute masterpiece.

But Rollins's greatest work for the label was still to come. On 22 September, Lion recorded him with only a rhythm section (Wynton Kelly, Doug Watkins and Philly Joe Jones) for company. Although this had been Rollins's preferred setting at Prestige, it may be that Lion was reluctant to go this route: he liked the feel of two or three horns in the front line, and might have been concerned about letting a maverick improviser such as Rollins go it alone. But the resulting album, *Newk's Time*, is remarkable.

For some, Rollins had already laid down the greatest recorded music of his career. The combination of power, acuity, inspiration and daring which characterises the best of the Prestige albums is probably unique in the jazz literature. Every saxophone player has aspired to that kind of intense achievement ever since. While Coltrane, Rollins's only serious rival in this and virtually any other post-Parker period, was always in search of something, encouraging his listeners to follow him in the journey, Rollins suggested a man who was already at the summit and was delivering on the promise of his enormous abilities. There was the huge, ironclad tone, the sweeping command of dynamics, the baleful depth of oratory, the insistent stalking of some ever more Olympian result. What Max Harrison once called 'his union of emotional candour, great art, and civilised irony'[6] was something entirely individual, even in a field which was full of aspiring individualists. Nobody in jazz has ever reconciled the heart, the mind and the soul with such unmitigated strength as Rollins.

Even so, he could still suggest a humane uncertainty, even if it hardly counted as vulnerability. *Newk's Time* is full of that. Frank Wolff's cover photograph shows a supercool gladiator: the hawk-like visage masked in dark glasses, the saxophone held like an archer's bow. Wynton Kelly, Doug Watkins and Philly Joe Jones are a classic Blue Note rhythm section – they support, and don't get in the way. One might wish from moment to moment that Kelly were a little more forceful in underlining some of the harmonies – his typical deftness is almost too cute for such rigorous, masculine music-making – but the point of all this is to follow Rollins, and more specifically the way he reacts to Philly Joe's drums. Jones doesn't have the slyness or the capacity to provoke which Blakey has, and he isn't the polyrhythmic specialist which Elvin Jones would become, but throughout *Newk's Time* it's his crashing cymbals and snare which Rollins feeds off most directly. Inevitably, it comes to the fore on 'Surrey With The Fringe On Top', which is a duet between Rollins and Jones. With no bass in support, it would be tempting for a saxophonist to play such a piece too quickly, yet Rollins actually holds himself back from either overplaying or going too drastically out of time. Interestingly, the results sound nothing like anything which was produced in later years by John Coltrane with Elvin Jones, and it is down to Rollins's reluctance to let go of his customary uses of space and syntax. His interest in shaking what he can out of the melody line, instead of quickly departing from it and focusing on the harmonies, stamps all this material.

For all its strengths, *Newk's Time* is, in the end, disappointingly short, even unfinished: the record doesn't break the thirty-five-minute barrier, the closing

'Namely You' is the briefest of set-closers, and 'Wonderful! Wonderful!' is a typical Rollins appropriation of an unlikely tune which, for once, doesn't entrance. But there was more bounty to come, in the shape of a recording of a day's work (3 November) at the Village Vanguard, one set from the afternoon with Donald Bailey and Pete LaRoca, and another from the evening with Wilbur Ware and Elvin Jones. Although Van Gelder took down at least twenty separate pieces, Lion only issued a single LP, *A Night At The Village Vanguard* (BLP 1581). It is Rollins *in excelsis*.

The surviving material amounts to almost two and a quarter hours of music. Long after the original LP appeared, some of Michael Cuscuna's recovery work in the seventies provided enough for a double LP of 'new' material, and in its current CD incarnation there are sixteen tunes and some amusing banter between Rollins and his audience (particularly when they try to identify the Broadway source of 'Old Devil Moon'). The saxophonist plays throughout this typical day's work with titanic force, the tone almost frost-bitten in its intensity, the phrasing an endless variation. The two surviving pieces with Bailey and LaRoca are excellent, but it's the evening music which really grips. Ware's bass lines, which stand in Van Gelder's mix like a relentless juddering motion, are the point of contact to Earth, while Rollins sculpts one cryptic ingenuity after another out of the air. Jones, meanwhile, is torrential with his cross-rhythms, dividing and remoulding the time while working as a percussionist – a continuous hiss of cymbals – and a kit-drum colourist. The absence of a piano might have contributed to the freedom of the leader, but one feels that Rollins would have been magnificent in almost any circumstance, and Jones and Ware simply add to the riches.

It is an early example of Rollins as a leader of his own group, since he had spent much of the previous few years with Max Roach, and it speaks of a man embracing his moment: but Blue Note, alas, would take down no further music from him. Unable to make Rollins a significant offer to keep him on, Lion had to watch as the saxophonist went on to record for Riverside, Contemporary and Metrojazz, before the first of his famous sabbaticals in 1959.

Clifford Jordan was another tenorman to make a Blue Note debut during 1957. His point of origin isn't difficult to divine from the title of his first album: *Blowing In From Chicago* featured him in a two-tenor line-up, alongside John Gilmore, who subsequently spent much of his career in Sun Ra's Arkestra. Jordan joined Horace Silver's band in 1957, and Silver plays on the session with Gilmore, a hot, exciting contest if not quite as brazenly pugilistic as some of the two-tenor records which Johnny Griffin and Lockjaw Davis would go on to make. Although he acquits himself well, Jordan's subsequent discs suggest that this kind of blowout wasn't really his thing. Both *Clifford Jordan* (BLP 1565) and *Cliff Craft* (BLP 1582) are almost laid-back in comparison. The septet of the first – with Lee Morgan, Curtis Fuller and altoist John Jenkins in the front line – is nicely tuned, but the music is often little more than an amiable ramble. For *Cliff Craft*, a quintet was assembled with Art Farmer, Sonny Clark, George Tucker and Louis Hayes. Farmer's romantic playing sits well alongside the thoughtful leader, who sometimes sounds like Rollins on a very low flame: they do some original bebop in 'Confirmation' and 'Anthropology', but it is bop delivered as a smiling memory.

Although Blue Note were frequently adding new names to their roster, the 'family' aspect of the line-ups was becoming more obvious. Rhythm sections would be run up from the same pool of expert players. The horns would appear in certain configurations, sometimes in an experimental aspect, often in what was already a tried-and-true – perhaps one player added to or subtracted from a previous personnel. But Lion didn't always persevere. Jordan's three albums are interesting, but hardly world-beaters, and their sales showed no terrific public response. So after three different kinds of session, Lion let him go (Jordan went on to record for Riverside and Jazzland). After his tempestuous debut, Johnny Griffin made *A Blowing Session* (BLP 1559) with Hank Mobley and John Coltrane, the kind of good-natured fisticuffs which were more familiar from Prestige dates than Blue Note sessions, before *The Congregation* (BLP 1580), a quartet set with Sonny Clark, Paul Chambers and newcomer Kenny Dennis on drums. *The Congregation* is arguably the best of the three, even if Dennis is no match for his obvious mentor Art Blakey and the title piece sounds like an attempt to play a jazz hit. But there's already a sense that Griffin had done all that he would do at Blue Note, of a circle closing. Griffin moved to Art Blakey and then to Thelonious Monk's group, and began making records for Riverside.

The most obvious examples of 'Blue Note men' among the horn players were Hank Mobley and Lee Morgan. Mobley cut *Hank* (BLP 1560), *Hank Mobley* (BLP 1568), a quintet date unreleased until the 1980s eventually titled *Curtain Call*, and a sextet date which went similarly neglected until its eventual issue as *Poppin'*. Mobley's albums of the fifties aren't especially outstanding, yet his own playing is always curiously satisfying, the work of a man who felt entirely settled and at home in his surroundings. The unruffled mobility of his playing can sometimes seem facile to the inattentive, but time after time his solos repay close listening, often full of guileful touches that show what a shrewd, resourceful improviser he was. That said, his greatest works lay just ahead of him. Mobley was a particular influence on many British players, who eagerly attempted to get their hands on his latest Blue Notes as they appeared.

Morgan, too, seemed to be growing up at Blue Note. In 1957, he led *Lee Morgan Vol. 3* (BLP 1557), *City Lights* (BLP 1575), *The Cooker* (BLP 1578) and *Candy* (BLP 1590), a formidable year's work, to set alongside numerous sideman appearances.

The major initiative during 1957, however, was the continued recording of Jimmy Smith. The organist recorded no less than nine sessions for Blue Note during the year, although not all of them were issued. With a couple of club recordings already behind him – the 'Club Baby Grand' sessions, made in the unlikely setting of Wilmington, Delaware, the previous August – Smith had already been set down both live and in the studio. Three days of recording in February 1957, with horns and without, resulted in a string of records, and a date made up of standards on 8 May was released under the title *Jimmy Smith Plays Pretty Just For You* (BLP 1563). An unsatisfactory trio date in August was followed by a session with horns in September which, again, only found a release across several records many years later. In November, Lion and Van Gelder went back to the club where the Blue Note boss had first heard Smith, and cut two albums under the heading *Groovin' At Small's Paradise Vols. 1 & 2*. A final trio date in November, scheduled for release as *Lonesome Road*, was again never issued.

Lion's activity with Smith is particularly interesting. Clearly, he wanted to record this exciting new discovery as frequently as possible. He was already trying several settings – a standards record, live albums, trio-plus-horns situations – with an eye on Smith's bankability. A title such as *Plays Pretty Just For You* was hardly conceived with posterity in mind. Yet the fact that three sessions made during the year were deemed unsatisfactory suggests that Lion was quickly aware how fragile his artist's success rate might be. The organ-combo fad had barely begun, yet already Lion was calculating what

Smith's most successful elements were likely to be. As much as Smith had seemed like a breath of fresh air on his arrival, it already looked as though Lion was going to have to be careful about over-exposing him too fast.

In the end, though, that was pretty much what happened. Smith shifted units - in modern industry parlance - better than most of his Blue Note colleagues, and Lion and Wolff needed the kind of fast turnover which Smith's albums supplied. Whether Smith's albums appeal depends to a considerable extent on whether his whole methodology appeals beyond its initial novelty. Although the later Blue Notes do suggest a winnowing-down of his style to its most effective ingredients, at this stage his albums do have a knack for sounding proudly similar to each other, a trait which, even in the setting of hard-bop convention, had to lead to listener fatigue. But that would be a long-term problem. For now, *A Date With Jimmy Smith, Groovin' At Small's Paradise* and even *Plays Pretty Just For You* must have seemed like manna to his new circle of fans.

Someone else who had something of a Blue Note comeback in this year was Lou Donaldson. His previous date had been back in 1954, but on 27 January he cut a quintet date (with Donald Byrd on trumpet), released as *Wailing With Lou* (BLP 1545). The avuncular bebopper returned with his vinegary style still undiluted by anything 'modern', and the opening head-clearing blast through 'Caravan' is typical of Lou at his liveliest, while the following 'Old Folks' is unfussy, unsophisticated heart-tugging. Donaldson's jazz is an entertainer's art, the flipside to Sonny Rollins's steel-backed art music, and with his numinous sessions for the label he stands as perhaps the more typical proponent of Blue Note's gospel. It's fitting that he was also the last to lead a session in 1957, with the excellent sextet date *Lou Takes Off* (BLP 1591).

Donaldson's comments on Alfred Lion's way of working bear repeating:

> See, man, Frank and Alfred were from Germany. They didn't know that much about our music. So they didn't bother you, you know what I mean? They wouldn't come out and say, 'Now you do this, you do that.' They'd come to the dates you're playing and it would be like, 'Finish?' And you'd be like, 'No, I'm not finished yet.' And so they sat there reading the paper. Then, they'd pay you your money and go. They'd say, 'Well look. Black people play this kind of stuff. They know what we're doing, so we let them play it.' That's why they made so much money.[7]

That may be how Donaldson remembers it, but other accounts have it rather differently. What most musicians tend to remember is the Alfred Lion dance. If a session wasn't going too well, Alfred would sit impassively in his seat, as if waiting for something to happen, but when the band finally hit a groove which he liked, he'd begin an ungainly shuffle around the control room, which Frank, if present, would eventually join in. The musicians knew that once Alfred had gone into his dance, they were on to something.

There was one other significant change for the label during 1957. The old Blue Note place on Lexington Avenue had become too small for a label that had outgrown its beginnings – not by that much, perhaps, but enough to demand a more substantial office. So, in the summer, they moved. The new address for Blue Note records was West 63rd Street, a midtown block that would be enshrined on the back of their LP covers: 'For Complete Catalog Write to BLUE NOTE RECORDS, 47 West 63rd St., New York 23.'

SEVEN

As the fifties began to run out, jazz seemed to be in a position of treading water. The death of Charlie Parker in 1955 had been the one real watershed of the decade: the symbolic passing of the bebop era marked by the demise of the man who had epitomised it, with no clear progression into something to replace it. Hard bop was bebop's natural successor, but it didn't seem like anything 'new', just a remodelling of principles which the last set of innovators had already established. As R&B and rock'n'roll commenced their unstoppable journey towards controlling the ears of a young listening audience, jazz began to seem - perhaps for the first time - old. The senior players, after all, were still around: Louis Armstrong, Duke Ellington, Benny Goodman; there were swing revivalists and New Orleans traditionalists. In Europe, 'trad jazz' was more popular than anything associated with bop.

Yet the music business was still a comparatively young and green industry. The idea of instant disposability, which would come to be an integral part of pop culture, had yet to overwhelm a business which was still finding its way and used to working comparatively slowly. Blue Note's jazz - the jazz of Jimmy Smith, Art Blakey and Horace Silver - was still working itself out and working its way forward.

For Horace Silver, who was now among Blue Note's most familiar and prolific presences, the hard-bop life was proving successful enough. Having built a reputation for his quintet, Silver had plenty of work and Alfred Lion was recording him regularly. But a revealing *Down Beat* interview with Dom Cerulli, from 1958, shows some of the difficulties of even a successful working life:

> For the last year, we worked pretty steadily. Our income has been, pretty generally, on the increase. But one of the troubles is that you go around and play the same clubs in the same towns over and over again. Cities can get over-exposed. For instance, Cleveland is a dead town for jazz. It had two clubs, and the first time I played there with the Messengers, the response was great. The last few times, though, the turnouts haven't been good. I asked to find out if it was me or my group or hard times. I found out that the people just aren't coming out any more.
>
> We play ['Senor Blues'] about three times a night. It's the most requested number in our book. The people holler for it. I think it's a good thing to play a tune a lot, although we sometimes get tired of it. I don't mind, because if the people like it, it must have some commercial potential. And it must be a musical thing, too. People probably dig it because it's simple, and it's easy to understand.
>
> The recording scene is very good at Blue Note. They treat me very well, and let me record what I want. When we draw up a contract, we talk it over and I tell them what I want in it. They're good on royalties, and we have a very good relationship. Al (Lion) doesn't push things on me, like some cats at other companies. I think I get a good break because the quintet is pretty important to the label.[1]

Silver's confidence in his label wasn't misplaced. It's doubtful if there was a more valuable musician - as leader and sideman - to the label than the pianist at this point. The sequence of records which he ran up at the end of the fifties was superbly effective. On 8 May 1957 he cut *The Stylings Of Silver* (BLP 1562); on 13 January 1958, *Further Explorations By The Horace Silver Quintet* (BLP 1589); on 1 February 1959, *Finger Poppin'*; and on 28 August 1959, the masterful *Blowin' The Blues Away* (BLP 4017). Although unassuming in terms of any kind of great statement, this is as fine a run of records as any regular jazz group has made.

As with several of the Blue Note mainstays - including Jimmy Smith, Hank Mobley and Lee Morgan - Silver's expertise deepened and he simply made better records as he went forward. He had never lacked confidence, but the experience of running a regular band and the disciplines of consistent work were honing his skills. While the Blue Notes suggest a mainstream of hard bop - which in turn implies a settling into a routine - their contents are actually original, diverse and very particular about avoiding clichés. *Further Explorations*, which has been rather neglected in reissue programmes (and only a single track merited entry in the otherwise excellent *Retrospective* survey issued by the label in 1999), is one of Silver's best records. The front line of Art Farmer and Clifford Jordan is beautifully balanced, Farmer's tactile elegance matched with Jordan's muscular but cooperative tenor. All but one of the tunes are Silver originals - no simple blues derivations or melodies dumped on to standard chord sequences. 'The Outlaw', which begins the record, is typical: shifting restlessly between Latin and swing sections, the complex theme is traversed so sweetly by the band that, for all its difficulty, the piece never seems intimidating. 'Melancholy Mood', played by the rhythm section alone, is one of Silver's best pieces of introspection. Everything on the record is a model of craftsmanship.

It was a band that had done a lot of roadwork, but the next edition of the Silver quintet would do even more. Trumpeter Blue Mitchell and tenor saxophonist Junior Cook enlisted in 1959 and stayed for several years. With Gene Taylor (bass) and Louis Hayes, this became Silver's most renowned outfit (Hayes would join Cannonball Adderley in 1960, and had various replacements). *Finger Poppin'* is not quite as fine as its predecessor, due in part to Mitchell and Cook, who as yet can't measure up to the standards set by Farmer and Jordan, but at least three pieces – the attacking blues 'Cookin' At The Continental', the almost 'proper' samba routine 'Swingin' The Samba' and the durable near-blues 'Juicy Lucy' – are at Silver's top level.

Blowin' The Blues Away is tremendous. The title track sets off at the tempo of a typhoon, and is apotheosised in Silver's frenetic solo. The ten-bar ballad 'Peace' is one of Silver's most-covered compositions, though it's rarely played as slowly and graciously as the original. 'Sister Sadie' became a hit choice for other bandleaders – Woody Herman's version is particularly strong – but, again, the Silver original is distinguished by its exacting delivery at what seems precisely the right tempo – up, but not overfast. With jazz on the cusp of a craze for so-called 'soul jazz', Silver was crystallising all the ingredients – gospel and blues templates allied with grooving beats – in such pieces and getting a near perfect result. 'The Baghdad Blues' is another of his tongue-in-cheek pieces of exoticism. To close the record, Silver went back to 'Melancholy Mood', but in an altered tempo and with changed voicings, a move inspired by Silver's fellow pianist Gil Coggins.

Silver's albums were outstanding because they worked *as albums*. As jazz had grown accustomed to the long-playing format, its LP records became more like entities and less like collections of tracks or jams or strings of solos. More than almost anyone else, Silver was fashioning balanced, cogent programmes of music, matched together for the forty minutes of a typical LP duration. It was more than just a question of dropping in the obligatory ballad or blues: without surrendering any of the variety he put into pace and colour, Silver saw to it that the music had a consistency of flow.

It was also music that won both commercial and critical success. Lion ensured that there was a steady sequence of singles released from the albums, including 'Sister Sadie', 'Finger Poppin', 'Juicy Lucy' and 'Swingin' The Samba', all the type of radio and jukebox favourites which kept Silver's name and music prominent. In the American jazz press, reviewers were for the most part similarly enthusiastic, although the critic's need to criticise inevitably came in from time to time. Martin Williams, in his review of *Further Explorations*, opined that Silver was engaged in 'the modernisation and elaboration of the kind of riff-blues-jump music of the 1930s and early '40s . . . he can enlarge it, has fresh things to say within it, and it is a conception which reaffirms and even asserts some very important and basic things about jazz. When he tries for other things (as in "Melancholy Mood"), he does not succeed.'[2]

By and large, the jazz media were kind to Blue Note, without indulging in any glad-handing. If the company's records were a notch ahead of any of their independent rivals, the reader of *Down Beat* and *Metronome* would hardly know it from their reviewers' reactions to the material. Good work was praised, but there was little evidence that future classics such as *Newk's Time, Further Explorations* or *Blue Train* were perceived as being much more than decent representations of work-in-progress. It's easy (and unfair) to use hindsight and be astonished at such a thing. But it does seem strange to look through the review columns of those times and see equal space being accorded to long-forgotten records by the likes of Dick Marx, the Dukes Of Dixieland and Angelo Pippo as to the masterpieces of the hard-bop era. Still, *Down Beat* was as embattled as anything else in the jazz business. A fortnightly, it was a very slim publication, and had to try and cover what was by then a diffuse and wide-ranging jazz scene. It may have been the golden age of hard bop, but there was more on, say, Stan Kenton in the magazine than on any of Blue Note's artists. The label also took only modest advertising: a third-page column was typical (Riverside, in contrast, was lavish in its advertising). In addition, the modern tradition of long-winded articles and in-depth reviews and interviews was something which had, so far, not invaded the music press.

Tirelessly, Alfred Lion and Frank Wolff went on recording and releasing. Blue Note recorded sixty-eight sessions during 1958–9, not all of them producing results which Lion deemed worthy of release, but still setting an extraordinarily high standard for the label. There were several new names to add to the leadership roster: saxophonists Tina Brooks and Jackie McLean, trombonist Bennie Green, trumpeters Dizzy Reece and Donald Byrd, and pianists Walter Davis and Duke Pearson. But the most important additions to the ranks were two groups.

One was the Three Sounds. The piano trio was becoming one of the most popular of jazz units. Small enough to offer the kind of closely focused sound which wouldn't deter listeners who didn't want to try too hard with their jazz, it was still able to carry all the sophistications which a more committed follower expected. At least two figures outside the hard-bop arena – Oscar Peterson and Erroll Garner – had won huge audiences with the format, often made up of people who rarely listened to any other kind of jazz (which is why Garner's *Concert By the Sea* album can still be found in old LP accumulations as a lone example of a jazz album). But besides Garner and Peterson, many younger pianists were following the format to considerable success, and soon every jazz label had at least one such trio on its books, playing what was often a kind of hip cocktail music: Red Garland at Prestige, Ahmad Jamal at Argo, Bill Evans at Riverside (though Evans was perhaps more self-consciously 'artistic', he probably appealed to much the same people who bought the other records).

Blue Note hadn't gone too far in that direction, but when he heard the trio from Washington DC called the Three Sounds, Lion went after that market in a serious way. The group had made a single set for Riverside with Nat Adderley, and when they arrived in New York, Lion signed them and cut some initial sessions on 16 and 28 September 1958, eventually released as *Introducing The Three Sounds* (BLP 1600). The trio was Gene Harris (piano), Andrew Simpkins (bass) and Bill Dowdy (drums), and that is the group which eventually cut sixteen albums for Blue Note over a ten-year period (only later on were Dowdy and then Simpkins replaced). Although they had originally featured a saxophonist, it was when Harris took centre stage and began making the most benign and good-hearted improvisations on popular material that the Sounds began to click. Light, bluesy, discreetly swinging – Dowdy was a drummer who believed in gentle persuasion, not bullying or bravado – their music was almost a definition of jazz formula. Harris would state the melody, maybe out of tempo, maybe with his partners there; then take a chorus or two where he gradually built the genteel intensity and fashioned a modest improvisation, probably with some locked-hands touches along the way; then a return to the tune, with a tag at the close. The steady mid-tempo lope was the normal setting, but ballads – where Harris would really arpeggiate the melody line – might follow a funereal beat and double the duration.

As a result, all their records were the same. If you liked one of them, you'd like *any* one of them, and in one of those curious situations where the law of diminishing returns doesn't seem to apply, the Three Sounds sold consistently well over their Blue Note life. It didn't hurt that Lion released more than twenty singles off the various albums. As smart background music, the Three Sounds were as fine as anybody could wish.

Long after the trio ended, Harris continued as an old-school jazz entertainer, having spent most of his adult life pleasing crowds of one sort or another. The Scottish guitarist Jim Mullen, who toured with him in later years, recalled how it worked:

> Gene used to say that these people have come out to see us, and it's our job to give them a fantastic time. He used to say at the end of the evening, 'If you leave here with a smile on your face, remember that Gene Harris put it there.' I've never seen anyone turn a room of strangers into family that way. We never rehearsed. He'd do this big rubato solo piano introduction with no clue as to what's coming up. Then he'd just start playing and you had to be ready to jump in there. That's how he wanted it.[3]

The other group to arrive in 1959 was one which had already been a Blue Note outfit. Art Blakey had made records for Columbia, RCA, Atlantic and Bethlehem since the previous Jazz Messengers sessions of 1955, but this time he returned for a long stay. The first new Messengers Blue Note was cut on 30 October 1958, and was released under the title *Moanin'* (BLP 4003). In the line-up were Lee Morgan, the saxophonist and composer Benny Golson, pianist Bobby Timmons and bassist Jymie Merritt. Aside from Blakey himself, that made it an all-Philadelphia band, and they sounded like the most cohesive and understanding of groups. 'Moanin'' itself is the kind of melodic tattoo which is, once heard, never forgotten, and although it depended heavily on the backbeat which the drummer paraded throughout the track – with, for

Blakey, surprisingly little variation – it created a Messengers showpiece which stayed with the band for the rest of its days. The solos are long and multifarious: Morgan is at his cheekiest and most spirited, Golson gets himself into some impossible twists which he manages to throw off before the end, Timmons does some enjoyable showing off and even Merritt has some space.

Timmons was the composer of 'Moanin'', but the real compositional meat of the record comes in Benny Golson's four pieces, of which both 'Along Came Betty' and 'Blues March' are definitive. While Golson's style as an improviser is forbiddingly turbulent and at times even chaotic, his writing is unexpectedly serene and often disarmingly lovely: his threnody for Clifford Brown, 'I Remember Clifford', remains one of the finest of jazz ballads. 'Along Came Betty' is a melody line of comparable beauty, and here, carefully voiced for the horns and played with a sublime restraint, Golson offers up an unassuming masterpiece. 'Blues March', announced by Blakey in his drum-major guise, seems on first acquaintance like a cute chunk of shuffling blues, but again the impeccably arranged lines for the horns show how inventively Golson could repackage the most familiar of materials. For much of the record, the leader is given a somewhat conventional role for a man who was used to leading from the front, but Golson also came up with a showcase for the drummer called 'The Drum Thunder Suite'.

Some of the impromptu spirit of the first Messengers records has been lost at this point. Maybe the band would never again sound the way it did with Silver at the piano. But Blakey had nevertheless built a unit which could outface any changes in personnel and become a dynasty unto itself. What *Moanin'* offered was a blueprint for years of productive repertory. A writer in the band who would contribute a chunk of core repertoire to the band's book; young soloists who would attempt to bring something of their own to an established set list;

and the ominous volcano at the back of the stage, ready to start spitting fire if a musician in the front line wasn't doing the right thing. *Moanin'* was really the first 'proper' Jazz Messengers album.

Blakey had not been entirely absent from Blue Note's release schedules. In March 1957 he had recorded a curious session which resulted in two LPs of an *Orgy In Rhythm*. Although there were contributions from Herbie Mann, Ray Bryant and Wendell Marshall, most of the music consisted of various confrontational episodes involving Blakey and eight other kit drummers or percussionists. Blakey had spent two years in Africa in the forties yet always maintained that his experiences there left his drumming unaffected, and there are few hints of any kind of 'world jazz' in these rather aimless records. Blakey returned to this type of format in the later *Holiday For Skins Vols. 1 & 2* (BLP 4004/5), a similar but rather more focused occasion cut only a few days after *Moanin'*; yet these sessions – like the record released under the nominal leadership of percussionist Sabu Martinez, *Palo Congo* (BLP 1561) – are more symptomatic of the then-current vogue for exotic lounge music, rather than any genuine Afro-Jazz fusion.

The Jazz Messengers were recorded at Birdland once again on 15 April 1959, with Hank Mobley returning in place of the absent Golson. The music on *At The Jazz Corner Of The World, Vols. 1 & 2* (BLP 4015/6) suggests a band beginning to get comfortable with its routine – but it's quite a routine. Any band that could boast soloists as fit and sparkling as Mobley and Morgan – the trumpeter's firecracker solo on Mobley's tune 'M&M' is just one example of his thrilling sound – was going to be worth recording at every opportunity. Yet the finest Messengers records were still to come.

Of the newcomers to the label during this period, one of the most interesting was Harold Brooks, nicknamed 'Tina' since childhood. He had played mostly in R&B groups before moving into more boppish environs, but he didn't make a significant jazz appearance until he was booked to play alto on Jimmy Smith's 1958 date *The Sermon*. After that, Lion gave him three dates of his own, but Brooks was a star-crossed character and only one of them was even released during his lifetime: another casualty of narcotics, he made no further records after 1961 and died in obscurity in 1974.

His first date, on 16 March 1958, was eventually released in the 1980s as *Minor Move*. It is heavy company – Lee Morgan, Sonny Clark, Doug Watkins and Art Blakey – but Brooks acquits himself well. He takes the third solo on the opening blues 'Nutville', as if reluctant to push himself forward, but plays with handsome authority. Brooks had a light sound, somewhat in kinship with the stalwart Hank Mobley, and like Mobley he could get around changes and tricky constructions with a deceptive smoothness, as if he didn't want to make anything sound too difficult, either for himself or his audience. In the notes to his later *True Blue*, he says: 'I want to express myself rather than be a killer technically, but in order to do this I have to grow technically.'[4] In the age of Rollins and Coltrane, Brooks might have felt himself overshadowed, but there seems to be scarcely anything deficient in either his feel or his delivery.

Minor Move is a little unfinished – most of it is extended blowing on standards, and the title track is the only interesting compositional moment – which may be why Lion put that date in the can and waited until the June 1960 *True Blue* to issue a debut by Brooks. Brooks had already played on trumpeter Freddie Hubbard's debut record *Open Sesame*, and Hubbard returned the favour for this date, with Duke Jordan, Sam Jones and Art Taylor. It only needs a few bars of the opening 'Good Old Soul' – a mystifying title for such a dark piece – to show what a huge advance on the previous session this one was. Ira Gitler describes the track in his notes as 'down and dirty', an unfathomable judgement on what is a haunting, almost stately minor theme, beautifully handled by the horns. Brooks's long solo is a remarkable statement, labyrinthine but played out with enormous strength. He capitalises on the idiosyncrasies of his tone – an occasional honking low note or a creased, poignant high one – to superb effect. Hubbard, then coming into his own greatness, almost matches him, before the theme returns to wind down a stunning performance. One can only wonder at Brooks's modest appraisal of his technique, since throughout the record he builds solos of sometimes heroic strength. All six themes – each by Brooks apart from the closing standard 'Nothing Ever Changes My Love For You' – are individual pieces of writing rather than generic blues or bop lines, and even 'True Blue' itself plays tag with notions of boogaloo jazz. This is one of the forgotten masterpieces of the Blue Note catalogue.

As mentioned, Brooks had made his Blue Note debut on the Jimmy Smith date which produced *The Sermon*, recorded on 25 February 1958 (a makeweight track, 'J.O.S.', was added from a session made a few months earlier). The title track was, in Blue Note terms, unprecedented. Running just over twenty minutes, it occupied an entire LP side. There were a few other examples of that kind of marathon on Prestige, but as an extended jam it was the kind of thing which would normally have fallen outside Blue Note's accepted practice. For once, Lion let Smith and cohorts take as much time as they pleased, basing the music around the locked-in groove of Smith, Kenny Burrell and Art Blakey, with decorative solos from Lee Morgan, Brooks and Lou Donaldson. It is not an immortal performance – unusually, Lee Morgan runs a bit dry in his inspirations, and the ragged closing minutes are less than outstanding – but Brooks impresses, again, with his fresh thinking. 'The Sermon' fades off into the distance and underlines the never-ending aspect of Jimmy Smith at

Blue Note. He continued to be recorded by Lion at a prodigious rate, but several of the sessions during the period went unreleased, and *Softly As A Summer Breeze* and *Home Cookin'* were the only other Smith albums to be released before 1960. Brooks, meanwhile, had made two other appearances, both times on sessions led by Kenny Burrell. A two-volume set made in May 1958 called *Blue Lights* (BLP 1596/7) featured combinations of eight different players, while an evening recording date at New York's Five Spot Café on 25 August 1959 had Burrell with a rhythm section of either Roland Hanna or Bobby Timmons on piano, Ben Tucker on bass and Art Blakey, with Brooks playing on a few pieces. The studio date was another jam-session sort of event, the players stretching out on blues and standards, and that feel carried over into the Five Spot session, where for once the qualities of the room interfered with Rudy Van Gelder's precision work: the piano sounds clunky, and the surrounding acoustic seems drier and more closed. If *Blue Lights* was relatively ordinary, *On View At The Five Spot Café* is splendidly harmonious. It's a pity that the surviving material (several sets were recorded but they only yielded a single LP) only features Brooks on a couple of tracks, as he plays with typical plangency and imagination, especially on the Dizzy Gillespie blues 'Birk's Works'. Burrell figures strongly throughout the record. The main point of interest for some in *Blue Lights*, though, was the cover art, a rare example of Reid Miles commissioning a commercial artist to come up with some graphics. The artist in question, Andy Warhol, had already done a couple of Blue Note sleeves – Johnny Griffin's shirt-bedecked *The Congregation*, and the striking line figure on a previous Burrell set, *Kenny Burrell Vol. 2* – but he would later achieve somewhat wider fame (lasting considerably longer than fifteen minutes).

Donald Byrd had already made records as a leader – including the exceedingly rare album for Transition, *Byrd's Eye View* – and was already familiar as a Blue Note sideman when in December 1958, a couple of weeks after his twenty-sixth birthday, he made his first set as a group boss for the label with *Off To The Races* (BLP 4007). *Byrd In Hand* (BLP 4019, May 1959) and *Fuego* (BLP 4026, October 1959) were quick follow-ups. Byrd is one of the most difficult of Blue Note's long-standing players to assess without feeling exasperated at his predilections and choices. His early appearances on record suggest a super-competent but ultimately faceless hard-bopper, the kind of musician whose work would eventually be turned on and damned as repetitive and shallow. His latter-day music, which ultimately arrived at a pop-jazz fusion that seemed to suggest the end of Blue Note as a creative jazz force, turned away from so many of the principles of his early playing that he hardly seemed like the same man. Yet he was a thoughtful and generous figure in his field, involving himself heavily in educational work and pioneering jazz studies at a college level in the US.

Byrd's first Blue Notes are careful, enjoyable hard-bop sessions, and not a great deal more. There seems little to say about them since their smooth playability offers plenty to entertain and not much to remember once the discs are over. *Byrd In Hand*, with a bevy of fellow Detroit men in the line-up, might be the best of the first few.

They certainly didn't match the three albums produced by the Jamaican-born trumpeter Alphonso Reece: *Blues In Trinity, Star Bright* and *Soundin' Off*. Dizzy Reece had been a mainstay of the London jazz scene since the middle fifties. Tony Hall, who loved his playing and was convinced that he was a match for the best American trumpeters, persuaded Lion to take a chance on recording Reece in London, with Donald Byrd and Art Taylor sitting in on an otherwise all-British date. Hall managed to bring Byrd and Taylor over from Paris, where they were working, to a studio in north London (for many years, *Blues In Trinity* was listed as having been recorded in France, but it was only a subterfuge to get round the Musicians' Union ban on American players recording in Britain). 'I gave the studio caretaker a fiver to get him to clear off for the afternoon,' remembers Hall. With the brilliant young saxophonist Tubby Hayes, Terry Shannon on piano and Lloyd Thompson on bass, the Anglo-American cooperative worked through a fine session. Reece is outstanding as a soloist, avoiding expected paths and mixing bop virtuosity with a more thoughtful demeanour. The title track is a quite ingenious blues, the bassist working in double time, the drummer in *triple* time, which offers the soloist three different options for his own tempo. Byrd plays on only two tracks but is entirely overshadowed by Reece, and Hayes, the prodigy who became the best-loved figure in British jazz, is so quick and hearty in his playing that he can leave the unwary breathless. He demolishes another blues, 'Close Up', and has a splendid feature on 'Round Midnight'.

The subsequent *Star Bright* and *Soundin' Off* were made after Reece had gone to America (he still lives in New York), and both are full of imaginative variations on the hard-bop formula: yet the trumpeter never caught the imagination of any audience beyond that of his small cult following, and Lion didn't record him again as a leader. Like Kenny Dorham, Reece was a player who asked for patience and involvement from his audience, and he was unable to court a wider appeal.

Of all the new signings, the most important individual was Jackie McLean, an alto saxophonist from – a local man at last! – New York, who had been on the city's scene since the beginning of the fifties. McLean had had a difficult few years. Despite several high-profile stints with other leaders – including Miles Davis, Art Blakey and Charles Mingus – McLean had made no real headway as a leader himself. His records for Prestige were mostly spotty, unconvincing affairs (he later rounded on the company, comparing working for them to 'being under the Nazi regime and not knowing it'),[5] and trouble with the police over his use of narcotics had led to the dreaded loss of his cabaret card, the same problem which had afflicted Monk's progress. Yet, in 1959, he signed up with Lion and also began working with the cooperative Living Theatre, a freewheeling stage group which staged various 'events' from poetry to performance art, culminating in the production of a play by Jack Gelber, *The Connection*, which dramatised aspects of the jazzman's life.

McLean's first Blue Note as leader was *New Soil* (BLP 4013), made on 2 May 1959 (material from an earlier session was subsequently released out of sequence). Although pitched as a typical hard-bop quintet session (with Donald Byrd, Walter Davis, Paul Chambers and Pete LaRoca), the music might have puzzled the unwary. McLean brought two pieces to the date, 'Hip Strut' and 'Minor Apprehension' (often better remembered as 'Minor March', which was the title used by Miles Davis in his recording of the tune). 'Apprehension' is a useful word to describe the music. Although 'Hip Strut''s structure eventually breaks out into a walking blues, its most striking motif is the suspension on a single, tolling chord, over which the soloists sound ominously trapped. In this one, McLean suggests the patient, rather effortful manner of one of his acknowledged influences, Dexter Gordon, but in the following 'Minor Apprehension' he sounds like the godson of Charlie Parker, tearing through the changes with the scalded desperation of the bebopper locked in a harmonic maze. The rest of the record, dependent on several Walter Davis tunes, is less impressive, but McLean's mix of plangency and something inscrutable is very striking.

Not always, though, particularly likeable. McLean is a player whose music has often aroused admiration over warmth. The sense that he is always playing

Alfred Lion and
Francis Wolff

Rudy Van Gelder
with Alfred Lion
in 1960

Michael Cuscana

Bruce Lundvall

Art Blakey

Miles Davis

Dexter Gordon

Thelonious Monk

Bud Powell

Horace Silver

Hank Mobley

Greg Osby

slightly out of tune lends an insistent sourness to the tonality of his music, and it is the recurring problem within a diverse and often fascinating discography for the label. His fellow alto saxophonist Lee Konitz, who has also been accused of playing sharp, remembers a session with himself, McLean, Dexter Gordon and Ben Webster: 'After the session I shook Jackie's hand, thinking how nice it was to play with him, and then it occurred to me I was thanking him for playing sharp!'[6]

Swing Swang Swingin' (BLP 4024) gave McLean the limelight as the sole horn, with Walter Bishop, Jimmy Garrison and Art Taylor behind him. This session tends to restore the emphasis on McLean's bebop origins, with big, powerful improvisations such as those on 'Stablemates' and 'Let's Face The Music And Dance' – a standard which very few jazz players have chosen to cover – suggesting that he still had a lot of juice to squeeze out of his bop sensibilities. But McLean began to change, in part, perhaps, because of his experiences with the Living Theatre, and his Blue Note albums would come to document a personality with a high degree of artistic curiosity.

In 1958, Bud Powell recorded his final two dates for Blue Note, released as *Time Waits* (BLP 1598) and *The Scene Changes* (BLP 4009). The scene *had* changed, and not in Bud's favour. The following year, he would leave for Paris, and though he effectively came home to die in 1964, American jazz more or less forgot about him in the interim. Whatever the virtues of these two sessions – most apparent in his new compositions, with such titles as 'Monopoly', 'Cleopatra's Dream', 'John's Abbey' and 'Time Waits' full of melodic ideas – the music is let down by the memory of Powell's brilliant early work and the sometimes stilted execution of his later pieces. Some pianists might have been thrilled to come up with records like these, but Powell's genius is done little service by the reliance on rhythmic patterns and keyboard effects, which suggest that he was seeking to anchor a pianism which he knew he could no longer safely extemporise. The reader should take the opportunity – if it ever arises – to view the eerie 1963 short film made about Powell in Denmark, *Stopforbud*, an almost silent twelve minutes which is like a farewell glimpse of this sad, portly figure.

By contrast, Jimmy Smith was 'just getting started'. But although he recorded frequently during 1958–9, Smith seems to have been subject to stringent quality control by Lion, since several of the dates were either left in the can or pillaged only for a couple of singles. *Softly As A Summer Breeze* (BLP 4200 – the cover features Smith grinning devilishly under an open umbrella) was the principal album to emerge during this period and, as the title suggests, much of the music offered a pacific treatment of some standard ballads, a surprising engagement for Philly Joe Jones, whose only recorded encounter with the organist this was. Still, there was a fast, exuberant run through Monk's 'Hackensack' and a 'Blues For Philly Joe' which highlighted the drummer's skilful brushwork.

The year 1958 also saw another great one-off in the Blue Note catalogue. Julian 'Cannonball' Adderley had been having a difficult time with recordings under his own name, having experienced less than ideal situations at both Savoy and Mercury, for whom he'd previously made several albums. Having split up his own band to try and resolve various financial problems, he had joined the Miles Davis group at the end of 1957, and the trumpeter had advised him that Alfred Lion was one record company boss whom he could trust. In the end, Adderley went to Riverside, but his sole Blue Note set – *Somethin' Else* – is another singleton classic in the label's archive. The rhythm section featured the exemplary Hank Jones on piano, Sam Jones and Art Blakey; and joining Adderley was his new boss, Davis, who played far better on this date than he did on any of his own Blue Note sessions from earlier in the decade. The five pieces on the original release take their own time and find a spacious amalgam of Adderley's ebullient, bluesy playing and Davis's bony lyricism. Most commentators have suggested that Davis dominates the record; but that is only so if one sets out to devalue Adderley's burnished and singing improvising. He has been unfairly sidelined for too long in the appreciation of his own record.

In the summer of 1959, Rudy Van Gelder moved operations. His little customised studio at his parents' home in Hackensack had been used to set down dozens of sessions, for Blue Note and others, but for a couple of years Van Gelder had been planning to leave home. In July 1959, he finally left his optometry practice behind. After two years of plans and designs, he had a new studio ready, in Englewood Cliffs, New Jersey. The first Blue Note date there was on 20 July – although the titles recorded that day were ultimately rejected by Alfred Lion.

Van Gelder remembered his parents' home:

> It was a fairly modern house for its time. The ceiling was fairly high. And it had spaces off the room, so its actual size was enhanced acoustically because there was a hall leading out with an alcove on one side. So you'd be in a room of fixed dimensions, but there were additional spaces to use for the musical sound to get bouncing around.[7]

It was either a tribute to Van Gelder's meticulousness or to the quality of that original room, but the Englewood Cliffs recordings show no marked change in fidelity over their predecessors. In his new setting, where he continues to work and record into the new century, Van Gelder had another high ceiling and low lighting. One of the most marked changes, though, was in Frank Wolff's session photographs. No longer could you spot fragments of sofa or venetian blind, the accoutrements of a normal living space. After the move, Wolff's photos improved, if only because the photographer had more space and could make better use of the room's lighting.

The last session at Hackensack and the first at Englewood Cliffs involved the same musician: Ike Quebec. After his close association with the early 'modern' days of Blue Note, the saxophonist had drifted off the scene. He had continued to work for his old boss Cab Calloway into the beginning of the fifties, but his style was out of style, and by the middle of the decade he was driving a taxi. In 1959, back in practice and seeing his big sound and swing-to-bop manner beginning to assume a classic feel, Ike returned to Blue Note, not only as a recording artist but as an A&R man. For Alfred Lion, who had always felt close to Quebec, it was more than a happy homecoming. Since Quebec could read music and address particular musical points in ways which eluded Lion and Wolff, he could help sharpen sessions which might otherwise have been flawed. The Blue Note family was one man stronger again.

EIGHT

The start of a new decade is one thing, but music never changes to fit the calendar. At the beginning of the sixties, Blue Note and jazz were in the thick of a rich, diverse period of creativity; by the end, both would be all but foundering. For the first half of the decade, sessions were recorded at the rate of one a week: with the rehearsal time involved, other aspects of pre-production and the customary checking out of 'the scene' outside, it was a miracle that Lion and Wolff found time to do anything other than recording and A&R. Yet the company carried on - and from a new base. Once again, the Blue Note office moved, although only a few blocks, to 43 West 61st Street.

Their limited success was part of their burden. With no major hits on the label to pay for the less commercial projects, there was no time for reflection: Blue Note were obliged to make turnover by almost churning out records. The projects recorded in the first quarter of 1960 were typical: single albums by Donald Byrd, Sonny Red Kyner, Lou Donaldson, Hank Mobley and Horace Parlan; an album of music by the Freddie Redd Quartet, taken from the play *The Connection*, the event which had kept Jackie McLean on the scene; a Jimmy Smith sextet session, released across the albums *Open House* and *Plain Talk*; and a session by the new Jazz Messengers line-up with Lee Morgan and Wayne

Shorter, *The Big Beat*. Admirable as much of this music was, none of it (with the exception of the Blakey record) was either of significant artistic impact or great commercial bounty. While Blue Note's standards remained impeccable, its hard-bop-based routine was beginning to stratify.

Hindsight can make this seem a surprising judgement. Any jazz label of today would be proud to have releases of such calibre and such moment in their contemporary programme. But the fact that, say, *The Big Beat* received a particularly lukewarm reception in *Down Beat* suggests that an unfavourable wind was beginning to blow through what was still an uncommonly vital musical form.

This was partly because jazz was quickly moving on, if not away from the hard-bop players. Ornette Coleman's New York debut in the autumn of 1959 had turned every head on the local scene, even if many had belittled this maverick player's abilities. John Coltrane, who had signed to Atlantic in the same year, had begun to give evidence of the extraordinary strides he was making. Sonny Rollins had temporarily disappeared, but would eventually return to demonstrate again the breathtaking extent of his powers. Miles Davis had recently released what would become the most successful of all his records, *Kind Of Blue*, which suggested another way out of hard bop's chord-based improvising. Bill Evans, Charles Mingus, George Russell and Thelonious Monk were all making challenging small-group records; and with big bands, there were forward-looking recordings from the veteran but still very popular Stan Kenton and his former sideman Maynard Ferguson. None of these were Blue Note artists (at least, in the case of Coltrane, Rollins and Monk, not any longer).

Until the end of 1963, Blue Note's direction remained unswervingly on the hard-bop route. Whatever Lion heard in such seemingly disparate voices as those of Freddie Hubbard, Baby Face Willette, Stanley Turrentine and Grant

Green – all of whom came to the label during this period – their common ground was the intangible subtext of soulfulness. The rhythms which had thrilled Lion when he heard Sam Wooding in Berlin seem to have remained his touchstone for the kind of jazz he believed in. He may have respected the later work of Davis, Mingus and the others, but it is hard to imagine that music on Blue Note. Company policy called for a certain simplicity, almost an acceptance of formula, which discouraged maverick playing of any specific kind.

Within those parameters, though, it is possible to argue that far from entering into any kind of ossification of their intentions, Blue Note was moving through one of its most creative periods. The opening years of the decade saw a sequence of releases – by the Jazz Messengers, Hubbard, Green, Horace Silver, Jackie McLean, Joe Henderson, Dexter Gordon – which maintain a fabulous level of creativity. Part of it was due to what was going on in the rest of jazz. The liberating elements in the music of Coleman, Davis and Coltrane fed back into the sort of mainstream which Blue Note's school represented: a musician such as Joe Henderson, for instance, would have sounded quite different if Coltrane had never existed. Besides, it wasn't as if leaders such as Blakey and Silver could have only had two or three good records in them. They were still relatively young men and still sharpening their own skills. As exciting and precocious as the records of 1955–60 had been, many would hold that those of 1960–5 are even more compelling.

One of the key influences on the company's movements was the presence of Ike Quebec. Just as Quebec had sidled Thelonious Monk into Lion's hearing a decade and a half earlier, so he began a significant involvement with the next wave of Blue Note artists. Perhaps his most important move was to assist in bringing to the label one of his contemporaries, the giant, wayward tenor saxophonist Dexter Gordon (although the initial move on that artist may have come from the Three Sounds' booking agent, who told Lion that Gordon was back and playing again). Thirty-eight years old when he made his Blue Note recording debut on 6 May 1961, Gordon was emerging from a wretched spell. Ira Gitler's sleeve note for the album, *Doin' Allright*, is discreet: 'Veteran listeners will certainly remember him but younger fans probably will not although he was intermittently active during the Fifties.'[1] Gordon had served two separate prison terms during the previous decade, and had hardly figured in the recording studios. In a parallel with Jackie McLean, he had appeared in a Californian staging of Jack Gelber's *The Connection*, which had helped to stabilise his attempt at some kind of comeback. Yet Gordon had been a premier voice in the bop of the forties, even though he was more of a transitional stylist, favouring bop's harmonic complexities but partial to the gentler, less taxing rhythmical methods of swing. Frank Wolff's cover photo for *Doin' Allright* is a canny piece of packaging: under the optimistically resurgent title, Gordon is perched in the back of one of Manhattan's hansom cabs, his face lit up by a wide grin.

Pensive but swaggering, the record is close to a Blue Note classic. Mannerism invades much of even Gordon's best work: for many that would mean no criticism, as in, for instance, the completely predictable but unfailingly engaging playing of Ben Webster. However, Gordon's taste for quoting from other melodies in the course of an improvisation could become tiresome and often he would seem to doze on his undeniably impressive tone, big foghorn notes suddenly sounding out of the horn like a call to wake himself up. Lagging behind the beat on ballads and ducking tempos which he didn't quite trust – both, incidentally, very Websterian traits – often rob his music of its resilience. Yet his first Blue Note, at least, is still Romanesque in its grandly sculpted figures. *Doin' Allright* assembles a good group – Freddie Hubbard, Horace Parlan, George Tucker, Al

Harewood - which falls into Gordon's particular style from the off. The lazy, insouciant blues 'Society Red' typifies the date: smart solos just slightly undercut by the leader's insistence that we needn't put ourselves out. It is not a record of great solos or even great moments: it's the combination of Gordon's beatifically relaxed style with the more urgent moves of his colleagues which casts the particular spell of the session.

Gordon never surpassed the beautiful feel of *Doin' Allright* in what actually proved to be a brief spell at Blue Note. Three days after the debut he recorded a quartet session, *Dexter Calling*, and a little over a year later he again cut two albums inside a week, *Go!* and *A Swingin' Affair*, with the same rhythm section of Sonny Clark, Butch Warren and Billy Higgins. Even in the brief interim between the first sessions and these two, Gordon seems to have lost a degree of his mobility: he lumbers at slow tempos and the phrasing seems so deliberate that much of the pleasure for the listener has evaporated. Although he liked playing with Sonny Clark, one feels that he did best with another horn out front: as the solitary lead voice, he seems encumbered, even weary. Gordon's memory has accumulated much sentimental affection, but next to, say, Hank Mobley, his Blue Note work has not worn so well as many would have it. Two further albums made in Paris in 1963 and another pair cut on a return visit to New York in 1965 are similarly flawed.

Gordon was an anachronism for the Blue Note of the sixties, akin to Sidney Bechet and George Lewis recording for the label in the fifties. Quebec's patronage of the artist was perhaps born of a sentimental affiliation which has been mirrored in the critical reaction to the recordings ever since. Next to Quebec's own sessions for the label, Gordon's albums can sound almost tame.

Ike Quebec had himself matured into a musician of almost apologetic grandeur. He was five years older than Gordon, and his tone and delivery were less affected. With no real career or reputation to speak of, his records garnered little attention, yet remain enormously satisfying examples of Blue Note's releases in the period. As with several of the most artistically successful of Blue Note's roster – Andrew Hill, Wayne Shorter, Larry Young – Ike was untypical of many of his colleagues. He was one of the oldest leaders to record for Blue Note in the sixties and basically belonged to a generation before his label peers. He would not have been out of place with such Count Basie sidemen as Eddie Lockjaw Davis, but there were threads in his style which would anticipate the soul-jazz movement of the sixties. Even his album titles – *Heavy Soul, Blue And Sentimental* – suggest a truce between those old and new approaches. They were unambitious records, filled with standards and blues, and the most striking thing about them is the preponderance of slow tempos: most Blue Notes were upbeat for most of the time, but Quebec took a different path.

When he cut a few singles at his return session in 1959, Lion saw them 'as a sort of trial balloon, and I was delighted to find not only that many people still remembered Ike, but also that those who didn't know him were amazed and excited by what they heard. So recently I decided to jump into a full album session with new material to give Ike a complete new start.'[2] Some of that sounds like record man's banter, and it did take well over a year before Lion booked Quebec for another full session. But the resulting record, *Heavy Soul*, is a superb vindication. Although they used an organist, Freddie Roach, rather than a pianist, they still had Quebec's old friend from the Cab Calloway band, Milt Hinton, on bass, with Al Harewood on drums given little to do other than tick off the time. The leader chose some old-fashioned material: 'I Want A Little Girl', 'The Man I Love' and even 'Brother Can You Spare A Dime'. The minor 'Acquitted' is an interesting original. But the power is in the playing.

Roach is used sparingly, almost as a colourist, and he frequently drops out altogether. There's lots of space and air around the solos and Quebec plays the ballads at not much above a crawl. Yet the fat, sometimes bleary tone carries a suggestion of strength in reserve along with the gutsiness of the improvising. Only days later, the same team returned to cut *It Might As Well Be Spring*, and repeated the trick. 'Ol' Man River' sees Quebec rather lose himself in formula R&B riffs, but elsewhere the authority goes hand in hand with a certain desolation – 'Willow Weep For Me' is a very bleak reading. A week later, with a different line-up (guitarist Grant Green, Paul Chambers and Philly Joe Jones), Lion recorded what might be Quebec's masterpiece, *Blue And Sentimental*. The title song opens the record at a desperately slow tempo, and though 'Like' offers some uptempo relief, most of the session is deep, deep blue. Somehow, Quebec gets through it without sounding tired or overweight, the deadly flaw of so many ballad-orientated records.

Quebec cut six more sessions in 1962, but only one was issued at the time, *Soul Samba*, a Latin-coloured session which suited him surprisingly well (he admired Stan Getz, though he sounded nothing like him, and some of this material was the kind of thing Getz was about to take on so successfully). A date in January with Bennie Green and Stanley Turrentine was something of a potboiler (and was eventually released as *Congo Lament* in 1980) and another ballad-oriented session with an undistinguished group was similarly held back by Lion. On 16 January 1963, though, Ike Quebec succumbed to lung cancer. Lion, who had grown close to the saxophonist, was deeply affected by his passing. His brief sequence of albums is a memorial which should be far better known and acknowledged.

Quebec was not the only casualty of that month. Sonny Clark died a few days later (officially of a heart attack, although an overdose was the likely cause of death). Clark had cut one final Blue Note date of his own, *Leapin' And Lopin'*, just a few weeks earlier, on 13 November (and Quebec had guested on a single track, 'Deep In A Dream', a typically full-blooded ballad). The fact of his absurd death is all the more painful because *Leapin' And Lopin'* is so fine, easily the pick of Clark's group records and an exemplar of hard-bop style. The band is ideally balanced: Tommy Turrentine on trumpet is bright and not too smart, Charlie Rouse on tenor saxophone is peppery and not too amenable. The young Butch Warren plays unobtrusive bass, yet draws out some very constructive lines which a listener will take pleasure in following. Billy Higgins, on the way to becoming one of the best drummers of his time, bounces the group along. And there is Clark himself, his touch more immaculate than ever. All the tunes are strong: Turrentine's amiable 'Midnight Mambo' and Warren's clever 'Eric Walks' are good vehicles, but they bow to Clark's own three originals – the blues paraphrase 'Somethin' Special', a modally inflected theme called 'Melody For C' and his farewell classic, 'Voodoo', a haunting thirty-two-bar theme that sticks irresistibly in the mind. In the middle of the first side, 'Deep In A Dream', with Quebec's rapt commentary, emerges almost as a bonus. So perfectly harmonious are all the ingredients – characters, tunes, solos, sound, plus one of Wolff's most striking close-ups of the leader on the sleeve – that this bids to be one of the most quintessential discs in the label's catalogue. Yet it is not 'important' for any kind of innovation or breakthrough; more a summation of one man's contribution to his language. Ira Gitler's final words in his sleeve note – 'Sonny Clark has come of age'[3] – are a cruel irony.

Jackie McLean might have shared a similar fate, but his stint with the Living Theatre had stabilised his professional life and he eventually overcame his addiction. McLean's Blue Notes are a sometimes problematical lot and the string of dates he made for the label in the sixties continue an intriguing if often difficult sequence. *Capuchin Swing*, made on 16 April 1960, is a sometimes rowdy affair which shows up how awkward it could be to accommodate McLean even within a group of his own leadership. His solos on 'Francisco' (named for Frank Wolff) and 'Condition Blue' make a glaring contrast to those of his bandmates. The tension in McLean's records from this period lies in a sometimes aggravating contrast between himself and his fellow horn players in particular. Michael James is quoted on the sleeve note to *Capuchin Swing* to the effect that 'there aren't more than a handful of jazzmen . . . who sound as passionately involved in their music',[4] but McLean's passion often seems to have more to do with being *outside*, rather than being involved. Mclean himself later said: 'A lot of my performances have been very emotional because I wasn't putting any work into it.'[5] *Bluesnik*, recorded the following January, has some of the same intensity, though apparently under more control: in what is actually a rather dull programme of blues pieces (the title track must have taken all of five minutes to 'compose'), the saxophonist's fast, biting solos shred the skilful and comparatively genial playing of Freddie Hubbard.

A Fickle Sonance, recorded the following October, assembled the same band which would record *Leapin' And Lopin'*, with McLean in for Charlie Rouse. It is, again, the trouble-making McLean who makes all the difference: where Clark's session would be elegant and composed, this one seems taut and angular. 'Five Will Get You Ten', once credited to Clark but now thought to be an otherwise unclaimed Monk tune, and the chilling title piece, where the alto leaps and twists against a modal backdrop, are strange, rootless settings for playing which can seem by turns anguished, stark and sneering. McLean's next record, *Let Freedom Ring*, would make a more explicit pact with matters removed from his bebop history.

* * *

Graduates from the Blakey and Silver schools of hard bop continued to make records for Blue Note, and in some cases turned in their best work during the period. This was especially true of Hank Mobley, whose albums as a leader turned from solid to outstanding. Mobley went on to record more than twenty albums for the label with his name out front, but for their sheer class and inventive spark, the sequence which he initiated with *Soul Station* in 1960 and ended with *Another Workout* in 1963 are in a finer league. The 'round sound' which he sought to perfect was at its most persuasive in this period. Yet he was unable to build on this artistic success, in part due to some personal difficulties: although he spent some time in the Miles Davis group in 1961–2, this was preceded and then succeeded by drug convictions and though he continued to work prolifically for Blue Note, his career had no momentum. All the more remarkable that he was able to set down music of the calibre that he did.

Mobley has always been a favourite among Blue Note collectors – perhaps *the* favourite musician in such circles. Though a journeyman rather than any kind of ground-breaking voice, he was more influential than jazz histories have often allowed. Many British musicians of the fifties and sixties would seek out his elusive records. If a figure such as Sonny Rollins was too overpowering a voice to be useful as an influence, the more diplomatic Mobley could offer more practical material to work with. His three great records are surely *Soul Station*, *Roll Call* and *Workout*. The first two benefit hugely from the presence of Art Blakey, at his most spirited, though still respectful of the point that this is Hank's date rather than his. *Soul Station* doesn't announce itself with daring material, but each of Mobley's four originals are neatly weighted to suit him, particularly 'This I Dig Of You'. 'Dig Dis' and 'Soul Station' itself are lines which anticipate soul jazz, but Mobley's fetching delivery of the notes has a songfulness in it. He's not preaching. 'Remember' and 'If I Should Lose You' were thoughtful choices for the two standards. Wynton Kelly is at his most dapper at the piano and Paul Chambers is customarily fine. What swings the record on to the top level, though, is Mobley's extraordinary understanding of how he makes time work for him. For such a relaxed sounding tenorman, with his unruffled, lean tone and curling melody lines, the way he can handle the beat, every inflexion in the line timed to go with an aspect of the pulse, is little short of amazing. Mobley's mastery is so complete that it often deceives the ear. He might seem to be lagging behind, or staggering slightly, yet there's never any need to right himself – he had it in the pocket all along.

Roll Call is by the same quartet, but adds Freddie Hubbard to the line-up, and to that end might be deemed to be not *quite* as strong. Hubbard plays handsomely, but it's Mobley we want to hear. On *Workout*, recorded in March 1961, Hubbard disappears, but Grant Green arrives, and Philly Joe Jones is in for Blakey. 'Workout' and 'Uh Huh' are functional rather than inspiring frameworks, and both 'Smokin'' and 'Greasin' Easy' aren't much more provocative than their titles, but again the session has the air of a routine fixture transcended by craftsmen who are grasping their moment. Mobley plays more aggressively on both 'Workout' and 'Uh Huh' than he ever had, while still harbouring enough of his own secret temperance to distinguish the improvising. For his standard choice, he again rivalled Sonny Rollins for his ability to surprise: 'The Best Things In Life Are Free' and 'Three Coins In The Fountain', the former especially providing one of his huskiest solos. *Another Workout* was recorded on 26 March 1961, but went unreleased until the eighties, depriving Mobley of the satisfaction of seeing his strongest work in its original sequence. With Kelly, Chambers and Jones again providing support, it once more carries the imprimatur of Mobley's most dedicated and fruitful playing.

* * *

Donald Byrd also set off on a string of dates: *Fuego, Byrd In Flight, The Cat Walk, Royal Flush* and two live records, *At The Half Note Café* and the inappropriately titled *Free Form*. Byrd's problem was that he was nearly always going to come off second-best on a label which had trumpeters of the calibre of Lee Morgan, Freddie Hubbard and Kenny Dorham. As accomplished a technician as he was, Byrd rarely impressed any special individuality on his solos. He had become one of the most recorded sidemen in New York by this time, and his very dependability told against him. His other characteristic was in picking up on a development when the innovative work had already been done. That is true of many jazz players, of course, but in Byrd's case (as with something like the *Free Form* date, cut in December 1961) it seemed more like opportunism than creative curiosity. The most valuable thing about some of these records is the space they give to some of the other players: Pepper Adams, otherwise rarely sighted on Blue Note in this period, and Herbie Hancock, who made his label debut on *Chant*, a session unreleased until many years later, and *Royal Flush*.

The return of Blakey to the company fold was, though, one of the most energising aspects of this period for Blue Note. The notion of a Jazz Messengers dynasty was by now firmly in place. From *The Big Beat* onwards, Blakey hardly changed his musical clothes. In 1980, he said:

> Yeah, you get tired of playing things like that, tired of playing 'Blues March' and playin' 'Moanin', but that's your bread and butter music, that's what it is. To keep from getting tired of it is to have different cats come in, play different versions of it. There're other kids that come along that need a break, put the old guys out there

> on their own. It keeps the group live and fresh, keeps it from getting stale.[6]

The 1960 edition of the Jazz Messengers was a quintet that could have humbled most of its rivals: Blakey led the team of Lee Morgan, Wayne Shorter, Bobby Timmons and Jymie Merritt, and the sheer class and expertise of the band powers through both their live and studio records. Like Miles Davis, perhaps his greatest rival as a small-group leader, Blakey didn't really write himself, and he relied on the input from at least one 'musical director' in his front line. In this case, although Morgan came up with some strong pieces, it was Wayne Shorter. The saxophonist had been with Blakey for several months prior to *The Big Beat*, having worked in various situations including the Maynard Ferguson Orchestra, and was already demonstrating his extraordinary gifts as a composer. The track which emerged as the hit of the album was Bobby Timmons's 'Dat Dere', itself a sequel to the very hummable 'Dis Here' which Timmons had already put in the band's book. But what stood out on the record were three Shorter compositions: 'Sakeena's Vision', 'The Chess Players' and 'Lester Left Town'.

Shorter's composing was to become one of the most fertile areas for jazz musicians: there's nothing rote or formulaic or even familiar about his writing in this period. So 'The Chess Players', built on a sequence of fourths, is subtly jointed around a sense of starting, stopping to think, and then moving on again, suggesting the scenario of the title. 'Sakeena's Vision', with its foreshortened bar structure, has a point which Shorter described as 'like an eclipse'[7] melding together the second eight measures with the bridge. Above all, there is the extraordinary 'Lester Left Town', in homage to Lester Young, who'd died a year earlier. The descending line which forms the hook of the melody seems to approximate Young's own slightly fey gait, and in turn reminds one of an inversion of another tribute piece, Monk's 'In Walked Bud'. But the bridge section is a complex bit of wrangling which must have taxed the players. Some indication of the difficulty of Shorter's pieces is hinted at by the solos of the normally cocksure Morgan. On 'The Chess Players' especially, which has space for two long improvisations by the horns, his customary swagger is undercut, and the last section of his solo is oddly stilted, as if he is drying up.

Morgan did, in fact, leave this Messengers line-up a year later. But that was still time enough for him to record another string of albums with the group – *A Night In Tunisia*, *Like Someone In Love*, both volumes of *Meet You At The Jazz Corner Of The World*, *Roots And Herbs*, *The Witch Doctor* and *The Freedom Rider*. Lion was continuing to record his favoured artists at a pace which meant that even excellent sessions such as *Roots And Herbs* could stay on the shelf for years. The calibre of these records is consistently electrifying. While the albums may have an occasional piece of formula business – a blues or a standard used to make up the numbers – the combination of Morgan and Shorter, a rare mixture of physical and intellectual strength, is consistently fascinating. It's not as if Morgan is the pugilist and Shorter the bookish type: actually, next to the trumpeter's streetwise, sassy playing, the saxophonist can often sound lumpen and even clumsy. He is both like and unlike Coltrane in this period: there's a similar weight of tone and a penchant for stepping down hard on the strong beats in a line. But his taste for thematic playing, and a flicker of faintly gothic humour, set him aside from Coltrane's ongoing developments.

Coached by the drummer, the horns set formidable standards. But as freely as Morgan and Shorter played, this remained a tight-knit group, with Blakey always reminding the listener that he set most of the tempos and the temperatures. The humid, furious title track of *A Night In Tunisia* might almost be a parody, so relentless is the thunder coming out of the drum kit, but for all the bonhomie which Blakey implies, he's serious about the business of playing jazz. *Roots And Herbs* wasn't released until 1970, but it has one of the most interesting track listings, since all six compositions are Shorter originals: 'Ping Pong', which bounces between two chords for the core of its theme; 'Look At The Birdie', which seems to take off from a Monk line; and 'Master Mind', which might almost be a rewrite of 'Milestones', suggest that Shorter was able to be both entirely original and capable of borrowing from contemporary jazz materials.

It was a remarkable sequence, but if anything the next group of Jazz Messengers albums might be even stronger. In the spring of 1961, Freddie Hubbard and trombonist Curtis Fuller replaced Morgan, expanding the group to a sextet for the first time. Hubbard had already made several Blue Note dates of his own, and Fuller was similarly no stranger to the label. Although there was some live recording done earlier at the Village Gate club, Lion recorded the new group for the first time in the studio on 2 October 1961, for the *Mosaic* album. After that came *Buhaina's Delight*. The bigger line-up afforded a grander sonority to the ensembles and Hubbard's arrival lent a fresh ingredient too. Where Morgan was perhaps the cooler personality, in terms of his strutting persona, Hubbard had an even finer command of the trumpet and was more obviously versatile: he could carry off ballads with poise and a sort of searching finesse, and while his power-playing was steelier than Morgan's, he seemed to look further ahead in his solos.

Besides the two new horns, there was a change on the piano seat, with Cedar Walton arriving for Bobby Timmons. This brought another important composer into the group: Walton's music rivalled Shorter's for its ambitious construction, even if he didn't quite have the saxophonist's level of inspiration. Both *Mosaic* and *Buhaina's Delight* have a large-scale feel, with longer tunes and the fatter sound of the sextet holding sway. But these were, for the time being, the final

Jazz Messengers dates for Blue Note, since Blakey took the group to another label for a spell. He did, though, cut another album of multiple drums for the label in January 1962. *The African Beat* featured eight different drummers and percussionists (including Curtis Fuller on timpani!), plus the exotic reed specialist Yusef Lateef and bassist Ahmed Abdul-Malik. With Solomon Ilori's penny whistle providing much of the melodic material, the music unfortunately comes across as a tourist's guide to pan-African rhythm and song. Whatever the leader got out of these adventures isn't clear. Certainly, his own groups played resolutely American music, no matter how much of Africa was in there all along. In the sleeve notes, Blakey says that 'Now I know I'm going to have to add African drummers to my regular band.'[8] But he never did.

Freddie Hubbard's contributions to the Messengers records were unimpeachable. But his own albums for Blue Note had already portrayed the work of a young master. *Open Sesame* was cut on 19 June 1960, a few weeks after Hubbard's twenty-second birthday. Freddie had come from Indianapolis – where he'd played with Wes Montgomery and his brothers – to New York two years earlier, and soon made a name for himself. The fanfare solo on the first, title track of *Open Sesame* is stunningly accomplished, and reminds of why the progress of hard bop seemed to consist of the arrival of one brilliant young voice after another. Hubbard's bubbling tone went with a very exacting rhythmical sense, where he could essay long lines which seemed to have each note precisely punched out. Double-time passages flood out of him as the fancy takes him, and his lip trills only heighten the virtuoso element in his work. It was a very tough style to sustain – which is why Hubbard's latter-day work, beset with technical difficulties, seems so disappointing next to his own golden age. *Open Sesame* has the added bonus of Tina Brooks in top form, while *Ready For Freddie* puts him alongside both Wayne Shorter and the new John Coltrane rhythm section of McCoy Tyner, Art Davis and Elvin Jones. 'Birdlike', from that date, shows the telling difference between original bebop and hard bop's sublimation of the form: over two extended solos, both Hubbard and Shorter annihilate the licks-based improvising of bebop routine, the trumpeter with extended, sparkling lines, the saxophonist with patterns which eventually break up into coughing, honking bits and pieces. *Goin' Up* is more conventionally based, with Hank Mobley as Hubbard's front-line partner, but both this and *Hub Cap*, which mirrors the Messengers' sextet instrumentation, benefit from the leader's decisiveness about his talents and how he wants to situate them. Hubbard would take some routes which didn't, finally, suit him that well, as in his work with Ornette Coleman and Eric Dolphy: as technically assured as he was, he still played at his best in a relatively conservative idiom. His fifth Blue Note set, *Hub-Tones*, with its naggingly ingenious title track, was made in October 1962 and presents Hubbard at his most effectively 'out': his tremendous improvisation on that piece in particular is a fiery advance on hard-bop rhetoric, yet not so remote as to step into any kind of free jazz.

Blue Note had some other new stars too. One whom Alfred Lion seemed particularly proud of was the guitarist Grant Green, a native of St Louis who had, like so many others, sought to try his luck in New York in 1960. Lou Donaldson had heard him in St Louis and seems to have more or less ordered Green to go to New York, where Donaldson gave him an introduction to Alfred Lion. Surprisingly, Lion began by giving Green his own date, before even using him as a sideman, but the debut session (16 November 1960) was apparently deemed unsatisfactory, since it was put on the shelf (and finally released - in 2001! - as *First Session*.) There is not, admittedly, much in the date which really begs one to sit up and take notice. Wynton Kelly, Paul Chambers and

Philly Joe Jones play smartly enough, and Green's fluency is only compromised by a certain weediness of tone, which might have more to do with the recording than anything else. But Lion was undeterred from using Green as a regular Blue Note man, and if anything he set an exceptional precedent: the following year, 1961, Green appeared on fifteen different sessions for the label, including his own 'proper' debut, *Grant's First Stand*, set down on 28 January, as well as the subsequent *Green Street, Sunday Mornin'* and *Grantstand*. Green's biographer Sharony Andrews Green asked Ruth Lion why he was so popular at the label:

> I think [it was] because when Alfred liked somebody, he recorded them as much as he could because he didn't know how long they would be around. Guys had to travel to keep working . . . Grant got nicely established, especially with Alfred, and that meant a lot in those days. If Al liked you, that meant that the other people were going to like you, too.[9]

The guitar was still a comparatively insignificant instrument in jazz. Compared to trumpeters, saxophonists and pianists, the guitarist was a second-class citizen. Most took up a role which was awkwardly cast between rhythm player and soloist. The guitar had yet to be subjected to the battery of electronic effects which would eventually set the tone for rock's use of the instrument, and the jazz guitarist would have to impose what personality they had on an otherwise bland, open tone. Guitars had featured in plenty of trios, such as those led by Nat Cole, Art Tatum and Red Norvo, but they tended to take up a tasteful sort of position, as if playing for a lounge audience. R&B and rock'n'roll groups changed all that, turning the guitar into a weapon of assault, but jazz players seemed unsure how to respond.

Green was largely self-taught, an unfussy and straightforward stylist. He liked a clean, clear tone and eschewed the superfast techniques of Tal Farlow or Jimmy Raney. Blues playing came very easily to him. Most of his records are unambitious in their choice of material and execution, but as with Kenny Burrell's countless sessions, they're curiously satisfying: the 'soulful' quotient which Lion set such store by persists through all of Green's early sixties dates, and it's easy to see why Lion liked him so much. *Green Street* is as good a place as any to hear him at his best. With the bare-bones support of Ben Tucker (bass) and Dave Bailey (drums), Green calmly makes his way through six pieces that don't so much tax him as offer some nourishing food for thought. His treatment of Monk's 'Round Midnight', by now one of the most overexposed pieces in the jazz canon, will refresh any coming to it for the first time: he works simple, guileful variations out of the theme and reinstates the lovely sonority in Monk's original inspiration. The opening blues, 'No. 1 Green Street', seems at first to rely too much on repetitions and well-worn riffs, but over the progress of the piece his ideas gather conviction because he seems to be enjoying the music so much. 'Grant's Dimensions' is more subtle than it first appears, Green using chunky chords in his delineation of the theme, and again a sequence of modest ideas builds into something strong and flexible. Green is often characterised as an aggressive player, but that description hardly squares with the serenity of his most personal performances.

Green built on this early session, both in his own playing and in the kind of surroundings which Lion moved him through. *Grantstand* allies him with Yusef Lateef and organist Jack McDuff, and the movingly beautiful *Born To Be Blue* has him alongside Ike Quebec and Sonny Clark, an association which fate decided would not be repeated. Although it looks from the outside like a suspiciously calculated occasion, *Feelin' The Spirit*, made in December 1962, required Green to play on traditional gospel themes, and the spirit is felt with unexpected candour and real feeling. As time went on, Green played harder and drew his lines with a degree more complexity, but he always remained the pacifying sort underneath.

Green also often found himself in the organ-combo situation which Blue Note continued to set up as a regular part of their schedules. Following the sensation surrounding Jimmy Smith's early appearances, organ players and organ-based groups became a critical part of the jazz economy. While their work tended to operate at a tangent to the music which was adjudged as the jazz mainstream, it played a major role in sustaining what had started to lose heart, or at least interest: the core jazz audience.

Hard bop's growing maturity, as documented in Blue Note's catalogue and in the releases by such contemporary labels as Riverside and Prestige, is at this distance fascinating to follow. At the time, though, audiences must have been less patient and less willing to absorb the steady progress of, say, Horace Silver's output: that is the luxury of scholars and collectors with plenty of time on their hands. And Silver was one of the most communicative of the hard-bop bandleaders: he was positively down-home next to the almost fearsome challenge offered by such contemporaries as the George Russell Sextet. For audiences seeking a little freshness and some visceral excitement in their jazz, the organ bands were undeniably attractive. For one thing, they used a lot more electricity. Rock'n'roll was electric music which almost instantly consigned the classic hard-bop format – two or three horns and a rhythm section – to a kind of yesteryear. The organ groups, with their electric keyboards and amplified guitars, at least met the rock and R&B players on their own terms. Like the most effective rock musicians, they also relied on effects as often as on musical, improvisational embellishment to make their point: repetition, the locking into a single groove and other bits of business which in some ways recalled the bar-walking saxophonists of the late swing era. The rocking riffs and gutbucket blues playing of Smith and his contemporaries might seem almost infantile next to the scathing brilliance of a Sonny Rollins solo, but in the neighbourhood clubs in which that music thrived, it made a lot more sense.

Jukebox business and radio programming also favoured this new music. On what came to be called the 'chitlin circuit' – black clubs in the major eastern cities – the organ combo was king. If Blue Note lit the fuse for that music in record-industry terms, the other labels were quick to chase down bands of their own in the style, and at Prestige, in particular, the whole tenor of the label switched over to this new soulful jazz. Besides Smith, there were Brother Jack McDuff, Shirley Scott, Johnny Hammond Smith, Jimmy McGriff, Richard 'Groove' Holmes and others, each trying to find their own wrinkle on what had been formulaic from the start.

While Smith remained Blue Note's premier organ man, Lion tried recording others in the style. The most renowned, even though very little is known about him, was Baby Face Willette, who cut two albums in January and May 1961 and then disappeared (his pair of albums for Argo are even more obscure than his Blue Notes). Willette bore a slight resemblance to Little Richard and Reid Miles's cover for *Face To Face*, the first of the two albums, is an arresting portrait, Willette seeming to loom up into the right-hand half of the sleeve. He came from New Orleans, and had been working since his teenage years in various touring R&B bands before Lou Donaldson heard him and recommended him to Lion. By this time, Willette was twenty-eight and had a developed style which was lighter and airier than the accepted Smith norm. But it was not so compelling. Both *Face To Face* and the subsequent *Stop And Listen* managed only poor sales (original pressings are extremely rare and enormously sought-after). Grant

Green and drummer Ben Dixon were on both sessions (Willette made his sole date as a Blue Note sideman on Green's *Grant's First Stand*), and Fred Jackson added some serviceable tenor to the first date; but Willette's failure to make any impact suggests how difficult it was for the merely capable exponents of the genre to find a following. Forty years later, his records change hands at prices that would surely make Baby Face gape. He is perhaps the ultimate collectable name on the label.

Freddie Roach was another hopeful organist. His first appearances were on Ike Quebec's *Heavy Soul* and *It Might As Well Be Spring*, and soon afterwards he was awarded his own name debut with *Down To Earth*, recorded on 23 August 1962. Roach suffered the same problem as Willette: he was solid enough, but not so distinctive that he would stand out from the Hammond pack. In the end, Roach made five albums for Blue Note, none of which made any major impact. But Roach's output suggests the alternative side to Blue Note's efforts with Jimmy Smith. While Smith clearly built on a bebop vocabulary and was a committed improviser, Roach was less concerned with pushing his own personality. On his third record, *Good Move*, he was set in a more or less traditional Blue Note hard-bop setting, with Blue Mitchell and Hank Mobley doing their usual thing, and his playing seems almost deferential. But the follow-up, *Brown Sugar*, was his most impressive effort, cut in March 1964. With his usual team of Eddie Wright (guitar) and Clarence Johnston (drums), Roach set to work on a programme which consisted entirely – with the possible exception of Quincy Jones's 'The Midnight Sun Will Never Set' – of soul tunes. Ray Charles's set piece 'The Right Time' is given a beautiful, simmering reading, the organist building thick layers of sound out of the chords. This was music more in the tradition of the R&B stylist Bill Doggett than in Smith's lineage, and it suited Roach handsomely. The saxophonist on the date was, surprisingly, Joe

Henderson, who'd already asserted that he wasn't this sort of player on two Blue Notes of his own - yet he *had* played in this kind of setting as an apprentice performer. Still, it's amusing to hear that Henderson, a jazz superstar of the nineties, is in this context no more creative than his predecessors on Roach dates, the now forgotten Percy France and Conrad Lester. 'A few ounces of black plastic with the mood of an evening spent playing the blues',[10] as Roach's own sleeve note had it.

'Big' John Patton, who also arrived at Blue Note in this period, seemed to find a middle ground between Smith's and Roach's approach. The opening track on his first album, 'The Silver Meter' from *Along Came John*, sums up almost everything one needs to know about Patton. Over a fat, growling bass riff, the tenor saxophonist grumbles his way through the simplest answering line. Once heard, it's not forgotten, although to sum up a career in one track is probably injustice to Patton, who actually proved himself a nimble improviser in the style of one of his favourite influences, Wynton Kelly. His other albums, with titles like *Oh Baby!* and *Got A Good Thing Goin'*, tend to follow a very straight path.

What about Jimmy Smith himself? It needed a patient ear to make the point, but his own playing underwent a steady evolution during the early sixties. The inflamed performer whom Wolff and Lion heard that night at Small's didn't so much lose his fire as bring it under a more scrupulous control. Some might complain that the scattershot exuberance of Smith's early records was the best thing about him, and it's true that as formulaic methods invaded the whole organ genre, Smith was as vulnerable as anyone else to pattern-playing and cliché. But as Lion recorded him in different contexts, Smith began to develop differing relationships with his playing companions. One of the most beneficial was with Kenny Burrell, a partnership which has proceeded on and off to this day. On the excellent 1959 date *Home Cookin'*, Smith and Burrell work out an interdependent dialogue which carries through the entire record. With Stanley Turrentine, on what were two of Blue Note's biggest sellers of the period, *Midnight Special* and *Back At The Chicken Shack* (both 1960), Smith found the ideal tenorman to offer a complementary voicing to his hard-nosed, bluesiest playing.

In one way at least, Lion reined in some of Smith's more adventurous work. *The Sermon*, the 1958 set which had yielded the enormous, side-long title track discussed earlier, running at just over twenty minutes, was an expansive piece of production which Smith didn't return to. Although carefully judged – none of the solos offers the kind of overwrought climax which would have buckled the performance before it had reached its close – it still stood as one of Smith's most dramatic efforts. To pitch a track of twenty minutes at any audience was pretty extraordinary at this point in the jazz LP's history, but for an artist whose records were selling via jukebox and radio exposure it was even more remarkable. Still, Smith never went for broke in that way again.

His later Blue Note sessions are actually an anti-climax after his earlier work. There is a complete hiatus between June 1960 and January 1962 (aside from a stray unreleased session), then Smith cut the session released as *Plays Fats Waller*. After that, the organist made four further albums in 1963, one (*Rockin' the Boat*) with Lou Donaldson, one (*Prayer Meetin'*) with Stanley Turrentine and two trio dates (*I'm Movin' On* and *Bucket!*) This apparent drift into neglect can be explained by the fact that Smith had actually switched affiliations: in 1962, he started making records for Norman Granz's Verve operation, which offered him the budget to make *Bashin'*, an album featuring the organist in the midst of orchestral charts by Oliver Nelson ('Walk On the Wild Side', which for some is Smith's finest hour, came out of these sessions). The final Blue Note dates look like contract fillers. But perhaps Smith had done all he was going to do at Blue Note already.

The label's great stalwart, Horace Silver, continued to make outstanding records during this period. With the Blue Mitchell-Junior Cook front line, Silver released *Horace-Scope*, *Doin' The Thing*, *The Tokyo Blues* and *Silver's Serenade*. While none of these is a dud, *The Tokyo Blues* is especially fine. Written following a trip to Japan, where the quintet was treated like incoming royalty, the music offers some of Silver's most inventive writing, with modal themes set against Latin rhythms. The title track seems to hint at some kind of oriental voicings without making anything explicit, and neither this nor 'Sayonara Blues', from the same date, is actually a blues. Silver's composing became sparer, even oblique: as busy as his group could sound, at other moments it had a sense of quiet contemplation, even on an up-tempo piece.

It was a period of enormous activity for the label, yet it coincided with hard bop's validity coming into question and with the start of the most serious decline in the jazz audience for many years. Then, in March 1962, one Blue Note album opened the door to the label's next wave of jazz recording.

NINE

Jackie McLean had become as much a Blue Note regular as Hank Mobley (by the end of his tenure with the original company, he had played on nearly fifty sessions), but he was one hard-bopper who had begun to question his own ground. For the sleeve of his 1962 *Let Freedom Ring* album, McLean asked to write his own notes: 'Jazz is going through a big change, and the listener or the fan, or what have you, should listen with an open mind. They should use a mental telescope to bring into view the explorers who have taken one step beyond, explorers such as Monk, Coltrane, Mingus, Cecil Taylor, Kenny Dorham, Sonny Rollins, Miles Davis, Ornette and, of course, Duke Ellington.'[1] McLean doesn't choose to be very specific about how he feels his own music is changing, other than expressing a general dissatisfaction with chord-based improvising, but earlier in the essay he does say: 'Ornette Coleman has made me stop and think. He has stood up under much criticism, yet he never gives up his cause, freedom of expression. The search is on.'[2]

What was this search? Perhaps McLean himself was not so sure, since most of *Let Freedom Ring* is a frequently awkward truce between his bebop roots and the new freedoms which Coleman had been putting on display in his music. But Coleman, too, had a debt to Charlie Parker and to blues playing. Why does

McLean sound, in comparison, to be struggling with his 'freedom'? It may be that he is, in effect, trying too hard. Listening to Coleman's music of the same period, one is constantly taken aback by how unselfconscious the playing is, as if the musicians in Coleman's famous quartet were free-at-last. McLean takes a much sterner route: if his earlier records sounded intense, this one is practically boiling. He seems unsure as to how best to use his tone, whether it should be flattened or made even sharper than normal, and there is both overblowing in the high register and a deliberate emphasis on oboe-like low notes. His three originals are open-ended and exploratory, but the one ballad, Bud Powell's 'I'll Keep Loving You', is a distinct contrast, with the saxophonist playing it in a way which sounds in this setting weirdly direct and unadorned. Although the pianist, Walter Davis, was a near contemporary of McLean's, the other players were young men: bassist Herbie Lewis and drummer Billy Higgins.

McLean's decision was not so much a conversion as a progression. Many of his generation had been scathing about Coleman's new music, while at the same time being uneasily aware that the Texan saxophonist was on to something. No experienced musician who heard the music of Coleman's first Atlantic recordings of 1959 could have been under the impression that the guiding hand was some kind of charlatan, even if they didn't agree with his methods or his way of expressing himself. At this distance, it seems odd that Coleman's music could even have excited so much controversy: not only does it sound light, folksy and songful, its accessibility follows a clear path down from bebop roots (a point best expressed in Coleman's first two recordings for Contemporary, with 'conventional' West Coast rhythm sections. The music there gives drummer Shelly Manne no rhythmical problems at all, but the two bassists involved, Percy Heath and Red Mitchell, both later remembered asking the leader about harmonic points which Ornette more or less waved aside).

In 1963, McLean built on the work of *Let Freedom Ring* by forming a new and regular band, with players who could accommodate what he saw as his new direction. Three of them were individuals who would have their own Blue Note engagements soon enough: vibraphonist Bobby Hutcherson, trombonist Grachan Moncur and drummer Tony Williams. All three featured alongside McLean on his next released session, *One Step Beyond* (although three other sessions which took place in between were shelved by Lion at the time). What is awkward about *One Step Beyond* – and the subsequent *Destination . . . Out!* – is that McLean is the one who sounds like the backward player. Just as Miles Davis found himself initially perplexed by Williams (who joined the Davis band in 1964), so did McLean struggle with the language of his younger sidemen.

It was a problem which some of McLean's contemporaries were also tussling with. Sonny Rollins, having emerged from a brief sabbatical at the end of the fifties, re-entered the recording scene with his intriguing *Our Man In Jazz* session for RCA, where he met Don Cherry, the trumpeter from Ornette Coleman's quartet. Although Rollins could be accredited as one of the most free-thinking of the hard-boppers, it was not the same kind of freedom as that evinced by Cherry and his compatriots, and Rollins never really came to terms with the clean-slate approach of the new-wave players.

At first, Lion and Wolff gave little sign that they were going to undertake the sort of wholesale change of policy which they had chosen when they signed on Thelonious Monk, some two decades earlier. They were still selling plenty of Three Sounds records, and still recording Blakey, Silver and the rest of their loyal roster. But as signings such as Baby Face Willette proved to be a commercial dead end, and the rumblings about the death of hard bop grew louder in the likes of *Down Beat*, it was clear that something had to give.

There was, though, a major difference between bop's first stirrings and the emergence of this 'New Thing', as it was dubbed in some quarters. Bop was in some senses a reaction against both conservatism and commercialism. The new jazz of the sixties was driven by artistic and socio-cultural pressures, not economic ones: it was not as if hard bop had been colonised by any kind of 'sell-out'. It was a progression that grew entirely from within jazz, as younger musicians sought to do what every young musician wants to do - stake out some personal territory for themselves rather than replicate what had come before. Whether or not free jazz had any specific political climate to it - chiming with a time when the civil rights movement was a powerful, gathering force - its emphasis on a release from such concerns as chords, bar lines and rhythmical restrictions certainly had its counterpart in the tenor of the times.

When bop came along, there was also no real forum for debate on its merits or otherwise. By the sixties, jazz had assumed art-form status and had witnessed the growth of a culture of intellectual commentary to go with its every new step. The tonnage of sleeve notes and magazine articles, absent from the days when *Down Beat* was a mere newspaper, accompanied every new LP or New York debut. Writers as diverse as Leonard Feather, Nat Hentoff and Leroi Jones shadowed all this newness, as well as what had carried through from before. By the end of the decade, the debate would be so wearisome, it could have bored to death many jazz fans more interested in music than polemics; but this, too, was a sign of the times.

Blue Note's new A&R man was Duke Pearson, a pianist from Atlanta, Georgia, who'd already recorded two albums of his own, *Profile* and *Tender Feelin's*, for the label. After Quebec's death, Lion realised that he was going to miss the assistance of a musician, although according to Pearson, it was a pretty *ad hoc* situation: 'Donald Byrd turned me on to them and they heard me and liked me, and next thing I know I was producing for them. One thing led to another.'[3] Pearson was a private man, not much given to talking, and it seems likely that he followed his own instincts, although his description of what he was allowed to do seems fanciful: 'I was on my own, entirely on my own . . . [I could record] anything I wanted to do. I liked it and that was it.'[4] Still, Pearson gave little evidence that he was much interested in jazz's new direction. His own playing betrayed a conventional hard-bop style, and he liked to arrange for larger groups: some of his later records were among the few Blue Note sessions which adapted the house style to an orchestral setting.

The key players in Blue Note's new-wave documentation were pianist Andrew Hill, organist Larry Young, vibraphonist Bobby Hutcherson, saxophonist Sam Rivers and drummer Tony Williams. Although the label would also record the two principals in the birthing of free jazz, Cecil Taylor and Ornette Coleman, and set down the modal freedoms of Wayne Shorter and Herbie Hancock, it was those five whose work represented a significant canon of outward-bound jazz within Blue Note's family roster.

Andrew Hill is arguably the most important member of this group. Although it has often been claimed that he was raised in Haiti (a rumour to which Hill himself has sometimes seemed to contribute), he actually came from Chicago, where he was born in 1937. Like many black musicians from the city, his grounding came in the fertile local R&B scene, and with such boppers as Gene Ammons and Chicago hero Von Freeman. After a brief spell in New York in 1961, he worked for a couple of years on the West Coast, before returning east in 1963 and catching the attention of Alfred Lion. After he played as a sideman on Joe Henderson's session for *Our Thing*, cut in September 1963, Lion offered Hill his own date – and two months later, the pianist began a burst of recording activity which would result in five albums being set down in a little over seven months. Indeed, most of Hill's reputation rests on these five records.

They were, in order: *Black Fire*, a quartet with Joe Henderson; *Smoke Stack*, with the two bassists Richard Davis and Eddie Khan, plus drummer Roy Haynes; *Judgement!*, a quartet with Bobby Hutcherson, Richard Davis and Elvin Jones; *Point Of Departure*, a sextet session with the distinguished line-up of Kenny Dorham, Eric Dolphy, Joe Henderson, Richard Davis and Tony Williams; and *Andrew!!!*, with John Gilmore, Hutcherson, Davis and drummer Joe Chambers. It is as fascinating and distinctive as any sequence of records in the jazz LP era, and much of the credit for its existence must go to Lion, who wasn't even able to find space in his schedules for the *first* of them to be released before they'd got as far as *Andrew!!!*

Hill is a tough musician to classify. Although his one featured album prior to the Blue Note records – *So In Love*, made for the small Warwick label in 1956 – shows a fairly unsurprising kind of midstream hard bop, by the time of his sixties sessions he was very much his own man. There is no reliance on either standards or blues and little which could be placed in alliance with the music of Blakey and Silver, yet Hill was very much involved in hard bop as a source of his methods. As a pianist, he is remote from the new music of Cecil Taylor. Although he cited Monk, Bud Powell and Art Tatum as his three major influences, he also qualifies the assertion – on Powell, he said, 'his music is a dead end'[5] – and it is very hard to find any passages in his playing which seem like nods to those three masters. His only kinship is with some of his contemporaries, particularly Mal Waldron (especially Waldron's 1959 trio set for Prestige, *Impressions*). What Hill and Waldron share is an interest in the darkest sounds the piano can produce, and in pulses which don't suggest either up-tempo swing or mid-tempo funk. Also like Waldron, Hill liked to use repetition – of either single chords, motifs or harmonic subtexts – as a device which underscores much of his methodology.

The result of this is a jazz of atmosphere: Hill's music broods, and it broods on both itself and what its performers can do with it. It seems curious that Alfred Lion liked his work so much - and Blue Note continued to record Hill right through the sixties - when Hill's soulfulness is manifest only in the most enigmatic of ways. When he tries anything funky (he wrote 'The Rumproller' for Lee Morgan, which was intended as a jukebox hit and failed), he usually misses. The two 'hornless' albums, *Smoke Stack* and *Judgement!*, are very different to almost everything else released by Blue Note. Elvin Jones provides most of the urgency on *Judgement!*, in a session which would otherwise revolve around a sort of tempoless counterpoint between Hill, Hutcherson and Davis: the bass vamp which opens 'Siete Ocho' (Spanish for 'Seven-Eight') is more like a point of stasis than a rhythmic ingredient, and Hill's repetitions are used to nearly excessive lengths in both solo and accompaniment. 'Yokada Yokada', from the same date, is almost a satire on twelve-bar blues form; but that is the only shaft of humour in an otherwise dark session. There's no turbulence in it, but the refusal of the players to follow expected procedures is strangely troubling.

Smoke Stack is similarly difficult. The two bassists are used as a kind of yin and yang, with Eddie Khan taking a less obtrusive, more traditional role, alongside the soloistic, even violent sounds emanating from Richard Davis. Hill's seven originals seem like the sketchiest of sources for the players - has any other musician attempted to cover Hill's music of this period? - but exist as frameworks for what is as much an ensemble piece as any vehicle for solo improvisation. *Point Of Departure*, though, has remained the Hill album which is most familiar, mainly because of its all-star line-up of horn soloists. Composition for composition, the record is no stronger than any of its brothers in the five-album sequence, but with Dolphy on superb form, the thoughtful Dorham and the tough, vulnerable Henderson, it was the kind of front line which only a dunce could have misdirected. Equally, Davis and the mercurial Williams make an exceptional partnership, the jittery accenting of the drummer offsetting the similarly assertive virtuosity of the bassist. Hill took care to vary the solo sequences across the five compositions, and he introduces shifts of pulse and harmony and little bursts of ensemble playing which keep the music restlessly on the move. In the notes, he says: 'Until we got to "Dedication" the session had been extremely happy'[6] which must have been the elation of musical achievement: happiness is one thing the record scarcely projects. Tension and anxious apprehension are more appropriate descriptions. Then the final 'Dedication' does, indeed, cast a genuinely sombre mood – Hill admits that the original title of the piece was 'Cadaver'.

As outstanding as these albums were, they pointed up a discomforting paradox in the new jazz: the better it was, the less people liked it. Joe Chambers's verdict on Andrew Hill's playing – 'It's like psychoanalysis, you've got to check it out'[7] – wasn't likely to have crowds flocking to the pianist's next engagement. Whereas hard bop's great achievements could communicate to a wide audience, the new jazz called for a degree of connoisseurship which dismayed many potential listeners. Hill's Blue Notes, for all their acclaim (which included high praise in the contemporary press), have never done well at the jazz box office. In the compact-disc era, only *Point Of Departure* has been in steady circulation.

It was a situation which must have disheartened Lion: Blue Note never sold millions with Monk either, but at this stage of the game they were entitled to see the albums of an artist such as Hill pay their own way. Similarly, the records by Hutcherson, Rivers, Young and Williams also proved difficult to sell, though for a variety of reasons.

*   *   *

Bobby Hutcherson remained a Blue Note artist for longer than most: he was still making albums for the label at the very end of its original life in the seventies. Born in Los Angeles but raised in Pasadena, he arrived in New York in 1961 and made his Blue Note debut with Jackie McLean's *One Step Beyond* band. The vibes were an even less popular jazz instrument than the guitar, despite the high profile of both Lionel Hampton and Milt Jackson, and Hutcherson was (along with the lesser-known Walt Dickerson) the first to try and make something of the instrument in the new environment of the sixties. With no real precedents available to him, Hutcherson devised a vocabulary which allowed the vibes to work on several levels: textural sound, the use of contrapuntal and multiple-melodic parts, and a fresh utilisation of the instrument's percussive qualities. Although in his latter-day work he has made use of the 'prettiness' of the vibes, much of his playing in this period is intentionally anti-romantic, getting away from the glassy beauty of the instrument and substituting a kind of dry lyricism.

He made several important sideman appearances with Eric Dolphy and Andrew Hill before Lion gave him his chance as a leader on *Dialogue* in April 1965 (a 1963 session was unreleased). *Dialogue* deserves to stand with the great records of the period, and with good reason: Hutcherson again assembled the best band Blue Note could have given him (Freddie Hubbard, Sam Rivers, Andrew Hill, Richard Davis, Joe Chambers), and the material - none of it by Hutcherson, the themes coming instead from Hill and Chambers - is an exceptional bridge between form and a kind of freedom, caught most effectively on Hill's 'Les Noirs Marchent'. Though the theme is played as a march, it then moves into what A. B. Spellman calls 'an essay in free group improvisation in which no one lays an apparently set role, in which there are no extended solos, but in which there is a mass evolution around some felt key'.[8] Ensemble and solo, form and freedom, this was a jazz which was stretching towards a very sophisticated development out of hard bop's language.

That brainy quality, though, was unfriendly enough to deter any but the most adventurous (as with Hill's output, Hutcherson's records have languished out of print for most of the CD era). Although this music was tonally conservative next to the contemporary outpourings of, for example, the saxophonist Albert Ayler, whose tumultuous music was just beginning to emerge on the independent New York label ESP, it was just as intimidating and didn't possess the visceral impact of Ayler's 'freak-out' music.

Sam Rivers was one saxophonist who might have appealed to some degree to Ayler's followers. By the time he came to Blue Note, he was already in his forties, born in Oklahoma in 1923. He had worked and studied in Boston and Florida in the forties and fifties, and had experience of R&B groups too – he was touring with the guitarist T-Bone Walker as late as 1962. But a spell with Miles Davis in 1964 brought him wider attention at last. The three dates which Blue Note released under his own name in the sixties offer an idiosyncratic view of the jazz past and present as it then stood. *Fuchsia Swing Song*, the first of the three, has the most conventional material, a rhythm section where the boppish Jaki Byard and Ron Carter clash effectively with the momentous Tony Williams, and solos by Rivers which are more shocking because they're set in such standard settings as a blues ('Downstairs Blues Upstairs'), an attractive thirty-two-bar theme ('Fuchsia Swing Song', where the distortions in the tenor improvisation are genuinely startling) and the ballad 'Beatrice', which has since entered the standard post-bop repertoire. *Contours* adds another horn (Freddie Hubbard) to the front line, and brings in Herbie Hancock and Joe Chambers for Byard and Williams, and here the material is more abstract and challenging. The title of the final piece of the four, 'Mellifluous Cacaphony [*sic*]', sums up Rivers's approach. As freely as he could improvise, Rivers was a composer-arranger – at the end of the century he would reassert that role with two outstanding big-band recordings – and was as interested in what he could do with structure as with liberty from form. It was the sort of halfway house which the sleeve-note writers for his albums welcomed as a respite from free-jazz aggression, although in less imaginative hands the music would have ended up sounding half-cooked. The third record, *A New Conception*, seemed like a capitulation, since it consisted of seven familiar standards with a rhythm section that 'really feels this kind of pleasant mood'.[9]

Tony Williams was quickly snapped up by Miles Davis for the trumpeter's new group in 1963, but he managed to play on thirteen sessions for Blue Note and helm two dates of his own. Williams was the ideal drummer for the freedom-with-form jazz of the sixties. Born in 1945, he had already appeared on several of the major jazz records of the period before he turned twenty. Unlike Sunny Murray and Milford Graves, two drummers who were crucial to the free playing of the time, Williams didn't altogether discard the tradition built up by Kenny Clarke, Max Roach and Philly Joe Jones. Basically, he souped it up. Everything Williams played was fast, very fast, whether it was a 4/4 time articulated with absolute crispness or a free-ranging pulse illuminated by his cymbals and developed via an seemingly endless variety of patterns played on all of his drums. The bop tradition of closing the high-hat cymbal on the second and fourth beats was soon bypassed by Williams, who preferred to keep the basic time with his ride cymbal, and used the high-hat for colour and emphasis. Listening to him is like hearing a sustained shower of sparks, some dazzling, others glinting through the sound of wood and skin. Whereas

Murray seemed to make his rhythm go forward in waves, rising and receding and rising again, Williams was always pushing hard, and straight ahead.

In some ways, Williams spent too little time at Blue Note. His later music saw him trying to reconcile his jazz time with a kind of virtuoso rock beat, the sort of drumming which would power most of the fusion music of the seventies, and it would have been intriguing to hear him attempt to meld his free style with the Blue Note funk of the later sixties. *Life Time*, made in August 1964, was a sampler of some of the approaches which the concerned young avant-gardist was interested in: the all-out rush of 'Tomorrow Afternoon', which was what one might have expected to fill up the whole date, balanced against the more skeletal music of 'Two Pieces Of One', the improvised trio piece 'Memory' and the duet between Herbie Hancock and Ron Carter, 'Barb's Song To The Wizard', which Williams doesn't play on at all. Without wishing to seem patronising, it is a rather amazing record for a nineteen-year-old drummer to have concocted, and confirmed the impression of many who'd worked with him that Williams was a very considerable musician even setting his drumming skills aside. The follow-up, *Spring*, wasn't set down until a year later, but is just as free from convention. Sam Rivers, Hancock and bassist Gary Peacock return from the earlier date, along with Wayne Shorter, who plays in tandem with Rivers on two tracks. 'Echo' is a drum solo by Williams and, like all drum solos, it means everything and nothing. Once again, there are parts of the record which are arhythmical, and the atmosphere of the music is doomy, dispersed only by the gripping playing of Rivers and Shorter. Graced with one of Reid Miles's sparest sleeve designs and given the rare distinction of a reverse with no sleeve notes of any kind, it was an enigmatic entry indeed, surrounded as it was in the recording ledger by sessions from Blue Mitchell, Freddie Roach and Lee Morgan.

* * *

That isolation says something about Blue Note's commitment to the avant-garde: not dilettantish, but cautious. It would be too easy to say that Lion was searching for musicians who could bridge the gap between Blue Note's standard hard bop and modal jazz and the New Thing, but there is a select number of Blue Notes of the period which appear to annex some middle ground. It would initially stretch credulity to see an organ player, of the same stripe as Jimmy Smith and John Patton, moving in that direction, but that was basically what Larry Young did. Young's most extreme music lay some way ahead, with the Tony Williams Lifetime group of 1969–70, yet his brief run of Blue Note dates in the middle sixties hint at a dramatic fusion of 'organ-combo' jazz with the more taxing ambitions of, in particular, John Coltrane.

Young had learned to play the organ in his father's nightclub in Newark, New Jersey. His first Blue Note engagement was as a sideman on Grant Green's *Talkin' About* session, and a few weeks later he made *Into Somethin'*, with Green, Sam Rivers and Elvin Jones, and a year after that the outstanding *Unity*, with Jones, the twenty-year-old trumpeter Woody Shaw and Joe Henderson. The latter date is a pristine example of the kind of album Blue Note made as an uncompromising mid-point between its established style and the newer developments. Shaw was a conservative who nevertheless was dedicated to what came after hard-bop trumpet. Henderson had already established himself as a flexible saxophonist, at ease in familiar and unexplored settings. And Jones, who was himself on the point of leaving the Coltrane quartet, had become one of the premier drummers in the music. It was a perfectly attuned band for Young's chosen milieu. The programme includes three originals by Shaw (including the first version of his signature piece, 'The Moontrane'), one by Henderson, Thelonious Monk's 'Monk's Dream', and one standard, 'Softly As In A Morning Sunrise'. The organist's own playing moves into the kind of territory which had more than one authority describe him as the John Coltrane of his instrument, but as with so many Blue Note dates, the group is the important thing: Shaw and Henderson play fierce, open-ended solos which explore the kind of terrain which Coltrane's quartet records had been mining, while Young is superbly accomplished, both in support of the soloists, in dialogue with the meteoric Jones and in his own solos, which are a working-out of a vocabulary which players such as Patton and Roach were not privy to. *Unity* is a timeless record which Young never quite matched again.

As a body of work, the recordings by these five musicians stand as a formidable part of Blue Note's original legacy. Yet most of them, as already noted, actually sold poorly, even by Blue Note standards, and are relatively little known next to the principal 'name' items in the label's catalogue. The only disc with any sort of avant-garde bearings which has found a sustained popularity was the sole Blue Note offering by the multi-instrumentalist Eric Dolphy, *Out To Lunch*.

Dolphy had a very brief career in the jazz limelight, although he had years behind him in the music before he made his breakthrough with his own groups and with the John Coltrane band of the early sixties. As with *Blue Trane* some years earlier, *Out To Lunch* is the testimony of a major artist for once given a little time and space to prepare a major statement. Like so many of Blue Note's small school of radicals, Dolphy was actually more of a traditionalist than many of his colleagues. He liked to play on chord sequences, and although his phrasing was fast and loose and garrulously imprecise, he rarely strayed very far from the root of whatever structure he was playing on. On both the alto saxophone and the bass clarinet, which he uses to superb effect on his Monk tribute on the album, 'Hat And Beard', he managed a huge, larger-than-life tone which again made his choice of notes seem more outlandish than they often were. In comparison, his flute playing could be almost unbearably beautiful. 'Gazzelloni' from this date is particularly fine, although even this has to bow to his solo on Oliver Nelson's 'Stolen Moments' from the Impulse! album *Blues And The Abstract Truth*.

With Freddie Hubbard – the reader will by now have noted how often the trumpeter was present on so many of the major works of this era, even if he didn't exactly have a pivotal role in any of them – Bobby Hutcherson, Richard Davis and Tony Williams, Dolphy here led one of the greatest groups of the day. The feeling that this was still an ensemble finding its way underlines the paradox between the permanence of a recording and the transience of even a relatively well-prepared studio situation such as this. What else might this group have achieved in a studio? A few hours on 25 February 1964 yielded one of the most remarkable recordings of the jazz LP era; yet Dolphy was able to record for Blue Note just once more (on Andrew Hill's *Point Of Departure*), since he died in Berlin only a few weeks later. Many years later, Michael Cuscuna, who'd been transfixed by the album on its initial appearance, searched through the session tapes to see what else was there: 'The material is so goddamn difficult. How could they play those fucking time signatures, how do they know where they are? The mastery with which they execute it is really astonishing. I was hoping for some great alternate takes, but there weren't any – what there was made me feel a little more comfortable about these superhuman people. They were fucking up left and right until they got it! It wasn't as easy for them as it sounds!'

Every year, Frank Wolff took a vacation in Europe, which he often combined with a little work: hence the recording of Dexter Gordon's *Our Man In Paris* and *One Flight Up* sessions. Wolff went to Stockholm in 1965 and there he recorded the man who'd become the godfather of the new music. Ornette Coleman's albums for Contemporary and Atlantic had had a terrific impact on the direction of the music, but in 1965 he was without a contract and available, though mostly on terms which would have scared away most prospective labels: Coleman has always felt that whatever he asks for, he's worth it. A December 1962 concert recording made in New York's Town Hall was originally scheduled for a Blue Note release but instead came out on ESP (a situation which has never been properly cleared up. Blue Note purchased the original tapes and assembled them into two LPs, but what happened after that is obscure. Much of the music remains unissued). Wolff, though, made one of his occasional appearances as sole producer when he set down the music from two days of concerts at the Gyllene Cirkeln, a restaurant in Stockholm. At the time, Coleman was leading a trio of himself, bassist David Izenzon and drummer Charles Moffett. The cover photographs of *At The 'Golden Circle', Stockholm, Vols. 1 & 2* show the three men wrapped up against the freezing Scandinavian winter. It was an inspired piece of location recording, since Coleman's music was in one of its most fruitful periods. He had recently taken up both trumpet and violin, both of which he played in a manner as idiosyncratic as the rest of his music, and in Izenzon and Moffett he had one of his finest support groups, a pairing that could swing hard but was also able to trace an almost neoclassical backdrop for the altoist, Izenzon's arco lines and Moffett's ominous rumblings helping to turn pieces such as 'European Echoes' and 'Snowflakes And Sunshine' into small tone poems. Coleman would return to Blue Note later in the sixties, but his best work for the label had already been done.

While records by artists such as Coleman, Hill, Rivers and Hutcherson gained plenty of critical attention, Blue Note's business in the middle sixties was still being done best by its label mainstays, even if many of them were coming to be regarded as little more than the foot soldiers of hard bop. A. B. Spellman, in his notes to Hill's *Black Fire*, said that 'there has been until almost yesterday a sickening familiarity about the jazz mainstream, and the most apparent extra-musical value of Coltrane, Coleman and Taylor has been that they've made the jazz mainstream uncomfortable in its learned devices, and thereby liberated younger musicians whose main interest is finding their own voice through playing jazz'.[10] Spellman's point was well enough made, but it's natural enough that every mainstream is familiar, sickeningly so or otherwise. Many were unwilling to follow the new precepts, not because they were suspicious of revolution, but because their own playing didn't have to trumpet innovation over individuality. Freddie Hubbard, the 'straight man' on so many of the major avant-garde dates of the period, only rarely tried such territory in his own recordings, yet his ten Blue Note albums as leader are a strong and vital sequence of Blue Note recordings.

Stanley Turrentine was one figure whose records have been largely ignored in jazz histories, yet they retain a prodigiously satisfying quota of creative jazz playing. Turrentine was nobody's torch-bearer for jazz progression. He often recorded with his then wife, Shirley Scott, and most of their records are programmes of blues, standards and simple bebop progressions. The two volumes of *Up At Minton's*, *Dearly Beloved*, *Never Let Me Go* and the others present a menu of meat-and-potatoes blowing that might have been the kind of thing which bored writers such as Spellman. In the usual cyclical way of these things, years later it would be these kinds of sessions which would be held up as more profoundly soulful, next to the sometimes 'pretentious' experimentation of some of the label's more demanding players. Not only Turrentine: there were also Hank

Mobley and Lou Donaldson carrying on as they were, and a further number of newcomers who fitted right in to the traditional Blue Note bag – saxophonists Harold Vick, George Braith and Don Wilkerson, and trumpeter Johnny Coles.

Donald Byrd had been trying something new – well, almost new, since yet again he was following up an earlier initiative. Max Roach's 1962 *It's Time* set for Impulse! had set the drummer's small group alongside a chorale of voice directed by Coleridge Perkinson, and Byrd repeated the trick with *A New Perspective*, made in January 1963 (in Byrd's defence, he had apparently been lobbying Lion to make the album for some time before the label chief assented). Duke Pearson did the arrangements and besides Byrd there was a fine band including Hank Mobley, Herbie Hancock and Kenny Burrell. Blending hard-bop music with gospel strains was a tough call for anybody, yet in one track, at least, Pearson came up with a gem, the moving 'Cristo Redentor', which later became a frequently covered tune. It was altogether enough to turn *A New Perspective* into a Blue Note hit, although when they tried to repeat the trick with the far less inspired *I'm Tryin' To Get Home*, the record failed.

Two figures offered an interesting middle-ground position, comparable to Larry Young's. Herbie Hancock had made his Blue Note debut (with Donald Byrd) as far back as 1961, and by 1965, with his ongoing stint with the Miles Davis group to assist, he had plenty of attention of his own. The early records *Takin' Off, My Point Of View* and *Inventions And Dimensions* are remarkably mature and finished collections from a man only just into his twenties. Hancock's gifts as a composer are immediately evident on the debut's 'Watermelon Man', with its sumptuous Freddie Hubbard solo and irresistible gospel-based groove. The third set, *Inventions And Dimensions*, is self-consciously experimental, with only one of the pieces starting from anything written down and the others grown from germinal ideas like a time signature or a rhythmic motif. Next to Andrew

Hill's work this can sound naive, but Hancock has a compensating clarity and an almost luminous pianistic touch, which seems to shine a light through the unfolding music. If this was free jazz, why did it so seldom sound this transparent and idyllic?

Hancock was a natural pastoralist, and an almost instinctive ballad writer. His two masterpieces were set down in 1964–5, *Empyrean Isles* with Hubbard, Ron Carter and Tony Williams, and the follow-up *Maiden Voyage*, by the same band plus saxophonist George Coleman. Hancock knew these players well (all except Hubbard were Miles Davis bandmates) and there is as much delicacy and refinement in the playing as there is questing onwards. The irony of Hancock's popularity in the past twenty-five years is that it has been almost entirely based on his work in the jazz-funk idiom, while his most particular talent arguably lies in the inspiration which produced the lyric beauty of such tunes as 'Dolphin Dance', 'Maiden Voyage' and ' Oliloqui Valley'. 'Canteloupe Island' from *Empyrean Isles* was to become the basis of a sampled hit in the 1990s, but in its original incarnation it is a lazy, thickly voiced groove which simply rolls forward, tartly decorated by Hubbard. As distinctive as these records are, there is little in them which would predict the way Hancock's career would turn in the seventies.

Joe Henderson would have a long, unpredictable career ahead of him too, but in 1964–5 he was hitting a first peak as a group leader and soloist. If anyone on Blue Note could be presented as a counterpart to John Coltrane, it was this bespectacled, self-effacing, quietly spoken man from Lima, Ohio. His appearances and records with the Horace Silver Quintet were rather different to the music of his own dates, which were a good deal more turbulent and anxious. It is fascinating to hear him with McCoy Tyner and Elvin Jones on both of his two 1964 dates, *In 'N' Out* and *Inner Urge*. The long title track to *In 'N'*

Out is a typical Coltrane charge, which Henderson does his best to resolve in his own image, without quite convincing that he's doing anything much more profound than following John. It helps that Kenny Dorham is on the date too, since his more patient playing usefully cools off some of the aggression. *Inner Urge*, though cut only a few months later, finds Henderson more particular and more his own man. It starts with another long assault on the title track, but this time Henderson's phrase shapes are more individual, his tone more in focus. These were unglamorous and in some ways rather grim sessions, since the saxophonist isn't much interested in any melodious side to his music at this stage. But their accumulated power, even when inflected by the towering influence of Coltrane, is still gripping.

Kenny Dorham was one figure who could have blended old and new tropes better than most, but he had a largely luckless career (he eventually succumbed to kidney failure in 1972, at only forty-eight years old). Although he'd been around since the first days of bebop, he had a strikingly uncluttered style, even though he had worked in a wider variety of jazz settings than most. *Una Mas* (1963) and *Trompeta Toccata* (1964) both have Henderson in their respective quintets, and they were an unexpectedly seamless partnership, the young saxophonist's battery of twist-and-turn licks the counterweight to the fluent, bluesy streams that came out of Dorham's horn. They were the kind of records which should have won both critical and commercial success, but Dorham had suddenly come to seem like a man out of his time and from this point he began to drift into obscurity.

Reviewing the records discussed above makes it seem as if Blue Note were struggling to have any kind of commercial success. But in 1964, at last, that was far from the truth. It was, indeed, success which began to spell the end of the old Blue Note operation.

TEN

One important absentee from Blue Note in the early sixties was Lee Morgan, who'd made some records for Vee-Jay at the beginning of the decade. His low profile was due in the main to a narcotics addiction which lost him most of his regular work, but in 1963 he had cleaned up sufficiently to return to active duty. His comeback date as a leader for Blue Note took place on 21 December 1963, and it consisted of what was apparently a typical, no-frills Blue Note blowing date. Morgan headed up a quintet with Joe Henderson, Barry Harris, Bob Cranshaw and Billy Higgins. One notable aspect of the session was that, for the first time, Morgan brought an all-original programme of his own. Another was that the title theme, 'The Sidewinder', would be the biggest hit Alfred Lion had ever had.

On the face of it, there's nothing so different in 'The Sidewinder' to any number of funky, blues-based groove tunes which go on just long enough to suggest a marathon (or at least to cast a hypnotic state on a susceptible listener). Morgan's tune, though, was a peerless example of right place and right time. Split over the two sides of a 45 rpm single, it was the jazz track of choice on jukeboxes everywhere in 1964. The tune, with some modifications (an added strings section), would later turn up in the background of a Chrysler

TV commercial. And suddenly, Blue Note had an album which edged up to number 25 in the *Billboard* LP charts.

It would be fatuous to suggest that 'The Sidewinder' was actually the weakest track on the album. Still, 'Totem Pole', the fast waltz 'Gary's Notebook' and 'Boy, What A Night' do have more musical interest than the main theme. But 'The Sidewinder', with its elegant, gritty solos, ingenious Barry Harris fills and crisp Billy Higgins beat, worked out perfectly (next to Morgan's follow-up record, *Search For The New Land*, made a couple of months later, *The Sidewinder* seems positively lightweight; but *Search For The New Land* sat on the shelf for several years and is, in comparison, a virtually unknown record). It was also not the only hit album which Blue Note recorded in 1964.

Horace Silver, the most dependable of all of Lion's team, finally gave way to an idea which his father had put into his head some time before, and decided to try and stew a little of the Portuguese music which he'd heard as a boy in with his patented funky hard-bop style. 'Song For My Father' was the end result, one of Horace's catchiest pieces and the title track of one of his strongest Blue Notes (in honour of the occasion, Frank Wolff took a photo of a beaming John Tavares Silver for the cover). The album was actually something of a mishmash of several sessions: the long-standing Silver line-up with Blue Mitchell and Junior Cook was coming to an end (Silver even recalled that, during one less than successful session, Lion advised him to seek a fresh personnel), and the key tracks on the record were done with a new front line of Joe Henderson and trumpeter Carmell Jones. Henderson's barnstorming solo on 'Song For My Father' remains one of his great moments, and it helped both the single release and the album to sell in quantities which even Silver's other albums had failed to get near.

A breakthrough, for sure. But Lion and Wolff soon realised that the success brought a still small company more headaches too. Most record labels would see a single Top Thirty placing in a year of releases as a pretty indifferent result, but after two and a half decades of selling next to nothing, such a situation impacted on Blue Note like an earthquake. For once, distributors would be clamouring for more – not only of the original hit, but for more records which *sounded like* the original hit. The hand-to-mouth existence which many labels have to go through, if not entirely live by, made it all the more difficult to adapt to any sudden success. The careful balance which Frank Wolff had maintained to keep the company afloat was in jeopardy through the one thing which they hadn't really bargained for: a hit.

Michael Cuscuna, the Blue Note scholar *par excellence*, sees it like this:

> Once you have success and are an independent label of any kind of music, you go through a series of independent distributors that cover different geographic areas, and you ship them records, and you want them to sell them so you ship them more, and they won't pay you for the last release until you have a new release that they want. It is really a game of chasing your own tail. So the more successful he was, the more Alfred had to go out on a limb economically, and the more pressure there was to match the success.[1]

In the short term, at least, Blue Note responded as best they could. Advertising, never exactly a priority for the company, began to be more visible (and audible: there was a significant presence of Blue Note ads on the radio for the first time). One thing Lion seemed to do from that point was try and get another 'Sidewinder' out of a likely-looking date, so there were plenty of long, start-up blues grooves on many of the albums recorded over the next couple of years. But the biggest consequence of *The Sidewinder* was a logistical one. Most Blue Notes might ship no more than four or five thousand copies and with the returns system available to distributors, it would be some time before a clear picture of the relative success of a typical Blue Note LP could be determined. Solid catalogue items like the Monk and Rollins records, or recent Blakey and Silver albums, could tick along at a steady pace, with occasional repressing as the stock situation determined; a Baby Face Willette album might languish altogether and eventually end up as a deletion. In the case of *The Sidewinder*, though, repeat orders, which for a previous Lee Morgan album might have been in the scores or hundreds, ended up in the thousands.

Although most of the same problems of independent distribution still exist today for any number of small labels, the modern record industry then was still relatively young and unsure of itself. Many record executives were unconvinced of the staying power of rock music and were waiting to go back to a world of Perry Como and Frank Sinatra records. The rock album had yet to make any serious impact: pop was the stuff of singles and singles didn't make as much money as albums did. Modern jazz had no commercial clout as such, but the channels for its exposure did still exist: there was a reasonable amount of it on the radio and there were still thousands of what the industry now calls 'Mom And Pop' record stores, independent, localised retailers who stocked what they felt would go down well in their neighbourhood. Even people with no sentimental or emotional attachment to the music still regarded jazz as an important part of their business.

Looking through the lists of sessions which Blue Note embarked on during 1965 and 1966, there's little indication that Alfred Lion had lost any of his appetite for his beloved hot music. He continued to record sessions that were almost a commonplace in the Blue Note chronology, yet which any jazz producer of today would have been more than proud to have put their name to. After a quarter-century, though, Lion was suddenly tired. His own health had been giving Ruth and him cause for concern, with worries over his heart condition – not the kind of problem which suits a lifestyle involving endless late nights, fifteen-hour days and innumerable balancing acts over finances and distribution. Lion had earlier turned down an offer for Blue Note from Atlantic. In 1965, he started talking to Al Bennett, the boss of Liberty Records.

The advantage which any big, pop-orientated label enjoys over any jazz label is simple: cash and resources. Liberty had cash to invest and jazz was an area that caught Bennett's eye. In 1965, he did a deal with both Richard Bock of Pacific Jazz – which had got off to a tremendous start with Gerry Mulligan's quartet sessions of the early fifties, and now was again doing well with Les McCann and the Jazz Crusaders – and Alfred Lion.

'The hardest thing about having a jazz label,' says Michael Cuscuna, 'is that you never have enough money to pay yourself and you don't have the reserves to grow the business. You take every cent that comes in and put it into pressing-plant money or making new records. There's no time to sit down and think, or put money aside for anything.' When he did the deal with Liberty, Lion at last had the reserves and the resources. But it was the beginning of the end for his own involvement. It's not clear how much Bennett paid for Pacific Jazz and Blue Note, but it seems likely that it was a lot less than each catalogue was worth. When Bob Weinstock sold his Prestige label in 1970, both Bock and Lion grumbled that he got more than a million dollars; clearly, they got nothing like as much.

At least Lion and Wolff were able to carry on as before, in terms of recording who they wanted and in the style they wanted. The recording-sessions list for 1966–7 is full of challenging material. The most extraordinary arrival was Cecil

Taylor, the New York pianist who was an even more forbidding figure than Ornette Coleman in the avant-garde scheme of things. Taylor's titanic self-belief had seen him through years when he was still washing dishes in restaurants to survive, even as he managed to make occasional recordings, and in 1966 he made two albums for Blue Note, *Unit Structures* and *Conquistador!* Compared to some of his work in the later sixties, these were relatively temperate and approachable recordings, although next to almost anything else in the Blue Note catalogue, they are devastatingly isolated. From the curt horn unisons which commence the title piece of *Conquistador!* the music launches into a superbly organised pandemonium. In Taylor's own words:

> There is no music without order – if that music comes from a man's innards. But that order is not necessarily related to any single criterion of what order should be as imposed from the outside. Whether that criterion is the song form or what some critic thinks jazz should be. This is not a question, then, of 'freedom' as opposed to 'nonfreedom', but rather it is a question of recognising different ideas and expressions of order.[2]

A summary which could function as an apologia, if one were needed, for the whole free-jazz movement.

The surprise here is that Lion should have considered recording Taylor at all, when his music is seemingly a diametric opposite to all the verities which the producer considered important in jazz. There is no 'groove' in Taylor's music, unless it is an endless one. Michael Cuscuna has also pondered this curiosity:

> It had to have a groove, whether it was 'Milneburg Joys' or 'The

> Sidewinder', everyone says that about Alfred and Frank – if it got to them, if they were dancing around, then it was a good performance. I remember one comment that led me to believe that he was really looking for these kind of records to be adventurous. There was one take of a piece on one of the Andrew Hill sessions, it was a very good take, but for the second one, which was the chosen one, he made the note, 'this one much less orthodox'. So he was looking for adventurous and uncharted waters, although he got into it late, by New York standards.
>
> If you ask Rudy Van Gelder, he'll say that the avant-garde and the temperament of the musicians drove Alfred out of the business. And yet, when I called him [Lion] about doing the *One Night With Blue Note* concerts, he said, you've got to get Cecil Taylor. I would have made the assumption that he just felt he had to keep up with the tenor of the times. When he signed Ornette Coleman and Cecil Taylor, I noticed that it was the first time he was signing an established person instead of creating a new talent, and I thought that was a bit odd for Blue Note.

Van Gelder, at least, did his usual impeccable job on both of Taylor's sessions. In a period when most of the pianist's music was poorly recorded in both live and studio settings, Van Gelder's expertise left us two vintage examples of Taylor at a period where there is otherwise very little documentation of what he was doing.

Besides Taylor, though, there were plenty of other reasons for the contemporary-jazz listener to keep following Blue Note. Lion's final great series of recordings were arguably those he made with Wayne Shorter. Since leaving Art Blakey and going to the Miles Davis group, Shorter had become a pivotal figure in terms of both his visibility and his composing, and the albums under his own name which emerged during the middle sixties all belonged to Blue Note. After the relatively orthodox *Night Dreamer* in 1964, there followed *Juju*, *Speak No Evil*, *The All-Seeing Eye*, *Adam's Apple* and *Schizophrenia*, plus two sessions which lay unreleased until much later, *The Soothsayer* and *Etcetera*. All bar *Schizophrenia* were recorded in an extraordinary eighteen-month period beginning in August 1964. Although many of the sessions which Blue Note regulars were booked to play came about more because of the artists putting pressure on the label for some regular work and a royalty advance, this was a case where the musician genuinely had a great deal to document in a short space of time. *Juju* positioned him with Coltrane's team of McCoy Tyner, Reggie Workman and Elvin Jones, but although Shorter was as questing a spirit as Coltrane in his way, what comes out is altogether different: the younger man had a more quizzical, even surreal streak to his make-up, which comes out sometimes as blackly humorous, sometimes as a kind of painful melancholy. The great energy of his playing is still wonderful to hear, and the comparative coarseness of tone of his earliest records has been softened, or perhaps mollified.

Speak No Evil, with Freddie Hubbard, Herbie Hancock, Ron Carter and Elvin Jones, is a blissful listening experience. Shorter's six originals are a distilled blend of ingenuity and expressiveness, edging round the boundaries of freedom but maintaining one solid foot in hard bop's compositional field. It was a perfect gig for Hubbard and Hancock, giving both as much scope as they wished without asking them to go too far. *Etcetera* and *Adam's Apple* were quartet dates with Hancock, Joe Chambers and bassists Cecil McBee (on the first) and Reggie Workman (on the second). Shorter's purple patch as a composer continued unabated through these sets, with pieces such as 'Footprints' entering the post-bop repertory almost at once, and some of his loveliest writing coming through on ballad lines such as 'Penelope'. Some of the quirkiness has moved away for the time being, but there remains a degree of poignancy which this elusive, unique jazz musician always seems to have close to hand. *The All-Seeing Eye* is Shorter's grandest and most difficult record, worked out as a kind of suite for eight musicians, moving through 'The All-Seeing Eye', 'Genesis', 'Chaos' and 'Face Of The Deep', before closing with the coda of brother Alan Shorter's 'Mephistopheles'. Parallels with some of Coltrane's big-scale pieces are again suggested, but there is little in the course of the record which freaks out, and nothing of the raging, unending trauma in Coltrane's music. Debussy and Sibelius play larger roles in Shorter's music of the period: it's a romantic kind of conflict.

Schizophrenia was the last of his records to be produced by Lion. With a sextet this time, it lacks some of the concentrated drama and creativity of the earlier discs: Curtis Fuller and James Spaulding (a sterling second banana on many Blue Notes of the period) are used more to fill out the sound than take meaningful roles for themselves, and though 'Tom Thumb' and 'Miyako' confirm that Shorter's writing was still blooming, the record seems almost tame.

Don Cherry, the trumpeter who'd appeared on Ornette Coleman's Atlantics and had also worked with both Sonny Rollins and Albert Ayler, cut three Blue Note dates of his own: *Complete Communion*, *Symphony For Improvisers* and *Where is Brooklyn?* (it still seems like a good question). Cherry was a musician who took his playing seriously, while unable to resist introducing a certain impishness into his work, every time. Thus the title piece of *Complete Communion* is 'to connect the overall oneness, which makes up our complete communion', yet for much of the record that kind of portentous seriousness is spelled by cheekily boppish lines and musical nudges and winks of all kinds. Cherry's records sit more oddly in the Blue Note catalogue than perhaps anybody else's: next to the macho humour which tended to be the label's stock gesture when it wanted to lighten up, Cherry's music is the work of an unruly gremlin.

Lee Morgan, Donald Byrd, Hank Mobley and Horace Silver continued to record albums that sounded exactly in sync with what their audiences expected. In the case of Morgan, he was for a time almost imprisoned within a routine of attempting to replicate *The Sidewinder*, with albums such as *The Rumproller* and track titles like 'The Double Up'. Slowly, Morgan's work began to atrophy, but he was such a fine player to begin with that the records still secured a high professional standard.

Jackie McLean formed a new group with pianist Larry Willis which sounded like a retrenchment of his more boppish approach, as if he'd been to freedom and back again, slightly the wiser. (Somewhat an exception was his 1967 date *New And Old Gospel*, where he played in a quintet with Ornette Coleman on trumpet. It is an odd blend of backwards and forwards.) Lion continued to give opportunities to new leaders: Blue Mitchell, having departed from the Silver quintet, made several Blue Notes of his own, in an agreeable if hardly shattering hard-bop style, and McCoy Tyner, who'd made several discs as a leader for Impulse!, made the excellent *The Real McCoy* in 1967, easily the best record under his own name up to that point and yet another instance of Blue Note finding the best in a young talent already exposed elsewhere.

Lion's last great success in commercial terms was with another old stalwart of the label, Lou Donaldson. *Alligator Bogaloo* was made in April 1967 and featured Lou alongside trumpeter Melvin Lastie and two important new elements, organist Lonnie Smith and guitarist George Benson. Donaldson had rarely exerted himself in the composing department and the threadbare material of *Alligator Bogaloo* was no exception; but the title piece had a naggingly catchy riff which won a wide audience, and although both Smith (developing some interesting directions out of the Jimmy Smith template) and Benson (making a very effective use of the Grant Green style) play some excellent things, the record sold via the beat. In the end, sales of the album were pushing up towards the six-figure mark.

On the cover, a heavily made-up white woman was displayed in a Reid Miles photo montage. Miles had begun to take cover pictures himself, departing from the Frank Wolff manner, and perhaps it suited a new, younger and ultimately more pop-orientated marketing method. Another line had crept in under the faithful Blue Note logo, which still otherwise declaimed 'The Finest In Jazz Since 1939': now it also said 'A Product Of Liberty Records' (in the same way that, in the nineties, the proud group of independent labels, including Verve, MPS, MGM and the like, now have their logos disfigured on reissue CDs by the words 'A Universal Company', reminding us all that corporate vanity is alive and well).

Alfred Lion produced his final recording session on 28 July 1967, a date featuring Stanley Turrentine playing what looks like an undistinguished set of mostly contemporary pop tunes (the session was never released). The master of Blue Note had had enough. As Michael Cuscuna remembers:

> Alfred said, 'I couldn't communicate with these people. I do things my way, and suddenly there were too many people and there were all these rules and procedures.' He had a very bad time of working with Liberty. It wasn't an issue of taking orders from above because they pretty much had carte blanche. If you look at those years, he was still doing Cecil Taylor and Sam Rivers, but he had to interface with all these people over promotion and how label copy had to be input into the system,

> and it just drove him nuts. While the daily finances were relieved, the whole system just dragged him down.

After almost thirty years, Alfred Lion relinquished the reins of his label and, watched over by Ruth, went into a retirement which continued uninterrupted until the 1980s. Troubled by his heart problems, he disappeared altogether from the jazz industry. The friendly but tough German had found himself an important niche in an art form which he had worked as hard as any jazz musician to look after, even if it was his business as well as his love. Horace Silver, thinking back to the countless hours he must have spent in Lion's company, said that 'what I learnt about making a record, I learnt from Alfred Lion'.[3] In one of the most oft-quoted remarks about Wolff and Lion, Bobby Hutcherson said that 'Alfred and Frank were more like jazz musicians than record executives. They loved to hang out and have a great time. They loved the music and had a real feel for it.'[4] In an age when corporate faces were taking over the business of music in all its popular forms, Alfred Lion was a company man of a different kind, and his Blue Note musicians had good cause to be grateful to the stocky Berliner, who never lost his thick German accent, his big-rimmed spectacles or his swept-back hair.

Frank Wolff, though, carried on. As a parting gift to Alfred, he packed his entire inventory of Blue Note session photographs into a case and sent them down to the Lions' new home in Cuernavaca, Mexico. It must have reminded Alfred of the several times when he had to shout at the photographer, 'Frank, you're clicking on my record!' The unobtrusive other half of the Blue Note team knew only one life: if small-label guys were workaholics by the nature of their calling, then Frank Wolff almost defined the term. Tony Hall, who knew both Wolff and Lion, remembers Alfred as 'very quick, very sharp, and Frank was more the quiet, down-to-earth sort'. With an even greater degree of responsibility, Wolff had to forego many of his photographic pleasures and focus on production and business even more. Reid Miles, too, stepped away from his design duties as the Liberty marketing people took a larger involvement. With Lion no longer there, perhaps the old Blue Note style had in any event run its course. There was surely scope for a productive change.

But change had been visited on jazz already, and not to its best interests. The hard bop which Blue Note had spent so many years documenting was in complete recession. In a scant few years, the audience for the music had shrunk to almost nothing. The jukeboxes which had once boasted a stock of Blue Note singles alongside new soul and R&B hits had pushed out the straight-ahead jazz material: if it wasn't funky, it didn't fit. The clubs which had once housed a thriving community of audiences and musicians alike, in a mutual appreciation of modern jazz, had faded away, except in the most significant urban centres.

Much of the blame has been put on the avant-garde, for making music too difficult for audiences to accept. But that was only a part of the story. Jazz had lost significant audience numbers from all sides, not just from those who were fed up with the noise-making of the New Thing. As black neighbourhoods began to change, with the advances of greater integration and better civil rights, so did the black music audience. Just as some bop musicians had rejected the blues as redolent of a time of oppression, so many now found the hard-bop mainstream an old-fashioned and unflattering environment or soundtrack. The new soul music of Marvin Gaye, to take one totemic example, managed to combine profundity and musical elegance with immediacy; and what black jazz musician was as cool as Jimi Hendrix, the premier rock guitarist? Even Miles Davis had to bow to him. It wasn't hard for many to decide which kind of music they preferred.

Young white audiences, too, found little in jazz to interest them. Although there were a few isolated examples of jazz success with this sector of the market, such as the beatific Charles Lloyd group with Keith Jarrett, college-age whites were turning to the new genre of album rock, with singer-songwriters such as Bob Dylan holding down one end and bands of the order of Country Joe and The Fish, Jefferson Airplane and the Butterfield Blues Band holding up the other.

Between 1967 and 1971, Frank Wolff and Duke Pearson fought what was basically a losing battle against these signs of the times. Compared to any earlier period in Blue Note's history, the results were not so much inauspicious as indifferent. There were still some fine records recorded and released. But almost nothing had any especial impact on either the marketplace or the critical standing of the label. Many of the long-standing Blue Note artists seemed to continue on a kind of automatic pilot. In the context of the time, a lot of the records sound almost anachronistic. Suddenly devoid of a context, plausible straight-ahead albums such as Hank Mobley's *Hi Voltage* or Lee Morgan's *The Sixth Sense* have a pointless demeanour, as if they're proudly irrelevant. John Patton is a good example of a Blue Note lifer gradually losing his way. His 1968 *That Certain Feeling* has characteristically muscular tenor from Junior Cook and solid back-up from Jimmy Ponder and Clifford Jarvis, but Patton is doing nothing that different to what was going on on *Along Came John*. Later in the year, he cut *Understanding*, which sets him alongside the interesting Harold Alexander, a saxophonist who seemed to be mixing R&B licks with an avant-garde edge, although Patton himself seems oblivious to his altered surroundings. His final date, *Accent On The Blues*, was made in 1969 and featured guitarist James Blood Ulmer, later to be a crossover star of the eighties, and the fairly wretched playing of saxophonist Marvin Cabell. Like so many of Blue Note's dates in this period, the records were neither very successful nor very good.

Wolff hadn't lost his taste for hearing new music, and Michael Cuscuna, who spoke to him at the time, felt that he had an agenda that went beyond merely keeping the ship afloat: 'I remember calling him up once, because I had an album by [guitarist] George Freeman I was trying to place, and Frank called me back and said, "I like the record, he's a good player, but I'm swamped right now - and if I were to sign a guitar player like that, it would be Jimmy Ponder." So he had an agenda, he had things in mind.'

Wolff and Pearson also brought in some straight-ahead players who made some genuinely excellent records. Perhaps the major sequence of outstanding material in the period were the sessions made by the groups led by drummer Elvin Jones, starting with a trio featuring Joe Farrell and Jimmy Garrison: *Puttin' It Together* and *The Ultimate Elvin Jones* date from 1968 and highlight not only Jones's mastery, but also the overlooked compositional skills of bassist Garrison and the talents of multi-reedman Farrell. Some strong studio dates followed in 1970–2, with the group expanding to various sizes, and saxophonists such as George Coleman and Frank Foster taking a role, but the triumphant coda was the three sets recorded at the famous Lighthouse Club on California's Hermosa Beach in September 1972. Although much of the material lay unissued for years, the Mosaic edition of Jones's complete Blue Note sessions, released in 2000, established what a powerhouse band this was, with mesmerising work from the young saxophonists Dave Liebman and Steve Grossman atop the Gene Perla-Jones rhythm section. Grossman had come off a stint with Miles Davis and Liebman would join that group the following year, but in this acoustic situation they essay the virtuoso styles which the younger reed players were using as a matrix of ideas in the aftermath of Coltrane. The long solos act almost as a working manual of ideas and techniques, just the kind of record which could have acted as a counterpart to a Blue Note classic of a generation earlier, influencing another new breed of players. But the original *Live At The Lighthouse* was bypassed by listeners more interested in something with electricity or funk.

The old Blue Note had never been able to afford any big-band dates, but at Liberty they tried a few. Thad Jones hadn't led a session for the label since 1957, but in 1970 he made *Consummation*, with the big band he had been co-leading with drummer Mel Lewis for several years (some German concert recordings from the year before were also released on the label). Produced by Sonny Lester across three different sessions, the album was a handsome showcase for the elegance of Jones's writing and the crisp, confident section work of what was a top-drawer orchestra. However, its release went almost unnoticed. Rather more important to the label was the bigger-scale work of Duke Pearson, who had been quietly putting together an impressive and multifarious body of work. Pearson's records are, in comparison to the more famous names in the roster, not much remembered (and he is another artist who has not been well served in the CD era). In their undemonstrative way, they display a thoughtful and individual vision, managing to almost surreptitiously put some straight-ahead content into the label's mainstream releases.

Pearson was especially proud of his big-band albums, *Introducing Duke Pearson's Big Band*, with its wonderful arrangement of 'A Taste Of Honey', and *Now Hear This*, which mixed Pearson originals such as 'Amanda' and 'Minor League' with a catholic choice of cover material. Chick Corea, who contributed a tune to the earlier set, was represented by a treatment of his 'Tones For Joan's Bones'. Yet Pearson also tried other idioms. *How Insensitive*, made in May 1969, was a charming Latin-inflected date which now sounds like a striking forerunner of Chick Corea's acoustic music with Return To Forever (later in the year, Pearson also made Blue Note's one entry into the Christmas album stakes).

Corea himself made some important early recordings for Blue Note. *The Song Of Singing* was made in 1970 with Barry Altschul and Dave Holland, and later in the year he made a session (unissued until later in the seventies) with Holland and reedman Anthony Braxton, a dry run for their work together as Circle (the earlier *Now He Sings, Now He Sobs*, although often packaged as a Blue Note album, is strictly speaking a session made for the Solid State imprint). Another musician who'd have an association with the early Miles Davis electric bands, Corea's brief spell at Blue Note must be counted as a missed opportunity for the label, since he would make some of the most successful acoustic and then electric jazz albums of the early and middle seventies.

The opportunities they did take were with talents which tended to be in the second division: Tyrone Washington, Reuben Wilson, Eddie Gale, Jack Wilson, the Contemporary Jazz Quintet (a lofty name for a group which lasted two records). Jack McDuff and Jimmy McGriff, two organists who had made their names earlier at other labels, turned in some perfunctory sessions which sought a middle ground between vintage organ-combo jazz and a kind of middle-of-the-road arranged music. Several of the veterans of the label continued to record at a great pace. Lee Morgan, Hank Mobley, Stanley Turrentine and Donald Byrd recorded frequently, as did Andrew Hill, although the inspiration of his profound earlier records had started to desiccate and many of his sessions stayed in the can. Wayne Shorter added three further records – *Super Nova*, *Odyssey Of Iska* and *Moto Grosso Feio* – to his discography and, as with Hill, the extraordinary power of the earlier records had been dispersed as the saxophonist sought new directions.

Bobby Hutcherson was an even more extreme example of a master musician going relentlessly down a dead end. Hutcherson's string of mid-sixties Blue Notes were quiet classics of writing and playing, but as the decade closed and the new one began, he seemed to lose his way entirely. He began co-leading a group with saxophonist Harold Land in 1968, which lasted for three years, after which the vibesman stayed largely on the West Coast; but his records became soupy, muddled affairs that seemed to be stretching towards some kind of agreement with electronic and soft-focus orchestral textures that was never going to suit such a sophisticated performer. *Now!* (1969), with its gang of cooing vocalists, and the bleary *Head On* (1971) suggest a disastrous downturn in his abilities, and until a magnificent return to straight-ahead music in the eighties and nineties, it seemed as if Hutcherson's capacity to play up to his strengths had deserted him.

Part of the problem for the 'new' Blue Note was that they had greater competition. Having moved alongside a major label, they were able to see that the era of every other rival looking up to Blue Note had effectively ended. George Benson and Wes Montgomery (who died in 1968) were setting a pace in jazz guitar which Blue Note couldn't answer. Grant Green, their lone guitarist-leader, had returned to the label in 1969, but his two records for Frank Wolff, *Carryin' On* and *Green Is Beautiful*, are very mixed – the leader's own playing is spirited enough but the repetitive and formulaic settings are a tragic climbdown for this gifted man (he made amends somewhat with the 1972 *Live At the Lighthouse*, but his moment was over, and he died practically forgotten in 1979). Freddie Hubbard, for so long Blue Note's key man in modern trumpet, had done well at Atlantic and was about to enjoy terrific success at Creed Taylor's CTI operation (playing, admittedly, the softest kind of instrumental pabulum). People did want jazz, or something like it, but it wasn't the kind which Blue Note were now peddling.

Frank Wolff eventually became ill. Always a modest and introverted man, he was loath to talk about his troubles, but Leonard Feather – who'd done so many sleeve notes for Blue Note in their glory days – noticed the change in him: 'When Frank came to California on a short visit late in 1970 and stopped over for dinner, I noticed that the perennial enthusiasm had started to fade. He seemed tired and drawn; but he knew of only one life and would continue to live it. He lived it right to the end. From his hospital bed, he remained on the telephone, taking care of details so meaningful to him that he could not bear the thought of delegating the responsibility to others.'[5] Frank Wolff died on 8 March 1971, of a heart attack, following surgery. Much of the old Blue Note died with him.

Between 1971 and 1979, the label floundered around in search of a direction. Even though there were a handful of commercial successes in the seventies, the music which the imprint recorded was full of noodling, posturing and modish idiocy. Scarcely any of the musicians who recorded for Blue Note during this period emerged with any real credit or credibility. Some of the old guard had finally bid adieu to the label with the demise of Wolff: Lee Morgan was shot and killed in an incident at Slug's nightclub in 1971; Hank Mobley disappeared; Stanley Turrentine and Andrew Hill moved on. Duke Pearson maintained some ties with the label, and though he signed to Atlantic, he kept an option to continue to record for Blue Note. But late in 1971, missing his children, he moved back to Atlanta. Even the labels on the LP pressings changed: a new, solid blue with black or white lettering, and 'The Finest In Jazz Since 1939' logo of old mothballed.

The man who benefited most from this third phase of Blue Note was certainly Donald Byrd. He had been experimenting with electric settings for his own playing, as had so many of his contemporaries, and this time it was – perhaps inevitably – the new electric music of Miles Davis which had caught his ear. Byrd didn't have Davis's magical touch with sidemen or feel for what really worked in these situations, and records such as *Electric Byrd* (1970) and *Ethiopian Knights* (1971) are very much hit-and-miss affairs. But in 1972 he met the arranger and producer Larry Mizell, and persuaded the label into letting Mizell produce a new project which eliminated virtually all traces of hard bop, put Byrd himself into the role of lead vocalist and backed all the front lines with a typical ensemble of expensive Los Angeles sessionmen, although Jazz Crusaders Joe Sample and Wilton Felder at least had some, er, soul. They called it *Black Byrd*, and with the perversity which seems to attend so many matters of record-industry business, it became one of Blue Note's all-time best-sellers.

Today, the record has a degree of charm, as do Byrd's increasingly silly follow-ups, *Street Lady* (1973 – a bit like a soundtrack to an imaginary sister-movie to *Super Fly*) and *Places And Spaces* (1974). But it is hard to recognise the man who had only a few years previously made sessions such as *The Cat Walk*. One of the difficulties of jazzmen taking on soul players at their own game was a fundamental awkwardness: next to bands such as the Ohio Players or Kool & The Gang, who had no pretence to playing scintillating solos but could lay down a terrifically tight groove, musicians like Byrd either sounded like they were slumming it or seemed comically self-conscious about trying to make their jazz-soul music work. After all, it wasn't as if musicians such as Marvin Gaye or Stevie Wonder were unworthy pop stars. They'd paid as many dues as most working jazz players.

Besides Byrd, Blue Note could boast a small nexus of plausible crossover figures. The flute player Bobbi Humphrey tootled her way through a few uneventful jazz-funk outings. The singer Marlena Shaw cashed in on a trend for outspoken 'soul women' with an album called *Who's This Bitch Anyway?* in 1974. Keyboard player Ronnie Foster, reedman Ronnie Laws and guitarist Earl Klugh all made records which had their jazz content almost vaporised by productions which were so polite and soft-focus that they sounded like they had been delivered freeze-dried to the record player. Instead of any kind of groove music, the label's values were being submerged in a sea of muzak-based candyfloss.

Here and there a project was scheduled to contain some sterner stuff. One example might be trumpeter Eddie Henderson's *Sunburst*, made in 1975. A glance at the personnel – Henderson, George Duke, Bennie Maupin, Julian Priester, Alphonso Johnson, Buster Williams, Bobby Hutcherson, Harvey Mason and Billy Hart – might whet the appetite for some quality playing, even with the trappings of mid-seventies fusion along the way. Despite some energetic moments, though, the record is entirely forgettable. Skip Drinkwater's production is glossily insubstantial, and the list of sleeve credits says much about how far away from Alfred Lion's Blue Note this current incarnation had come.

Lou Donaldson carried on more or less regardless. His final Blue Note album was *Sweet Lou*, cut in March 1974 (two sessions made a year later were never released). Titles such as 'Peepin'' and 'If You Can't Handle It, Give It To Me' sound like the old Lou, but the record was as strong as a wet tissue, drenched in overdubbed voices, brass and whatnot. Yet one Blue Note artist stayed resolute to the end. Horace Silver had become the longest-serving of all Blue Note performers, and it was fitting that he should be responsible for the final albums made in this era: *Silver 'N' Percussion* (1977), and *Silver 'N' Strings Play The Music Of The Spheres* (cobbled together between 1978 and 1979). These closing statements weren't exactly his finest hour, but Horace had otherwise kept his own faith (and probably his own counsel) when it came to the kind of music that was behind the otherwise increasingly faddish album covers and titles. As early as 1969, Silver had tried to sidle a sort of hippie philosophising into his albums, with *You Gotta Have A Little Love* a good example: the sleeve shows a beaming collective of representatives from different races. Inside, though, the music features an uncompromised Silver quintet, with Randy Brecker, Johnny Williams, Bennie Maupin and Billy Cobham. Admittedly, the pianist went down the road of introducing vocals, sometimes his own, into projects such as *That Healin' Feelin'* (1971), *The United States Of Mind, Phase 2: Total Response* (1971) and *Phase 3: All* (1972), but he still made sure that there was plenty of trumpet, saxophone and piano in there as well. *In Pursuit Of The 27th Man* (1973) is as good a record as any which came out of Blue Note in the seventies, and better than most: both of the Brecker brothers were in the band, and Silver also included some quartet tracks with vibesman Dave Friedman, an intriguing sideline to his regular work.

By 1979, Blue Note was finished as an active label. The music which had built the label in the LP era, hard bop, was at its lowest ebb and the company had found nothing to replace it. Acoustic jazz itself was somewhat in the doldrums, with the crossover music of jazz rock or fusion dominating what scene there was and groups such as Weather Report headlining the festival circuit. Even at the low point of the mid-late seventies, though, there were signs of an acoustic revival. The small German-based independent ECM, headed by Manfred Eicher, had secured some important successes with a mix of European and American artists, including Chick Corea, Keith Jarrett and Jan Garbarek. In New York itself, an enclave of small performing spaces had grown up, creating a movement known as 'loft jazz', where a mix of new voices (David Murray, Oliver Lake) blended with avant-garde veterans (Sunny Murray, Roscoe Mitchell). With his Studio Rivbea, Sam Rivers ran one of the most important spaces. It was the kind of initiative which one can easily imagine Alfred and Frank getting involved in; but there was no interest whatsoever from the rapidly fading new Blue Note and there were no further new recordings made after the final Horace Silver session of 2 November 1979.

There was, though, one thing the label did have going for it. Both jazz and the LP format had, by the middle of the seventies, been going long enough to have their own sense of history. It was a decade when the industry began to learn how to repackage the past: every genre of music could be sold a second time over, either to listeners who'd missed it the first time round, or to an audience that wanted it remodelled, perhaps through compilations or new editions. 'Catalogue' is what drives the business: if your back numbers are strong, you're already set up.

Nobody had a stronger catalogue of modern jazz than Blue Note, and given how little marketing it had ever been subjected to, much of it was hardly known even to its core audience. And then there were all the unissued sessions which Alfred Lion had put on the shelf, often not so much because the dates weren't good enough, but because there weren't enough spaces in the schedule (or the budget) to accommodate them all. Somebody was going to have to look at all this and do something about it.

ELEVEN

By his own admission, Michael Cuscuna had been 'banging on the door' to George Butler, the executive who was then in charge of Blue Note, as soon as Butler had started there in 1972. A garrulous, curly-haired, bearded enthusiast (he has held on to all those qualities in the interim), Cuscuna was twenty-four years old and already a veteran of the scene: broadcasting, journalism and a small amount of record production. His principal occupation at the time was working for Atlantic Records, the label which had once offered to buy out Alfred Lion and which was now a powerhouse of rock, soul and jazz. As a Blue Note collector himself, Cuscuna was rattled by the disrepair which the company's heritage had apparently fallen into. What was going on?

Cuscuna had become obsessed with the undiscovered Blue Note, having found out about various unissued sessions over the years from the musicians involved. He began keeping a diary of what he knew was there. Butler resisted his calls, but Cuscuna was persistent, although after a couple of years of meetings, phone calls and the like, he was just about ready to give up on it. In 1975, though, he went to a party for the launch of a Donald Byrd album, where he was introduced to another Blue Note executive, Charlie Lourie. 'I said to Charlie, "You know, there's a lot of interesting stuff there." He said, "Yeah,

I know, but a lot of it is on unmarked tapes and it can't be identified. We're thinking of getting UCLA students to listen and see if they can identify some of it." And I said, "Wait a minute. Can we have breakfast and talk?"'

The next day, Cuscuna showed Lourie the notes he'd managed to build up, and the Blue Note man took the idea away with him. As he was about to leave for California to master a Chico Hamilton record, Cuscuna got a call from Lourie, confirming that he had permission to go and check out the Blue Note tape vault, housed in Los Angeles. Cuscuna changed his ticket, arranging to stay longer than he'd intended.

> It was a very exciting first day, I can tell you. When they took me down the street to where the tapes were in this room, I was thrilled – until I realised what I was up against. Charlie was right, there was no paperwork to be found, and it was a very long process. I'd find Jimmy Smith tapes, with the date, and 'reel one', and that was it – no tune titles, no sidemen's names, nothing. Little by little I started to piece it together. There were some sessions which I listened to which were wonderful, but I was hitting a dead end as to who it was. One might have had Sonny Clark and Grant Green on it, but they were both dead, and we weren't sure who else was on it. With something like a Jackie McLean session, it was great, because I could send him a cassette and ask who it was. Bit by bit I pieced it together. With tune titles I could go to BMI and ask whose name it was registered in that year, things like that.

The awful pay-off lay a couple of years ahead:

> The Japanese company King, who'd been licensing the records for their

market, sent over a Xerox of this file of unissued sessions, where Alfred had written all the details with comments. I'd already put out about twenty albums the hard way, and suddenly there was all this information.

Cuscuna began releasing first a series of double albums of previously unissued sessions by most of the major Blue Note names of the sixties, then two further series of single LPs of similar material, up until around 1981. Long-time fans were both shocked and delighted at hearing new material from Jackie McLean, Hank Mobley, Lee Morgan and many others, and real buried treasure such as extra material from the Sonny Rollins Vanguard sessions. Although sales were sometimes relatively moderate, the series reminded many who might have forgotten that the label's contribution to documenting the jazz scene of that period was matchless, no matter how enfeebled it had become in the later 1970s.

During this period, Cuscuna would give copies of his 'new' Blue Notes to Horace Silver, to pass on to Alfred Lion. Silver was the only figure from his past life that Lion had any real contact with, and Ruth, still fearful for Alfred's health, protected him from any further involvement than that. Yet Lion was obviously curious. At the same time, Cuscuna and Lourie talked about commencing new recording for Blue Note again, but the response from senior figures at EMI – who by now controlled Blue Note, having swallowed up Liberty and United Artists some years earlier – was negative – for now. So they mused on what alternatives there were for the Blue Note catalogue. Cuscuna had discovered some fresh Thelonious Monk material, not enough for an entire 'new' record, but certainly significant tracks which deserved to be reunited with the issued material. What to do with it all? The answer was to license all the material for a limited-edition, deluxe set, sold via mail order, and cutting out middle-man distribution – the kind of thing which Blue Note itself had done at its inception. *The Complete Blue Note Recordings Of Thelonious Monk* was the first set produced by Mosaic, the company which Lourie and Cuscuna went on to form, in order to market the jazz recordings which, for one reason or another, the owning companies weren't prepared to handle in this way. The set was something of a model for every serious jazz-reissue programme ever since. It emerged in 1982, with the compact-disc era still some distance away, and the boom in jazz reissues yet to happen: but its rapturous reception gave some hint as to how a forgotten area of the music market could yet be revived.

When the set had been out for a while, Michael Cuscuna was surprised one day to receive a call he thought he'd never get: it was Alfred Lion. The Lions had moved to Rancho Bernardo, near San Diego, in 1979, still hidden away from the jazz world's view; but Alfred had gone over to a friend's house and made the circumspect call to Cuscuna, while Ruth was out of earshot. He had been curious about these guys who were putting out his old records in this way. Thereafter, Cuscuna would get the occasional call from Lion, though he was forbidden to initiate contact himself.

In 1984, there came an announcement which surprised the American record industry. Bruce Lundvall, a veteran career man who had been in the music business since 1960, was to move from his current post at Elektra to head up a new Blue Note Records, at EMI America. The ebullient Lundvall was delighted with his new job. Being in charge of a smallish jazz imprint doesn't seem like the career apogee of someone who'd held down as many important jobs as he; but he was a Blue Note man.

Lundvall is that rarity in the modern record industry, a genuine music man who's managed to endure the corporatisation of the subject he loves. When he was fourteen, he went to the Colony Record Shop in New York and bought a couple of new 78s – 'Criss Cross' by Thelonious Monk and 'Bags Groove' by Milt Jackson, two classic Blue Note releases. He was a confirmed modernist after this, and went through a typical teenage jazz fan's baptism, spending all his money on records or sitting in the peanut gallery of Birdland for a dollar. One night, he went to hear Art Blakey at the club and it happened to be the night that Lion was recording *One Night At Birdland* ('I remember a couple of tunes they played that didn't make the record, too'). When he got out of college in 1957, he decided that he wanted to be in the record business and the first company he went to was Blue Note: 'I just knocked on the door and went in. I remember Alfred being there, he gave me about five minutes, very politely said, "I'm sorry, we have no jobs – we do this business ourselves."'

In the end, after military service, Lundvall did get a position, at Columbia in 1960. He worked for Goddard Lieberson, the head of Columbia's music operations and one of the great industry figures of his day, from whom Lundvall seems to have acquired much of his philosophy about the trade: that while there is an obligation to business, there is also an obligation to music, as an art form. (Lieberson actually hired Reid Miles as an art director in 1963 – while still allowing him to do Blue Note covers, an extraordinary concession.) Lundvall eventually rose to become general manager of Columbia, and in the seventies, he was able to sign many major figures to what was otherwise a skimpy roster of jazz talent. In the first half of the decade, fusion had dominated Columbia's thinking, like everyone else's; but Lundvall brought in Stan Getz, McCoy Tyner, Woody Shaw and Max Roach. His proudest moment was bringing in Dexter Gordon. When it was announced, Ahmet Ertegun of Atlantic called him and said, 'You've done the greatest thing, you've signed Dexter Gordon!'

Lundvall tired of CBS after the company had gone through a bad spell of downsizing, and he moved over to Elektra, as president, and managed to found a new jazz imprint, Elektra Musician. Early in 1984, he was at a Recording Industry of America Association meeting and the chairman of EMI took him to one side and asked how he would like to start Blue Note over again. Not quite thirty years after he had knocked on Alfred Lion's door on West 63rd Street, Bruce Lundvall began running the new Blue Note in 1984.

> When I stepped into this thing, with all the enthusiasm in the world, stepping into Alfred's shoes was tough. We had this great legacy, but we had to add to it, and we had to make money. I'd like to have had a pure jazz label, but I knew that wasn't going to make money.

What Lundvall did, immediately, was diversify. Instead of turning over the jazz label to any kind of pop product, he established a 'boutique' operation called Manhattan that could work alongside Blue Note and help float the more venerable label (Manhattan's early roster included such adult-orientated rock acts as Natalie Cole and Richard Marx). But what the grand marque needed was something to make people realise that it was up and running again. The idea that Lundvall came up with was a celebration: a New York concert which would bring together as many of the old Blue Note giants as they could get. At this point, Lundvall had already hired Michael Cuscuna as a consultant to the new operation. When he floated the idea of the concert to Cuscuna, the latter sat down and began to sketch it out. Cuscuna remembers:

> When Bruce asked me it was one day in July 1984. In about an hour or so I'd sketched out what I thought would be the ideal groups and the key tunes, and within another three hours I'd talked to nearly all the

> artists and gotten their agreement – Herbie and Stanley and Freddie and everybody. Five years after that, it would have taken you five weeks to get all those people on the phone, and then you'd have to go through the managers and the schedules and stuff. What it really says is how little people were doing at that time, where they could all be accessible in an afternoon and I could book a date.

What Lundvall also knew was that he had to get Alfred Lion to the concert:

> I said, 'Look, we have to have Alfred, Reid Miles and Rudy Van Gelder as guests of honour.' Michael said, 'Well, Ruth won't allow him to come to New York City.' So I sent Alfred a telegram, on a Friday, saying, we're doing this concert, and you'll be the guest of honour. Next day I got a call at home. 'Bruce? This is Al. You got a pen? Write this down. You've got to have Dexter on tenor sax, you've got to have Hank – is he still playing? Now, alto – you must have Jackie McLean . . .' On every instrument, he wanted to have about a hundred people playing! And it was, 'Yes, yes, we will be there, I'll talk to Ruth!'

The concert itself, bannered as 'One Night With Blue Note', was an occasion more moving for its associations than for the music. New York's Town Hall was filled to capacity on 22 February 1985, and the line-up was almost as extraordinary as any wish-list could have had it: Art Blakey, Freddie Hubbard, Jackie McLean, Bobby Hutcherson, Joe Henderson, Curtis Fuller, Johnny Griffin, Cecil Taylor, McCoy Tyner, Tony Williams, Woody Shaw, Kenny Burrell, Lou Donaldson, Jimmy Smith. There were also spots for some of the new figures which Lundvall had signed: guitarist Stanley Jordan, flautist James Newton, pianist Michel Petrucciani and saxophonist Bennie Wallace. But there were some unhappy omissions: Hank Mobley was too ill to perform and Horace Silver, the most indispensable of all Blue Note's team, did not agree to play.

The music itself, as with most stage-managed great occasions, only intermittently caught fire. But the underlying theme was a homage to Alfred Lion, and in that respect the concert was a triumph. None of the musicians involved had seen Alfred since 1967 and the many reunions at the rehearsals were, even in the eyes of the hard-boiled Cuscuna, 'hard to watch'. A wave of emotion swept over the concert as Alfred, frail but beaming, was given an ovation.

It was also an important moment for what had become something of a revival in acoustic jazz in the 1980s. If Blue Note was poised to make a 'comeback', it was hardly in isolation: EMI had chosen their moment well. A new breed of so-called 'young lions' had been emerging who were more interested in playing in the hard-bop and post-bop styles of sixties jazz than in performing fusion, which had suddenly run out of steam as the wave of the seventies finally subsided. Premier among them, in record-business terms at least, was the New Orleans trumpeter Wynton Marsalis. Ironically enough, Marsalis had been signed to Columbia by none other than Bruce Lundvall. Although he did not take any credit for 'discovering' Marsalis, he took over the deal from a procrastinating George Butler, who was then at CBS. Lundvall heard Marsalis playing a sideman gig with Woody Shaw, asked him to come into his office next day, and did the deal there and then. The trumpeter had emerged from the ranks of Art Blakey's Jazz Messengers, along with his saxophone-playing brother Branford, and seemed equally at home playing jazz or classical music; but he was also a very articulate and outspoken critic of musicians who didn't respect the jazz tradition, and who didn't play up to the best of their abilities. As a result, he had become a jazz media darling in an age when there simply weren't any others, and both the industry and the audience began to take notice.

There were other reasons for jazz's ascendancy too. Perhaps the wheel had simply turned in its favour; but by now the music had been around long enough to have established its cultural credentials, so that there were college courses and arts subsidies and historical retrospectives and record companies suddenly remembering that they had a lot of unreissued jazz records in their vaults. Compared to pop records, jazz records were cheap to make and market. While the black audience still showed little sign of any new interest, a middle-class white audience had begun to investigate jazz once again. Some listeners who'd grown bored with rock - or now felt that they were too old for it - decided to check out jazz for a change.

Incredibly, there was even a cult beginning to gather around hard bop as a dance music. In England, a handful of alternative rock groups such as Pigbag and Rip Rig & Panic had been trying out an admittedly clumsy mix of jazz with indie-rock, and a few club DJs, perhaps tired of trying to find old soul records to enliven their retro nights, began sourcing beats from Jazz Messengers and Jimmy Smith records. Certain London locations, such as the Wag Club and Dingwalls, became known for their hardcore jazz nights, where these records appeared to be winning a new audience. (In reality, 'proper' hard bop played only a bit part in this movement. More ubiquitous were records with a strong Latin flavour, or more simplistic soul jazz by artists such as Boogaloo Joe Jones.) As word travelled back across the Atlantic, curious young Americans began to look for old Blue Note vinyl, which had previously lain mostly untouched in second-hand jazz bins.

Collectors were, indeed, also involved in this acoustic revival. The one territory which had not forgotten about acoustic jazz in the seventies was Japan, and throughout much of that decade and on into the eighties, King and other Japanese companies licensed Blue Note albums for reissue in superb facsimile pressings, using top-notch vinyl and generally treating them like immaculate first editions. More than any other jazz label, Blue Note had become a collector's delight: the different editions of each issue, from the early Lexington Avenue pressings, through the 'New York', 'Liberty' and 'Blue' label editions of later years, the use of 'deep-groove' vinyl, stereo and mono versions, and ever more minute minutiae, asked for a stamp collector's discipline in the study of these long-playing records. Scarce vintage pressings began to command hundreds of dollars, and later albums by the likes of Baby Face Willette or Fred Jackson became prized pieces to carry under the arm.

Into this climate, Lundvall pitched his first series of reissues, twenty-five of the most obvious classic titles, although their return on LP caused considerable interest. What mattered more, though, were the new artists and how they would do. Lundvall was lucky with several of his early signings. Stanley Jordan, a clever guitar technician whose methods involved playing melody lines by tapping along the neck of the instrument, sold close to half a million records with his debut, helped by a catchy version of 'Eleanor Rigby'. It wasn't that much more interesting than *Black Byrd*, but it gave the label its start. Lundvall brought in the improvising vocalist Bobby McFerrin, whom he'd previously signed to Elektra Musician, and while the first record did reasonably well, McFerrin scored an unlikely bull's-eye with the worldwide hit 'Don't Worry, Be Happy' off his 1988 record *Simple Pleasures*, a million-seller. These were the kind of figures which Lion and Wolff could only have dreamed about, and underlined that the newest Blue Note was part of a worldwide operation. But they were the near-pop records. What else could Blue Note do?

Lundvall also brought back several Blue Note lifers, although often it was only a brief second-time-around, as if none of them really belonged in the new era. McCoy Tyner did an uneventful album with Jackie McLean and went on to make three solo records which are among the finest things in his now huge discography. Tyner, though, disliked any one-label allegiance and eventually went elsewhere again. Stanley Turrentine and Freddie Hubbard came back, briefly, but they had both dissipated their talents during many years of soft-focus music, and Hubbard's decline in particular was dreadful. Tony Williams had emerged from numerous fusion-based adventures and gone back to an acoustic quintet, including Wallace Roney and Mulgrew Miller: there were some excellent records, but they didn't sell and the group couldn't find any impetus (Williams died suddenly in 1997, at only fifty-one). Dexter Gordon made a single record based around his appearance in the film *Round Midnight*, but he wasn't to live much longer, passing away in 1990. Jimmy Smith made *Go For Whatcha Know* in 1986, a disappointing set.

Some of the new artists, though, recorded some more than promising music. Bennie Wallace, a Southern saxophonist cast in the mould of the big, swaggering tenor players of a generation or two earlier, made some outstanding records; James Newton, a flute player once associated with the loft movement of the seventies, put together a remarkable set of Duke Ellington repertory for *The African Flower*, which came top in the *Down Beat* poll that year; and the diminutive French pianist Michel Petrucciani, one of the great discoveries of the eighties, embarked on a string of Blue Note albums which, though sometimes flawed, each had outstanding music.

The best of the returning artists, though, was Joe Henderson. The tough, quizzical player of the sixties had matured into an elder statesman whose music had lost little of its resilience or its craft. Two separate LPs called *The State Of The Tenor*, cut at the Village Vanguard in November 1985 with only

Ron Carter and Al Foster for support, reasserted both Henderson's own mastery and the timelessness of this format – a playing situation which Sonny Rollins had showcased to such devastating effect in the same venue for Blue Note some thirty years earlier. Alfred Lion liked Henderson's session so much that he insisted that it was the finest Blue Note date of all time.

In 1986, Alfred and Ruth took part in a further tribute when they went to Japan for the first time, for the Mount Fuji Festival, where another Blue Note homage had been organised. Despite appalling weather conditions, the event was an even more tumultuous occasion, since the Japanese audience were a knowledgeable and committed gathering that recognised how special the event was. When one of the assembled bands broke into the opening bars of Sonny Clark's 'Cool Struttin'', the roar of recognition from the crowd almost caused the band to lose their way in disbelief. Alfred, who had to be attended by a doctor and needed to have oxygen close by, was obviously finding the trip a strain, but he was almost completely overcome by the ovation which the audience gave him.

After this, the Lions went back into their secluded Californian life; but Alfred's heart was failing. He died on 2 February 1987. At his graveside, Ruth, Bruce, Michael and Gil Melle each stood and said a few words. Copies of some of Alfred's favourite albums were placed around the headstone: *The State Of the Tenor* was there, along with *Blue Train* and a few others. At the end, at least he had the satisfaction of seeing his extraordinary work honoured at last.

One thing Lion almost never did was work with singers: a single album by Sheila Jordan, *Portrait Of Sheila*, and one by Dodo Greene, *My Hour Of Need*, were the only ones which were released in his era. But Lundvall knew that he couldn't pass singers by: today, every jazz-orientated roster needs singers, which open a whole new market. His first signing after McFerrin, Dianne Reeves, was another success, selling 200,000 copies of her debut set.

As Lundvall said in 1999:

> We haven't had a year when we've lost money since we started. I say that with a slight question mark, because Blue Note was commingled with Manhattan for the first three years. Fortunately, I always had a very good financial person, and people who'd guide me along and let me know where my numbers were. I've had seven bosses in the fourteen years I've been here, and they were all supportive of Blue Note, they left me alone, let me sign who I wanted to sign, and if it was an expensive signing, they'd sometimes even help me.

What also helped Blue Note – and every other jazz catalogue of long standing – was the new medium of the compact disc, which by 1990 had transformed catalogue sales as every jazz collector retooled their libraries around the new format (one can only imagine how aghast Lion might have been, at the thought of yet another round of origination costs). As the great Blue Note library was once again remastered, this time for CD, the jazz business began to gather fresh momentum, across all the major labels. Not only Blue Note: Verve, which had been acquired by Polygram many years earlier, started to sign new acts and generally rev up a situation which for a long time had done little more than sell old Ella Fitzgerald records. Columbia continued with the Marsalis brothers and a number of Marsalis-school players such as Terence Blanchard, and began to look at refashioning their vast assemblage of Miles Davis recordings (a process which has sustained them to this day). The Warner Music organisation had the considerable holding of Atlantic Records, along with their own back catalogue, which held a trove of John Coltrane, Ornette Coleman, the Modern Jazz Quartet and more. RCA, under Steve Backer, began working through a vault which stretched all the way back to the Original Dixieland Jazz Band sides of 1917, alongside a new-artist programme that included several 'difficult' modern players such as Steve Lacy and Henry Threadgill.

RCA's rather muddled roster of players at the time shows how uncertain the big companies were about what might sell and what wouldn't; what was artistically credible and what would go down as a doomed bit of fashion-mongering. One player which RCA took on board, after Blue Note had seemingly missed out, was the Dallas-born trumpeter Roy Hargrove, who recorded his first RCA Novus album in October 1989, when he was barely twenty years old. Lundvall's recollections of his dealings with Hargrove are particularly instructive about the way the jazz business was changing with the times.

> I brought Roy to New York, straight from his high school band in Texas. He stayed with [trumpeter and producer] Don Sickler for about a week, and Sickler opened him up to people like Kenny Dorham and other trumpet payers he hadn't heard before. Don was doing an album for Toshiba Somethin' Else [the Japanese sister label to EMI Blue Note], because they wanted an album of Blue Note standards, which Don put together for them, and he used Roy as the second trumpet player. Then we brought Roy over to Mount Fuji, where he played with Bobby Watson, and he recorded with Bobby on *his* first record. At that point, I felt he wasn't ready to be signed. He had a scholarship offered to him by Berkeley School of Music, and Rufus Reid, who's the head of the jazz department at William Patterson, New Jersey, called me and said, This is a very gifted and natural player, he shouldn't be going to Berkeley, he

should be with us. Is there a way you could pay his tuition? I said, Well, that's difficult, he's not signed here. He said, We can pay his room and board, but not his tuition.

I went to Roy and said, Look, I want to make a kind of deal I've never made before – I want to sign you as a sideman, with an option to sign you as a leader, when you're ready. He liked it, his mother didn't. His high school teacher said to him, You'll be so important to these students – there were a lot of underprivileged kids there – if you get a scholarship to Berkeley, but no one's ever heard of William Patterson down here in Texas. So we were unable to do it. Then he hooked up with a manager, Larry Clothier. Then I brought him back when he was at Berkeley, because every Monday night we used to have a Blue Note night at the old Birdland on 115th Street, and I brought Roy down to play – he was good, but he still wasn't ready to be signed. I met with Larry Clothier, and he was looking for a ridiculously expensive deal, and I passed. Roy ended up at RCA. So we lost him. I thought Roy had a sound that was great, and hopefully he would develop. But . . .

Hargrove was about the same age as the young Lee Morgan when he first made records for Blue Note – but there were no mentors or managers involved then, no massive advances, and the career curve of a musician was less open to calculated long-term planning. Subsequently, Roy Hargrove made a string of records for Novus, and then another string for Verve, with only a modest impact.

It wasn't just the jazz business which had changed – it was the whole music industry. The stakes that had once been manageably low were becoming irresponsibly high for the new multinational record corporations. The old Blue

Note had never pretended to compete with its gigantic counterparts, but now it was part of a giant itself. The tough part for Lundvall was trying to preserve something of the original label's integrity in a corporate environment. But how could he? For Lion and Wolff, the music had always come first; for Lundvall, as with his old influence Goddard Lieberson, there was a duty to look after the art as well as the bottom line. Yet even that old-fashioned scruple was beginning to get lost, as the record business chased its own tail with sometimes disastrous consequences – at least, for anyone who cared about music.

For some years, the industry had been growing smaller, at least in terms of the number of big players. Even relatively major-minor labels like Virgin, A&M and Island had lost their independence, swallowed up by bigger music corporations. When MCA and Polygram merged in 1998, creating the monolithic Universal Music, and a proposed merger between EMI and Warner Music only just failed to happen, it looked as if the number of 'majors' on the playing field would be reduced to four. For all-conquering, Esperanto-like pop acts, that was nothing but good news. Multi-outlet record retailers welcomed the opportunity to deal with fewer and fewer suppliers, making it easier for them to offer punitive terms to small-scale distributors and maximise their own profit levels. Small, independent record stores died in vast numbers. At a time when a world of diverse music was becoming more available to consumers than ever before, a dreadful homogeneity was beginning to sweep through the dealings of the major record companies.

Lundvall did his best to build a roster that could combine credibility with sales. After the early flurry of records by returning veterans, he looked mostly for fresh or relatively unexposed names, as if asserting that the new Blue Note should be like the old one in spirit but not in kind. Various young players arrived for a few records, before leaving the label again: saxophonist Rick Margitza, guitarist

John Hart, trumpeter Marcus Printup, pianists Joey Calderazzo and Benny Green. The example of Green seems like a discouraging instance of how frequently jazz returns could not achieve parity with jazz finances. In the modern era, with the equation having to include recording, marketing and promotional costs, as well as a musician's advance, any jazz record on a major label has to recoup a lot of money – for a jazz record. As Lundvall sees it: 'I try to stay with an artist for at least three records. Greg Osby's had seven now and he doesn't make us much money. Benny Green made five for us and then we ended up dropping him as the records became more expensive. He was selling OK, but not enough to justify the escalating advances.'

On occasion, a successful artist still leaves a label because he or she thinks that, in the end, they can do better elsewhere. Guitarist John Scofield grew into one of the major jazz figures of the nineties during his time at Blue Note. As the guitar became ever more ubiquitous as a jazz instrument, and its major exponents became more influential and high-profile, Scofield's seven albums for the label between 1989 and 1995 established him as perhaps the premier figure on his instrument. Yet he then went to Verve.

There are perhaps three musicians who have emerged from Blue Note in the last decade that set the tone for the label's vitality: Cassandra Wilson, Joe Lovano and Greg Osby. Wilson is that rarity, an art singer who's managed to find a popular success. She spent most of the eighties on the independent JMT imprint, where a series of poorly produced albums succeeded in hiding a sometimes startling and lustrous voice in the middle of confusing electric band arrangements. The one record where she was able to get some clear space was the standards album *Blue Skies*, which she reportedly disliked. That was, though, the one record which Bruce Lundvall liked and wanted to build on, and in 1993 he gave her a deal.

> I signed Cassandra, and then I went to see her play at a restaurant in New York, and she was absolutely awful. She had this electric, M-Base type band, she'd sing a chorus and then turn it over to the band, they'd drown her out . . . awful. Michael Cuscuna was there, and he came over and said, Lundvall, you've made a mistake. Then she came in to the office, and I said, Cassandra, you're not going to like what I tell you. You can make any kind of record you want to make, but first of all get rid of that band. I couldn't hear any of the lyrics and I believe you're hiding behind the band. She was upset at first, but then she said, Well, there's a guy in my building called Craig Street – this was a guy who had been working in construction! – and he has some interesting ideas. So I let her do some demos with this guy, and she came back with this tape which had 'Tupelo Honey' and 'You Don't Know What Love Is' on it, just the way they are on the record. And I said, Cassandra, this is the entire plot!

Blue Light 'Til Dawn was a huge hit for Blue Note, crossing over into rock critics' review columns and accorded second-coming status by many. With its strange mix of material – Van Morrison and Robert Johnson and Joni Mitchell tunes next to each other – and Street and producer Brandon Ross's peculiar fantasy on string-band and country-blues forms, the record is a remarkable one-off, although already there are signs that Wilson's sometimes arch and self-regarding style is getting the better of her instincts, a situation exacerbated by the record's follow-up, *New Moon Daughter*. In 1999, she released a record based around the music of Miles Davis, *Traveling Miles*, which some saw as disastrous, others as perhaps her most original and accomplished work. More than any other musician on the label, Wilson has set a severe, art-music agenda in her own work; perhaps she is the Andrew Hill of this Blue Note generation.

Tenor saxophonist Joe Lovano might be Blue Note's most-liked performer of today. The drummer Peter Erskine had asked Lundvall to come and hear his new band at one of their gigs at New York's Sweet Basil Club: 'I went down, and Joe was in the band and he played the most incredible solos. I knew about Joe, but I hadn't heard him specifically for a while – and instead of signing Peter, I signed Joe.' Lovano's first record, *Landmarks*, was released in 1991, and since then he has recorded steadily for the label. His protean style seems perfectly in tune for the methods a modern jazz musician has to follow to keep an audience interested: different settings, diverse material, regular shifts of emphasis and colour. While he and his label haven't succumbed to the idiotic fad of turning every new record into some kind of concept album – a trend which many major musicians at work in the nineties for major labels will one day look back on and blanch – Lovano has 'met' with many of his label peers (Michel Petrucciani, Gonzalo Rubalcaba, Greg Osby), cut live and studio dates, with big, middleweight and small ensembles, and only once – with his delightful *Celebrating Sinatra* record of 1996 – hung the result on a specific peg. Just as his own playing style personalises many of the master players of the past fifty years, into a growling sound which takes unexpected melodic routes and still summons moments of honeyed sweetness, Lovano has guilefully appropriated plenty of the jazz-record settings of the LP and CD era into his own – for want of a better term – vision.

If one player stands out as 'important', however, it's the alto saxophonist Greg Osby. Like Wilson, Osby was a pivotal figure in the so-called M-Base movement of New York-based musicians who were trying to make something new out of a fusion of (broadly speaking) bebop licks and hip-hop rhythms in the eighties. As Osby himself says, of the latest school of young players: 'These cats were weaned on hip hop. They're of the hop hop generation, addressing

America's classical music. They have a whole lot of other things that will work its way through the music. It may not be very obvious, but there are rhythms and delivery. In hip hop, they lay back the beat, which we have accepted as the swing feel.'[1]

Osby's first few records for Blue Note were an astonishing muddle, as if he was trying to work out exactly what, from these various fields, he could pull together that would make sense for a contemporary saxophonist. *Man Talk For Moderns, Vol. X* and *3-D Lifestyles* already sound dated and encumbered by rhythmic stiffness and awkward juxtapositions. From *Black Book* onwards, though, Osby began sorting it out to much greater effect. His saxophone sound is pointed, anti-romantic: he uses little vibrato and seems to want to pierce the heart of a musical proposition. He can unspool long, Shorter-like lines of notes, or base an improvisation around jagged little riffs and motifs, either laying on the beat or spinning up and away from it. When the band is working with him, the music can be intoxicating in its power, as well as its modernity. If jazz ever needs to justify itself as a contemporary sound, Osby's current music would form an admirable text.

Certainly *Art Forum*, *Further Ado*, *Zero*, *Banned In New York* and *The Invisible Hand* form an exceptional body of work. But besides Osby's own contributions, he has also become an important central figure among several of the younger players who have graduated to their own new Blue Note records: vibraphonist Stefon Harris, saxophonist Mark Shim, drummer Brian Blade and pianist Jason Moran, all of whom have recorded outstanding debut sessions of their own for the label. Osby, Moran, Shim, Harris, bassist Tarus Mateen and drummer Nasheet Waits have also worked together under the band name New Directions, with their eponymous album an ingenious reworking of nine Blue Note standards such as 'The Sidewinder' and 'Song For My Father'. If there is a modern-day equivalent of Lion's repertory of Blue Note regulars, it is surely this circle of formidable young talents.

In 1999, the group also went out on tour, playing in non-traditional venues for jazz, and finding that a young crowd did come out and hear them. Searching for a new, young audience became one of the paramount issues for the jazz industry in the nineties. The music business as a whole likes to see itself as eternally youth-orientated, and with pop marketeers targeting younger and younger listeners, the idea of trying to sell records to an ageing audience was becoming anathema in record-industry culture. Jazz, along with classical music, suffered as a consequence. As older potential record buyers felt themselves increasingly disenfranchised by the environment and stopped visiting record stores, the business realised that it was losing many of the core buyers for its more difficult music.

One phenomenon at the close of the century offered some hope in snaring young listeners back. 'The jam bands', a small movement of groups, were small instrumental combos who were picking up the old cues of organ jazz, but putting it into some kind of rock situation. The premier example was the trio Medeski, Martin & Wood, who had built up a nationwide American following almost akin to the Grateful Dead, through touring endlessly and playing in small places which otherwise didn't hear much of this kind of music. Lundvall snapped them up for Blue Note, though in the face of some fierce competition from other labels. If this kind of music seemed novel and new, it was because the 'instrumental' element had almost completely deserted rock and pop over the past twenty-five or so years. Where most rock audiences would have been used to some instrumental jamming in the days of (to pick three otherwise quite disparate groups) Mountain, Soft Machine and Wishbone Ash, that strain of showmanship has fled from the mainstream. Whether Medeski, Martin & Wood and their ilk are of likely long-term importance is a question which this text cannot yet answer.

One phenomenon from earlier in the decade certainly didn't last – even though they turned out to become the biggest-selling artists in the history of Blue Note, selling two million records worldwide. As Bruce Lundvall remembers it:

> That was a tough decision, putting that record out. I felt Alfred might be rolling in his grave at first. David Field, who was working at Capitol, brought me this single called 'Cantaloop', which was full of Blue Note samples, by these guys called US3. I listened, and thought it sounded like possibly a left-field hit. I was out in LA with Tom Everard and we were driving around in the car and playing it over and over . . . I said, Tom, we can't put this out on Blue Note, it's got to be on Capitol. It's a pop record, a novelty. He said, Nah, it's got to be on Blue Note. I thought about it and – yeah, it has to be on Blue Note.
>
> So I met with these guys, Geoff Wilkinson and the others – they were nervous wrecks, they thought we were going to stop them putting out the record because it used all these Blue Note samples. I said, Not only do we want to put the record out, we want you to do an album, and you can sample whatever you want from the Blue Note catalogue. I thought they were going to faint.

US3 had a very lucky break when 'Cantaloop' (based around the piano lick from Herbie Hancock's 'Cantaloupe Island') was picked up as part of a major commercial campaign; ever since, the track has become irritatingly familiar from numerous drop-ins behind television trailers and the like. Lundvall's verdict that it was a novelty hit was, in the end, right enough. The second US3 record was not so successful. With Capitol somewhat in the doldrums at the time, Lundvall was forced into shipping 300,000 units of the record, subsequently taking back 225,000 in returns: 'That was why that was a bad year for us.'

Whatever else happened, there was always Blue Note's matchless catalogue to sustain them. Since catalogue always accounts for at least fifty per cent of the take in any sales year, labels have to keep their best eye on that important situation. As the CD boom died down and the collections of jazz fans stabilised, how would Blue Note keep the catalogue afloat? One answer was the 'Connoisseur' series, a sequence of releases of some of the more obscure titles in the catalogue, with each limited to a pressing of some 10,000 issues for the world. Artists such as Harold Vick and Bennie Green were never going to justify a regular place in the catalogue at a time when record stores were constantly downsizing their inventory and the worldwide glut of product continued to increase. But this was one way of answering the cries of diehard collectors.

The other was to try and figure out a way of refreshing catalogue areas which had become over-familiar. In the UK, a surprisingly successful series of themed compilations repackaged both the greatest hits of the label, as well as dance-floor obscurities, in a long-running 'Blue' series – *Blue Breakbeats, So Blue So Funky, Blunited States Of America* and so, endlessly, on. But more important was the continuous upgrading of CD technology. Many in the industry now admitted that the early days of CD resulted in much indifferent remastering, and record labels everywhere asked consumers to better their previous collections with a 'new edition' featuring what might have been only slightly superior sound.

The most recent initiative by Blue Note has been to enlist Rudy Van Gelder. The engineer has remained continuously at work, making jazz records, at his

Englewood Cliffs studio, but his association with Blue Note basically came to an end after Lion's retirement. Suspicious of bigger record companies, he continues to work for independent labels: 'The new Blue Note is not like the old Blue Note. Back then I was dealing with one person who was the owner of the company. The producer was paying all the bills and hired all the musicians. Now it's another world, another kind of business.'[2] Yet Van Gelder acceded to the request of the boss of Blue Note's Japanese arm, Hitoshi Namekata, to remaster many of his own vintage recordings (continuing a tradition of valuable work done by this side of the company. Throughout the nineties, on their Somethin' Else imprint, the Japanese also sponsored many valuable recordings which form a significant but in the main little known adjunct to the main Blue Note listing). Namekata wanted them in the latest twenty-four-bit remastering, but otherwise Van Gelder would work entirely from his own original tapes and deliver masters that would follow the pattern of the original LP – no out-takes or extra tracks. The perfectionist engineer was delighted and has so far delivered close to two hundred of his own remasterings for Japan. In the US, though, only fifty or so releases have emerged in this 'RVG Edition'. Warmer and more vibrant than ever, the new editions are a testament to his own remarkable skills, then and now.

Van Gelder's remarks sum up the view that everyone in this story seems to hold: it was different then, and it's very different now. The new Blue Note cannot be the same as the old one, just as jazz itself is not the same. As 2000 drew to a close, Bruce Lundvall sat in his office, looking out over Park Avenue South, and thought back on what had been a good year for the company. Cassandra Wilson and Medeski, Martin & Wood had enjoyed fine sales, there had been no disasters and catalogue was holding up well enough. But it had been a strange few weeks in the business. There had been rumours that Columbia's jazz department was about to be shut down altogether. The press was full of talk that straight-ahead jazz was being, basically, dumped by the major labels. Crossover, that refuge for marketing scoundrels everywhere, was touted as everybody's only solution to the ills in both the jazz and classical business.

> In the past, there were always jazz hits. But there are no jazz hits any more. If you think about the Benny Golson book, the Horace Silver book, Dave Brubeck's 'Take Five', 'Birdland', 'Chameleon', 'Rockit', it's been a long time since there's been an instrumental hit. Hit doesn't necessarily mean like a pop single, but a composition that becomes extremely popular. I remember, all through, you were listening to Erroll Garner and George Shearing, or Johnny Smith doing 'Moonlight In Vermont' with Stan Getz - you were buying jazz hits. The question in the mainstream area is, where are the people who are writing pieces which people, other than their fellow musicians, are interested in hearing? It's not really happening. I think it's incumbent for the artist to think in terms of the composition. It's been missing from acoustic jazz for a very long time.

In his sixties, Lundvall is in his twilight years in the business. One can only wonder if anyone else other than this portly, white-haired jazz fan could have kept as much of Blue Note's independent feel alive inside an otherwise massive corporation. But perhaps it is a mistake to even seek the same kind of independence within the Blue Note of today: if you are intent on it, better to look at one of the indie-jazz labels of this era. When Lion and Wolff began their work on behalf of jazz, they were almost alone in the field. Today, there are more than five hundred independent jazz labels, many with catalogues which approach the size and scope of the original Blue Note. Between them, they are documenting the work of thousands of players, each trying to make their own kind of hot music. Meanwhile, Bruce Lundvall continues his stewardship of the great original.

'That's what I want it to be, to still feel like Blue Note. I can't let Alfred down.'

NOTES

One

1 From 'The Commodore Story', essay with *The Complete Commodore Recordings Vol. 1* (Mosaic).

2 Ibid.

3 Quoted in notes to *From Spirituals To Swing* (Vanguard).

4 From *The Blue Note Years: The Jazz Photography Of Francis Wolff* (Rizzoli).

5 Ibid.

6 *Newsweek*, March 1985.

7 From *The Blue Note Years: The Jazz Photography Of Francis Wolff* (Rizzoli).

8 From *The Blue Note Label*, Cuscuna and Ruppli (Greenwood).

9 Ibid.

10 Margulis was, in fact, always a man with an agenda. He wrote for *The Worker* and was a left-wing activist whose political interests eventually dismayed Lion, who wanted simply to get on with the business of making records. In 1947, when Blue Note began getting into the new music of bebop, Margulis didn't want to have anything to do with it, and sold out his interest in the label to Lion.

Two

1 Quoted in *The Blue Note Years: The Jazz Photography Of Francis Wolff* (Rizzoli).

2 From Blumenthal essay in *Thelonious Monk: The Complete Blue Note Recordings* (Blue Note).

3 *Down Beat*, 21 April 1948.

4 Quoted in *Hear Me Talkin' To Ya,* Hentoff and Shapiro (Peter Davies).

5 *Metronome* magazine, 1947.

Three

1 Quoted in *The Complete Blue Note Recordings Of Thelonious Monk* (Mosaic).

2 Quoted in the notes to *Bud Powell: The Complete Blue Note And Roost Recordings* (Blue Note).

3 Quoted in the notes to *Gil Melle: The Complete Blue Note Sessions* (Blue Note).

4 Interview with Van Gelder on www.allaboutjazz.com, 2000.

5 Interview with Melle in *Blue Note: A Story Of Modern Jazz* (film).

6 Quoted in notes to *Horace Silver Retrospective* (Blue Note).

7 From *Miles: The Autobiography Of Miles Davis*, Davis and Troupe (Simon & Schuster).

8 Quoted in *The Blue Note Label*, Cuscuna and Ruppli (Greenwood).

Four

1 Sleeve note to *A Night At Birdland* LP.

2 Sleeve note to *Live Messengers* LP.

3 Quoted in the notes to *Bud Powell: The Complete Blue Note And Roost Recordings* (Blue Note).

4 Ibid.

5 Quoted in *The Blue Note Label*, Cuscuna and Ruppli (Greenwood).

6 Interview with Cuscuna by Lon Armstrong, *Doobop* Issue Five (2000).

7 Quoted in *The Blue Note Years: The Jazz Photography Of Francis Wolff* (Rizzoli).

8 Ibid.

9 He discusses it in the *Horace Silver Retrospective* booklet notes.

10 Quoted in *The Blue Note Years: The Jazz Photography Of Francis Wolff* (Rizzoli).

Five

1 Sleeve note to *The Herbie Nichols Trio*.

2 Essay by Frank Kimbrough and Ben Allison for *The Complete Blue Note Recordings* (Blue Note).

3 Quoted in essay on Nichols in *Outcats*, Francis Davis (Oxford).

4 Quoted in *Grant Green: Rediscovering The Forgotten Genius Of Jazz Guitar*, Sharony Andrews Green (Miller Freeman).

5 Ibid.

6 From Frank Wolff's sleeve note to *The Best Of Jimmy Smith*, 1968.

7 Ibid.

8 Quoted in *The Cover Art Of Blue Note*, Marsh, Callingham and Cromey (Collins & Brown).

9 Ibid.

10 Ibid.

11 Ibid.

12 Quoted in booklet notes to *Horace Silver Retrospective* (Blue Note).

Six

1 Quoted in *Hard Bop*, David Rosenthal (Oxford).

2 This story is from Michael Cuscuna.

3 Quoted in sleeve note to *The Ultimate Blue Train* (Blue Note).

4 Quoted in sleeve note to *Bud Powell: The Complete Blue Note And Roost Recordings* (Blue Note).

5 Ibid.

6 From *Jazz On Record*, McCarthy, Harrison, Morgan, Oliver (Hanover).

7 Quoted in *Grant Green: Rediscovering The Forgotten Genius Of Jazz Guitar*, Sharony Andrews Green (Miller Freeman).

Seven

1 *Down Beat*, March 1958.

2 *Down Beat*, 24 July 1958

3 *Jazz Review*, Issue 11, 2000.

4 Quoted in sleeve note to *True Blue*.

5 Quoted in *Four Lives In The Bebop Business*, A. B. Spellman (Limelight.)

6 *Jazz Review*, Issue 15, 2000.
7 Quoted in *The Blue Note Jazz Photography Of Francis Wolff*, Cuscuna, Lourie and Schnider (Universe).

Eight

1 Sleeve note to *Doin' Allright*.
2 Quoted in sleeve note to *Heavy Soul*.
3 Sleeve note to *Leapin' And Lopin'*.
4 Quoted in sleeve note to *Capuchin Swing*.
5 Quoted in *Jazz People*, Valerie Wilmer (Quartet).
6 From Blakey interview with Bob Rusch, *Cadence*, July 1981.
7 Quoted in sleeve note to *The Big Beat*.
8 Quoted in sleeve note to *The African Beat*.
9 Quoted in *Grant Green: Rediscovering The Forgotten Genius Of Jazz Guitar*, Sharony Andrews Green (Miller Freeman).
10 Sleeve note to *Brown Sugar*.

Nine

1 Sleeve note to *Let Freedom Ring*.
2 Ibid.
3 Pearson interview with Bob Rusch in *Cadence*, September 1980.
4 Ibid.
5 Sleeve note to *Black Fire*.
6 Sleeve note to *Point Of Departure*.
7 Quoted in the sleeve note to *Dialogue*.

8 Ibid.

9 Quoted in the sleeve note to *A New Conception*.

10 Sleeve note to *Black Fire*.

Ten

1 Interview with Cuscuna by Lon Armstrong, *Doobop*, Issue Five (2000).

2 Quoted in the sleeve note to *Conquistador!*

3 Quoted in *The Covert Art of Blue Note*, Marsh, Callingham, Cromey (Collins & Brown).

4 Quoted in *The Blue Note Label*, Cuscuna and Ruppli (Greenwood).

5 Ibid.

Eleven

1 From 'Blue Note: 60 Years And Still Counting Off', *Jazz Times*, April 1999.

2 Interview with Bruce Carovillano, *New Jersey Monthly*, August 1997.

All illustrations are reproduced by courtesy of Blue Note Records.

APPENDIX

The Blue Note Label

A basic discography of the classic period

This lists, in the order in which they were assigned catalogue numbers, the LP catalogue which Blue Note produced during the Lion–Wolff era.

The Modern Jazz 5000 Series: Ten-Inch LPs (the subsequent twelve-inch incarnations of this music are listed in [brackets]).

5001 Ike Quebec/Charlie Christian etc, *Mellow The Mood*

5002 Thelonious Monk, *Genius Of Modern Music, Volume 1* [BLP 1510/11]

5003 *The Amazing Bud Powell, Volume 1* [BLP 1503]

5004 Tadd Dameron/Fats Navarro, *Fats Navarro Memorial Album* [BLP 1531/32]

5005 *James Moody With Strings conducted by Andre Hodier*

5006 *James Moody and His Modernists*

5007 Errol Garner, *Overture To Dawn, Volume 1*

5008 Errol Garner, *Overture To Dawn, Volume 2*

5009 Thelonious Monk, *Genius Of Modern Music, Volume 2* [BLP 1510/11]

5010 Max Roach/Kenny Dorham Quintet, *New Sounds*

5011 Milt Jackson, *Wizard Of The Vibes* [BLP 1509]

5012 Howard McGhee's All-Stars + McGhee/Navarro Boptet

5013 Miles Davis, *Young Man With A Horn* [BLP 1501/02]

5014 Errol Garner, *Overture To Dawn, Volume 3*

5015 Errol Garner, *Overture To Dawn, Volume 4*

5016 Errol Garner, *Overture To Dawn, Volume 5*

5017 Dizzy Gillespie, *Horn Of Plenty*

5018 Horace Silver Trio, *New Faces, New Sounds* [BLP 1520]

5019 The Swinging Swedes/The Cool Britons, *New Sounds From The Old World*

5020 Gil Melle Quintet/Sextet, *New Faces, New Sounds*

5021 Lou Donaldson/Horace Silver etc, *New Faces, New Sounds* [BLP 1537]

5022 *Miles Davis, Volume 2* [BLP 1501/02]

5023 Kenny Drew Trio, *New Faces, New Sounds*

5024 Howard McGhee/Gigi Gryce etc, *Volume 2*

5025 Wynton Kelly Trio, *New Faces, New Sounds*

5026 Meade Lux Lewis/Charlie Christian etc, *Memorable Sessions*

5027 Benny Morton/Ben Webster etc, *Swing Hi, Swing Lo*

5028 *Jay Jay Johnson with Clifford Brown* [BLP 1505/06]

5029 Elmo Hope Trio, *New Faces, New Sounds*

5030 Lou Donaldson/Clifford Brown etc, *New Faces, New Sounds* [BLP 1526]

5031 Wade Legge Trio, *New Faces, New Sounds*

5032 Clifford Brown, *New Star On The Horizon* [BLP 1526]

5033 *Gil Melle Quintet, Volume 2*

5034 *Horace Silver Trio, Volume 2*/Art Blakey, *Spotlight on Drums* [BLP 1520]

5035 *Sal Salvador Quintet*

5036 Urbie Green Septet, *New Faces, New Sounds*

5037 Art Blakey Quintet, *A Night at Birdland, Volume 1* [BLP 1521/22]

5038 Art Blakey Quintet, *A Night at Birdland, Volume 2* [BLP 1521/22]

5039 Art Blakey Quintet, *A Night at Birdland, Volume 3* [BLP 1521/22]

5040 *Miles Davis, Volume 3* [BLP 1501/02]

5041 *The Amazing Bud Powell, Volume 2* [BLP 1504]

5042 *Tal Farlow Quartet*

5043 Frank Foster Quintet, *New Faces, New Sounds*

5044 Elmo Hope Quintet, *New Faces, New Sounds, Vol. 2*

5045 *George Wallington and His Band*

5046 Lionel Hampton, *Jazztime Paris*

5047 *Clifford Brown Quartet*

5048 Gigi Gryce/Clifford Brown Sextet

5049 Gigi Gryce/Clifford Brown, *Jazztime Paris, Volume 1*

5050 Gigi Gryce/Clifford Brown, *Jazztime Paris, Volume 2*

5051 Gigi Gryce/Clifford Brown, *Jazztime Paris, Volume 3*

5052 The Cool Britons, *New Sounds From Olde England*

5053 Julius Watkins Sextet, *New Faces, New Sounds*

5054 Gil Melle Quartet, *New Faces, New Sounds, Volume 3*

5055 *Lou Donaldson Sextet, Volume 2* [BLP 1537]

5056 Jutta Hipp Quintet, *New Faces, New Sounds From Germany*

5057 *The Eminent Jay Jay Johnson* [BLP 1505/06]

5058 *Horace Silver Quintet, Volume 1* [BLP 1518]

5059 Conte Candoli/Herb Geller etc, *Best From The West, Volume 1*

5060 Conte Candoli/Herb Geller a.o., *Best From the West, Volume 2*

5061 *The Swinging Fats Sadi Combo*

5062 *Horace Silver Quintet, Volume 2* [BLP 1518]

5063 *Gil Melle Quintet, Vol. 4: Five Impressions Of Color*

5064 *Julius Watkins Sextet, Volume 2*

5065 Kenny Dorham Octet, *Afro-Cuban* [BLP 1535]

5066 *Hank Mobley Quartet*

5067 *Lou Mecca Quartet*

5068 *The Prophetic Herbie Nichols, Volume 1*

5069 *The Prophetic Herbie Nichols, Volume 2*

5070 *The Eminent Jay Jay Johnson, Volume 3* [BLP 1506]

Blue Note 1500 series: The Twelve-Inch series

Most of these were issued in both monaural versions (BLP series) and artificial stereo versions (BST 81000 series).

1501 Miles Davis, *Miles Davis, Volume 1*

1502 Miles Davis, *Miles Davis, Volume 2*

1503 Bud Powell, *The Amazing Bud Powell, Volume 1*

1504 Bud Powell, *The Amazing Bud Powell, Volume 2*

1505 J. J. Johnson, *The Eminent J. J. Johnson, Volume 1*

1506 J. J. Johnson, *The Eminent J. J. Johnson, Volume 2*

1507 Art Blakey and The Jazz Messengers, *Cafe Bohemia, Volume 1*

1508 Art Blakey and The Jazz Messengers, *Cafe Bohemia, Volume 2*

1509 *Milt Jackson*

1510 Thelonious Monk, *Genius Of Modern Music, Volume 1*

1511 Thelonious Monk, *Genius Of Modern Music, Volume 2*

1512 Jimmy Smith, *A New Sound, A New Star, Volume 1*

1513 Thad Jones, *Detroit–New York Junction*

1514 Jimmy Smith, *A New Sound, A New Star, Volume 2*

1515 Jutta Hipp, *At the Hickory House, Volume 1*

1516 Jutta Hipp, *At the Hickory House, Volume 2*

1517 Gil Melle, *Patterns In Jazz*

1518 Horace Silver, *And The Jazz Messengers*

1519 Herbie Nichols, *The Herbie Nichols Trio*

1520 Horace Silver and Art Blakey, *Sabu*

1521 Art Blakey, *A Night at Birdland, Volume 1*

1522 Art Blakey, *A Night at Birdland, Volume 2*

1523 Kenny Burrell, *Introducing Kenny Burrell*

1524 Kenny Dorham, *'Round Midnight at the Cafe Bohemia*

1525 Jimmy Smith, *The Incredible Jimmy Smith, Volume 3*

1526 Clifford Brown, *Memorial Album*

1527 Thad Jones, *The Magnificent Thad Jones*

1528 Jimmy Smith, *At Club Baby Grand, Volume 1*

1529 Jimmy Smith, *At Club Baby Grand, Volume 2*

1530 Jutta Hipp, *With Zoot Sims*

1531 Fats Navarro, *The Fabulous Fats Navarro, Volume 1*

1532 Fats Navarro, *The Fabulous Fats Navarro, Volume 2*

1533 Johnny Griffin, *Introducing Johnny Griffin*

1534 Paul Chambers, *Whims of Chambers*

1535 Kenny Dorham, *Afro-Cuban*

1536 *J. R. Monterose*

1537 Lou Donaldson, *Quartet/Quintet/Sextet*

1538 Lee Morgan, *Lee Morgan Indeed!*

1539 Horace Silver, *Six Pieces Of Silver*

1540 Hank Mobley, *With Donald Byrd And Lee Morgan*

1541 Lee Morgan, *Volume 2*

1542 *Sonny Rollins*

1543 Kenny Burrell, *Volume 2*

1544 Hank Mobley, *And His All-Stars*

1545 Lou Donaldson, *Wailing With Lou*

1546 Thad Jones, *The Magnificent Thad Jones, Volume 3*

1547 Jimmy Smith, *A Date With Jimmy Smith, Volume 1*

1548 Jimmy Smith, *A Date With Jimmy Smith, Volume 2*

1549 Cliff Jordan/John Gilmore, *Blowing In From Chicago*

1550 Hank Mobley, *With Farmer, Silver, Watkins, Blakey*

1551 Jimmy Smith, *At The Organ, Volume 1*

1552 Jimmy Smith, *At The Organ, Volume 2*

1553 [Number not used]

1554 Art Blakey, *Orgy In Rhythm, Volume 1*

1555 Art Blakey, *Orgy In Rhythm, Volume 2*

1556 Jimmy Smith, *The Sounds Of Jimmy Smith*

1557 Lee Morgan, *Volume 3*

1558 Sonny Rollins, *Volume 2*

1559 Johnny Griffin, *A Blowing Session*

1560 Hank Mobley, *Hank*

1561 Sabu Martinez, *Palo Congo*

1562 Horace Silver, *The Stylings Of Silver*

1563 Jimmy Smith, *Plays Pretty Just For You*

1564 Paul Chambers, *Quintet*

1565 *Cliff Jordan*

1566 Lou Donaldson, *Swing And Soul*

1567 Curtis Fuller, *The Opener*

1568 *Hank Mobley*

1569 Paul Chambers, *Bass On Top*

1570 Sonny Clark, *Dial "S" for Sonny*

1571 Bud Powell, *The Amazing Bud Powell, Volume 3 – Bud!*

1572 Curtis Fuller, *Bone And Bari*

1573 John Jenkins, *With Kenny Burrell*

1574 Hank Mobley, *Peckin' Time*

1575 Lee Morgan, *City Lights*

1576 Sonny Clark, *Sonny's Crib*

1577 John Coltrane, *Blue Train*

1578 Lee Morgan, *The Cooker*

1579 Sonny Clark, *Trio*

1580 Johnny Griffin, *The Congregation*

1581 Sonny Rollins, *A Night At The Village Vanguard*

1582 Cliff Jordan, *Cliff Craft*

1583 *Curtis Fuller/Art Farmer*

1584 Louis Smith, *Here Comes Louis Smith*

1585 Jimmy Smith, *Groovin' At Small's Paradise, Volume 1*

1586 Jimmy Smith, *Groovin' At Small's Paradise, Volume 2*

1587 Bennie Green, *Back On The Scene*

1588 Sonny Clark, *Cool Struttin'*

1589 Horace Silver, *Further Explorations*

1590 Lee Morgan, *Candy*

1591 Lou Donaldson, *Lou Takes Off*

1592 Sonny Clark, [unissued]

1593 Lou Donaldson, *Blues Walk*

1594 Louis Smith, *Smithville*

1595 Cannonball Adderley, *Somethin' Else*

1596 Kenny Burrell, *Blue Lights, Volume 1*

1597 Kenny Burrell, *Blue Lights, Volume 2*

1598 Bud Powell, *The Amazing Bud Powell, Volume 4 – Time Waits*

1599 Bennie Green, *Soul Stirrin'*

Blue Note 4000 Series

A continuation of the Modern Jazz series. Many releases were issued in both monaural versions (BLP series) and stereo versions (BST 84000 series). Beginning with 4258, all subsequent LPs were issued only in stereo, with the exception of numbers 4263, 4264 and 4265. A few later numbers were used for first-time editions of previously-unissued music, released in the 1980s. In addition, some later numbers were also assigned to records which were eventually released under a different number altogether: Hank Mobley's *Far Away Lands*, for instance, was assigned both 4367 and 4425, but actually appeared as LT-1045.

4001 Sonny Rollins, *Newk's Time*

4002 Jimmy Smith, *House Party*

4003 Art Blakey and the Jazz Messengers, *Moanin'*

4004 Art Blakey, *Holiday For Skins, Volume 1*

4005 Art Blakey, *Holiday For Skins, Volume 2*

4006 Dizzy Reece, *Blues In Trinity*

4007 Donald Byrd, *Off To The Races*

4008 Horace Silver Quintet, *Finger Poppin'*

4009 Bud Powell, *The Amazing Bud Powell, Volume 5 - The Scene Changes*

4010 Bennie Green, *Walkin' And Talkin'*

4011 Jimmy Smith, *The Sermon*

4012 *Lou Donaldson with the Three Sounds*

4013 Jackie McLean, *New Soil*

4014 The Three Sounds, *Bottoms Up*

4015 Art Blakey, *At The Jazz Corner Of The World, Volume 1*

4016 Art Blakey, *At The Jazz Corner Of The World, Volume 2*

4017 Horace Silver, *Blowin' The Blues Away*

4018 Walter Davis, *Davis Cup*

4019 Donald Byrd, *Byrd In Hand*

4020 The Three Sounds, *Good Deal*

4021 Kenny Burrell, *At The Five Spot*

4022 Duke Pearson, *Profile*

4023 Dizzy Reece, *Star Bright*

4024 Jackie McLean, *Swing, Swang, Swingin'*

4025 Lou Donaldson, *The Time Is Right*

4026 Donald Byrd, *Fuego*

4027 Freddie Redd, *Music From "The Connection"*

4028 Horace Parlan, *Movin' And Groovin'*

4029 Art Blakey and the Jazz Messengers, *The Big Beat*

4030 Jimmy Smith, *Crazy Baby*

4031 Hank Mobley, *Soul Station*

4032 Sonny Red, *Out Of The Blue*

4033 Dizzy Reece, *Soundin' Off*

4034 Lee Morgan, *Leeway*

4035 Duke Pearson, *Tender Feelin's*

4036 Lou Donaldson, *Sunny Side Up*

4037 Horace Parlan, *Us Three*

4038 Jackie McLean, *Capuchin Swing*

4039 Stanley Turrentine, *Look Out!*

4040 Freddie Hubbard, *Open Sesame*

4041 Tina Brooks, *True Blue*

4042 Horace Silver Quintet, *Horace-Scope*

4043 Horace Parlan, *Speakin' My Piece*

4044 The Three Sounds, *Moods*

4045 Freddie Redd, *Shades Of Redd*

4046 Duke Jordan, *Flight To Jordan*

4047 Art Taylor, *A.T.'s Delight*

4048 Donald Byrd, *Byrd In Flight*

4049 Art Blakey and The Jazz Messengers, *A Night In Tunisia*

4050 Jimmy Smith, *Home Cookin'*

4051 Jackie McLean, *Jackie's Bag*

4052 Tina Brooks, *Back To The Tracks*

4053 Lou Donaldson, *Lightfoot*

4054 Art Blakey and the Jazz Messengers, *Meet You . . ., Volume 1*

4055 Art Blakey and the Jazz Messengers, *Meet You . . ., Volume 2*

4056 Freddie Hubbard, *Goin' Up*

4057 Stanley Turrentine with The Three Sounds, *Blue Hour*

4058 Hank Mobley, *Roll Call*

4059 Kenny Drew, *Undercurrent*

4060 Donald Byrd, *At The Half Note Cafe, Volume 1*

4061 Donald Byrd, *At The Half Note Cafe, Volume 2*

4062 Horace Parlan, *Headin' South*

4063 Kenny Dorham, *Whistle Stop*

4064 Grant Green, *Grant's First Stand*

4065 Stanley Turrentine, *Comin' Your Way*

4066 Lou Donaldson, *Here 'Tis*

4067 Jackie McLean, *Bluesnik*

4068 Baby Face Willette, *Face To Face*

4069 Stanley Turrentine, *Up At Minton's, Volume 1*

4070 Stanley Turrentine, *Up At Minton's, Volume 2*

4071 Grant Green, *Green Street*

4072 The Three Sounds, *Feelin' Good*

4073 Freddie Hubbard, *Hub Cap*

4074 Horace Parlan, *On The Spur Of The Moment*

4075 Donald Byrd, *The Cat Walk*

4076 Horace Silver Quintet, *Doin' The Thing*

4077 Dexter Gordon, *Doin' Allright*

4078 Jimmy Smith, *Midnight Special*

4079 Lou Donaldson, *Gravy Train*

4080 Hank Mobley, *Workout*

4081 Stanley Turrentine, *Dearly Beloved*

4082 Horace Parlan, *Up And Down*

4083 Dexter Gordon, *Dexter Calling*

4084 Baby Face Willette, *Stop And Listen*

4085 Freddie Hubbard, *Ready For Freddie*

4086 Grant Green, *Grantstand*

4087 Leo Parker, *Let Me Tell You 'Bout It*

4088 The Three Sounds, *Here We Come*

4089 Jackie McLean, *A Fickle Sonance*

4090 Art Blakey and the Jazz Messengers, *Mosaic*

4091 Sonny Clark, *Leapin' and Lopin'*

4092 Kenny Clarke, *The Golden Eight*

4093 Ike Quebec, *Heavy Soul*

4094 Fred Jackson, *Hootin' 'N' Tootin'*

4095 Leo Parker, *Rollin' With Leo*

4096 Stanley Turrentine, *That's Where It's At*

4097 Art Blakey, *The African Beat*

4098 Ike Quebec, *Blue And Sentimental*

4099 Grant Green, *Sunday Morning*

4100 Jimmy Smith, *Plays Fats Waller*

4101 Donald Byrd, *Royal Flush*

4102 The Three Sounds, *Hey There*

4103 Ike Quebec, *Congo Lament*

4104 Art Blakey, *Buhaina's Delight*

4105 Ike Quebec, *It Might As Well Be Spring*

4106 Jackie McLean, *Let Freedom Ring*

4107 Don Wilkerson, *Preach Brother!*

4108 Lou Donaldson, *The Natural Soul*

4109 Herbie Hancock, *Takin' Off*

4110 Horace Silver, *The Tokyo Blues*

4111 Grant Green, *The Latin Bit*

4112 Dexter Gordon, *Go*

4113 Freddie Roach, *Down To Earth*

4114 Ike Quebec, *Bossa Nova Soul Samba*

4115 Freddie Hubbard, *Hub-Tones*

4116 Jackie McLean, *The Jackie McLean Quintet*

4117 Jimmy Smith, *Back At The Chicken Shack*

4118 Donald Byrd, *Free Form*

4119 Charlie Rouse, *Bossa Nova Bacchanal*

4120 The Three Sounds, *It Just Got to Be*

4121 Don Wilkerson, *Elder Don*

4122 Stanley Turrentine, *Jubilee Shout*

4123 Kenny Burrell, *Midnight Blue*

4124 Donald Byrd, *A New Perspective*

4125 Lou Donaldson, *Good Gracious*

4126 Herbie Hancock, *My Point Of View*

4127 Kenny Dorham, *Una Mas*

4128 Freddie Roach, *Mo' Greens Please*

4129 Stanley Turrentine, *Never Let Me Go*

4130 Big John Patton, *Along Came John*

4131 Horace Silver, *Silver's Serenade*

4132 Grant Green, *Feelin' the Spirit*

4133 Dexter Gordon, *A Swingin' Affair*

4134 Horace Parlan, *Happy Frame Of Mind*

4135 Freddie Hubbard, *Here To Stay*

4136 Solomon Ilori, *African High Life*

4137 Jackie McLean, *One Step Beyond*

4138 Harold Vick, *Steppin' Out*

4139 Grant Green, *Am I Blue*

4140 Joe Henderson, *Page One*

4141 Jimmy Smith, *Rockin' The Boat*

4142 Blue Mitchell, *Step Lightly*

4143 John Patton, *Blue John*

4144 Johnny Coles, *Little Johnny C*

4145 Don Wilkerson, *Shoutin'*

4146 Dexter Gordon, *Our Man In Paris*

4147 Herbie Hancock, *Inventions And Dimensions*

4148 George Braith, *Two Souls In One*

4149 Hank Mobley, *No Room For Squares*

4150 Stanley Turrentine, *A Chip Off The Old Block*

4151 Andrew Hill, *Black Fire*

4152 Joe Henderson, *Our Thing*

4153 Grachan Moncur III, *Evolution*

4154 Grant Green, *Idle Moments*

4155 The Three Sounds, *Black Orchid*

4156 Art Blakey and the Jazz Messengers, *The Freedom Rider*

4157 Lee Morgan, *The Sidewinder*

4158 Freddie Roach, *Good Move*

4159 Andrew Hill, *Judgment!*

4160 Andrew Hill, *Smoke Stack*

4161 George Braith, *Soul Stream*

4162 Stanley Turrentine, *Hustlin'*

4163 Eric Dolphy, *Out To Lunch*

4164 Jimmy Smith, *Prayer Meetin'*

4165 Jackie McLean, *Destination . . . Out!*

4166 Joe Henderson, *In 'N Out*

4167 Andrew Hill, *Point Of Departure*

4168 Freddie Roach, *Brown Sugar*

4169 Lee Morgan, *Search For The New Land*

4170 Art Blakey and the Jazz Messengers, *Free For All*

4171 George Braith, *Extension*
4172 Freddie Hubbard, *Breaking Point*
4173 Wayne Shorter, *Night Dreamer*
4174 Big John Patton, *The Way I Feel*
4175 Herbie Hancock, *Empyrean Isles*
4176 Dexter Gordon, *One Flight Up*
4177 Grachan Moncur III, *Some Other Stuff*
4178 Blue Mitchell, *The Thing To Do*
4179 Jackie McLean, *It's Time!*
4180 Anthony Williams, *Life Time*
4181 Kenny Dorham, *Trompeta Toccata*
4182 Wayne Shorter, *Juju*
4183 Grant Green, *Talkin' About!*
4184 Sam Rivers, *Fuchsia Swing Song*
4185 Horace Silver, *Song For My Father*
4186 Hank Mobley, *The Turnaround!*
4187 Larry Young, *Into Somethin'*
4188 Donald Byrd, *I'm Tryin' To Get Home*
4189 Joe Henderson, *Inner Urge*
4190 Freddie Roach, *All That's Good*
4191 Duke Pearson, *Wahoo!*
4192 Big John Patton, *Oh Baby!*
4193 Art Blakey and the Jazz Messengers, *Indestructible*
4194 Wayne Shorter, *Speak No Evil*
4195 Herbie Hancock, *Maiden Voyage*
4196 Freddie Hubbard, *Blue Spirits*
4197 The Three Sounds, *Out Of This World*

4198 Bobby Hutcherson, *Dialogue*

4199 Lee Morgan, *The Rumproller*

4200 Jimmy Smith, *Softly As A Summer Breeze*

4201 Stanley Turrentine, *Joyride*

4202 Grant Green, *I Want To Hold Your Hand*

4203 Andrew Hill, *Andrew!*

4204 Dexter Gordon, *Gettin' Around*

4205 Pete LaRoca, *Basra*

4206 Sam Rivers, *Contours*

4207 Freddie Hubbard, *The Night Of The Cookers, Volume 1*

4208 Freddie Hubbard, *The Night Of The Cookers, Volume 2*

4209 Hank Mobley, *Dippin'*

4210 Ornette Coleman, *Town Hall Concert*

4211 Ornette Coleman, *Town Hall Concert*

4212 Lee Morgan, *The Gigolo*

4213 Bobby Hutcherson, *Components*

4214 Blue Mitchell, *Down With It*

4215 Jackie McLean, *Right Now*

4216 Anthony Williams, *Spring*

4217 Andrew Hill, *Compulsion*

4218 Jackie McLean, *Action*

4219 Wayne Shorter, *The All-Seeing Eye*

4220 Horace Silver, *The Cape Verdean Blues*

4221 Larry Young, *Unity*

4222 Lee Morgan, *Cornbread*

4223 Jackie McLean, *Jacknife*

4224 Ornette Coleman, *At The 'Golden Circle', Volume 1*

4225 Ornette Coleman, *At The 'Golden Circle', Volume 2*

4226 Don Cherry, *Complete Communion*

4227 Joe Henderson, *Mode For Joe*

4228 Blue Mitchell, *Bring It On Home*

4229 John Patton, *Got A Good Thing Goin'*

4230 Hank Mobley, *A Caddy for Daddy*

4231 Bobby Hutcherson, *Happenings*

4232 Wayne Shorter, *Adam's Apple*

4233 Andrew Hill, *Involution*

4234 Stanley Turrentine, *In Memory Of*

4235 Jimmy Smith, *Bucket!*

4236 Jackie McLean, *High Frequency*

4237 Cecil Taylor, *Unit Structures*

4238 Donald Byrd, *Mustang!*

4239 John Patton, *Let 'Em Roll*

4240 Stanley Turrentine, *Rough 'N' Tumble*

4241 Hank Mobley, *A Slice Of The Top*

4242 Larry Young, *Of Love And Peace*

4243 Lee Morgan, *DelightfuLee Morgan*

4244 Bobby Hutcherson, *Stick Up!*

4245 Art Blakey, *Like Someone In Love*

4246 Ornette Coleman, *The Empty Foxhole*

4247 Don Cherry, *Symphony For Improvisers*

4248 The Three Sounds, *Vibrations*

4249 Sam Rivers, *A New Conception*

4250 Horace Silver, *The Jody Grind*

4251 Jack Wilson, *Something Personal*

4252 Duke Pearson, *Sweet Honey Bee*
4253 Grant Green, *Street Of Dreams*
4254 Lou Donaldson, *Lush Life*
4255 Jimmy Smith, *I'm Movin' On*
4256 Stanley Turrentine, *The Spoiler*
4257 Blue Mitchell, *Boss Horn*
4258 Art Blakey and the Jazz Messengers, *The Witch Doctor*
4259 Donald Byrd, *Blackjack*
4260 Cecil Taylor, *Conquistador*
4261 Sam Rivers, *Dimensions And Extensions*
4262 Jackie McLean, *New And Old Gospel*
4263 Lou Donaldson, *Alligator Bogaloo*
4264 McCoy Tyner, *The Real McCoy*
4265 The Three Sounds, *Live At The Lighthouse*
4266 Larry Young, *Contrasts*
4267 Duke Pearson, *The Right Touch*
4268 Stanley Turrentine, *Easy Walker*
4269 Jimmy Smith, *Open House*
4270 Jack Wilson, *Easterly Winds*
4271 Lou Donaldson, *Mr. Shing-A-Ling*
4272 Blue Mitchell, *Heads Up*
4273 Hank Mobley, *Hi Voltage*
4274 Tyrone Washington, *Natural Essence*
4275 McCoy Tyner, *Tender Moments*
4276 Duke Pearson, *Introducing Duke Pearson's Big Band*
4277 Horace Silver, *Serenade To A Soul Sister*
4278 Frank Foster, *Manhattan Fever*

4279 Herbie Hancock, *Speak Like A Child*

4280 Lou Donaldson, *Midnight Creeper*

4281 John Patton, *That Certain Feeling*

4282 Elvin Jones, *Puttin' it Together*

4283 Booker Ervin, *The In-Between*

4284 Jackie McLean, *'Bout Soul*

4285 The Three Sounds, *Coldwater Flat*

4286 Stanley Turrentine, *The Look Of Love*

4287 Ornette Coleman, *New York Is Now!, Volume 1*

4288 Hank Mobley, *Reach Out!*

4289 Lee Morgan, *Caramba!*

4290 Lonnie Smith, *Think!*

4291 Bobby Hutcherson, *Total Eclipse*

4292 Donald Byrd, *Slow Drag*

4293 Duke Pearson, *The Phantom*

4294 Eddie Gale, *Eddie Gale's Ghetto Music*

4295 Reuben Wilson, *On Broadway*

4296 Jimmy Smith, *Plain Talk*

4297 Wayne Shorter, *Schizophrenia*

4298 Stanley Turrentine, *Always Something There*

4299 Lou Donaldson, *Say It Loud*

4300 Blue Mitchell, *Collision In Black*

4301 The Three Sounds, *Elegant Soul*

4302 Kenny Cox, *Introducing Kenny Cox*

4303 Andrew Hill, *Grass Roots*

4304 Larry Young, *Heaven On Earth*

4305 Elvin Jones, *The Ultimate*

4306 John Patton, *Understanding*

4307 McCoy Tyner, *Time For Tyner*

4308 Duke Pearson, *Now Hear This!*

4309 Horace Silver, *You Gotta Take A Little Love*

4310 Grant Green, *Goin' West*

4311 Don Cherry, *Where Is Brooklyn?*

4312 Lee Morgan, *Charisma*

4313 Lonnie Smith, *Turning Point*

4314 Booker Ervin, *Back From The Gig*

4315 Stanley Turrentine, *Common Touch!*

4316 Frank Foster (unissued)

4317 Reuben Wilson, *Love Bug*

4318 Lou Donaldson, *Hot Dog*

4319 Donald Byrd, *Fancy Free*

4320 Eddie Gale, *Black Rhythm Happening*

4321 Herbie Hancock, *The Prisoner*

4322 Brother Jack McDuff, *Down Home Style*

4323 Duke Pearson, *Merry Ole Soul*

4324 Blue Mitchell, *Bantu Village*

4325 Horace Silver, *The Best Of Horace Silver*

4326 Lonnie Smith, *Move Your Hand*

4327 Grant Green, *Carryin' On*

4328 Jack Wilson, *Song For My Daughter*

4329 Hank Mobley, *The Flip*

4330 Andrew Hill, *Lift Every Voice*

4331 Elvin Jones, *Polycurrents*

4332 Wayne Shorter, *Super Nova*

4333 Bobby Hutcherson, *Now*

4334 Brother Jack McDuff, *Moon Rappin'*

4335 Lee Morgan, *The Sixth Sense*

4336 Stanley Turrentine, *Another Story*

4337 Lou Donaldson, *Everything I Play Is Funky*

4338 McCoy Tyner, *Expansions*

4339 Kenny Cox, *Multidirection*

4340 John Patton, *Accent On The Blues*

4341 The Three Sounds, *Soul Symphony*

4342 Grant Green, *Green Is Beautiful*

4343 Reuben Wilson, *Blue Mode*

4344 Duke Pearson, *How Insensitive*

4345 Jackie McLean, *Demon's Dance*

4346 Jones-Lewis Orch, *Consummation*

4347 Art Blakey and the Jazz Messengers, *Roots And Herbs*

4348 Brother Jack McDuff, *To Seek A New Home*

4349 Donald Byrd, *Electric Byrd*

4350 Jimmy McGriff, *Electric Funk*

4351 Lonnie Smith, *Drives*

4352 Horace Silver, *That Healin' Feelin'*

4353 Chick Corea, *The Song of Singing*

4354 Jeremy Steig, *Wayfaring Strangers*

4355 Joe Williams, *Worth Waiting For*

4356 Ornette Coleman, *Love Call*

4357 Candido, *Beautiful*

4358 Jack McDuff, *Who Knows What Tomorrow's Gonna Bring?*

4359 Lou Donaldson, *Pretty Things*

4360 Grant Green, *Alive!*

4361 Elvin Jones, *Coalition*

4362 Bobby Hutcherson, *San Francisco*

4363 Wayne Shorter, *Odyssey Of Iska*

4364 Jimmy McGriff, *Something To Listen To*

4365 Reuben Wilson, *A Groovy Situation*

4366 John Patton (unissued)

4367 Hank Mobley, *Thinking Of Home*

4368 Horace Silver, *Total Response*

4369 Elvin Jones, *Genesis*

4370 Lou Donaldson, *Cosmos*

4371 Lonnie Smith (unissued)

4372 Richard Groove Holmes, *Comin' On Home*

4373 Grant Green, *Visions*

4374 Jimmy McGriff, *Black Pearl*

4375 Ornette Coleman (unissued)

4376 Bobby Hutcherson, *Head On*

4377 Reuben Wilson, *Set Us Free*

4378 Gene Harris, *The Three Sounds*

4379 Bobbi Humphrey, *Flute In*

4380 Donald Byrd, *Ethiopian Night*

4381 Lee Morgan (unissued)

4382 Ronnie Foster, *Two Headed Freap*

4383–4412 [Numbers not used]

4413 Grant Green, *Shades Of Green*

4414 Elvin Jones, *Merry Go Round*

4415 Grant Green, *The Final Comedown*

4416 Bobby Hutcherson, *Natural Illusions*

4417 Hank Mobley, *Thinking Of Home*

4418 John Patton, *Memphis To New York Spirit*

4419 McCoy Tyner, *Extensions*

4420 Horace Silver, *All*

4421 Bobbi Humphrey, *Dig This*

4422 Marlena Shaw, *Marlena*

4423 Gene Harris, *Gene Harris Of The Three Sounds*

4424 Stanley Turrentine, *Z.T.'s Blues*

4425 Hank Mobley, *Far Away Lands*

4426 Lee Morgan, *The Rajah*

4427 Jackie McLean, *Tippin' The Scales*

4428 Clifford Brown, *Alternate Takes*

4429 Various Artists, *The Best Of Blue Note, Volume 1*

4430 Bud Powell, *Alternate Takes*

4431 Hank Mobley, *Another Workout*

4432 Grant Green, *Born To Be Blue*

4433 Various Artists, *The Best Of Blue Note, Volume 2*

4434 The Three Sounds, *Babe's Blues*

4435 Hank Mobley, *Straight No Filter*

The definitive listing of all Blue Note sessions, from 1939 to the present, can be found in *The Blue Note Label* by Michael Cuscuna and Michel Ruppli (Greenwood Press, second edition 2001).

Index